The Diary of an Unprofessional Soldier.
By the late Capt. T.A.H. Nash
16th. Bn. Manchester Regt.
1914 - 1918.

Being the true story of a
Front-Line Territorial Army Soldier
on Active Service in World War One.

Edited by Capt. T.A.M. Nash.

Captain Thomas Anthony Havelock Nash

First published in Great Britain by
Picton Publishing (Chippenham) Ltd. 1991
ISBN 0 948251 48 4

Text paper supplied by
James McNaughton Paper Group Limited, Bristol.
Printed in Great Britain by Picton Publishing,
Queensbridge Cottages, Patterdown,
Chippenham, Wilts. SN15 2NS

iii

TOUJOURS · FIDELE

Anthony Havelock Nash.

CONTENTS.

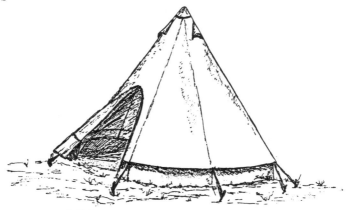

A Bell Tent usually for 12 men lying
with feet towards the centre pole.

Dedication.

Introduction.

There are a few points that need to be said in order to make my position as Editor of this Diary better understood, and your subsequent reading of it more enjoyable.

It was a little before the end of the First World War that my Father wrote the following:

"Foreword.

I have taken the trouble to record my experiences as a soldier because I hope to find during the dark days to come some solace in the remembrance of these epic years. It is astonishing to find how one's opinions alter in the course of a few years and in transcribing my old notes I have been sorely tempted to modify the expression of my views; I have resisted that temptation as I believe that the actual impressions at the moment of their reception are worth more than when qualified in the light of riper experience or kindlier judgement.

September 1917."

The transcription was two years before my elder brother was born and named Morton, and four years before I was christened Megson after two of his wartime pals. Their names were to be remembered at least for as long as we lived. My other godfather was General Sir John Shea who had been their Divisional Commander on the Somme.

About 1928 my Father took us two boys to see the Battlefields and later when at home we dug trenches and played with all sorts of weapons and uniforms, but we became no more blood-thirsty than any other lads who were less well armed. The photographs of bayonet, revolver and periscope have been included as it is thought they provide a tangible, material connection with the Author. His .450 Webley and Scott Revolver No. 173256 can now be seen at the Museum of the Manchesters having been with us since the earliest days and which we had always been told never to point at anyone - even if empty.

The next step nearer to me doing anything about the Diary, was when Gen. Sir John Shea gave me a farewell gift and a letter at the start of my working life on a Rhodesian Cattle Ranch. It said, "Your father was the youngest Company Commander in my division in 1916-17. He led his men well because he tried to understand their needs and always listened to them with sympathy however trivial their fancies or complaints. They knew this and so would follow him anywhere because they also knew that he never asked them to do a job he wouldn't do himself; and would never do anything which was mean or petty.

I tell you this because he has given you a shining example".

It seems strange to realise that 'Pop', as we knew him died shortly after my arrival abroad; and that that was fifty years ago. The Diary I had read before leaving home, but I remember it contained certain pages which no longer exist. However he was a copious writer who evidently greatly enjoyed setting down his thoughts whenever opportunity occurred. Virtually he wrote the story of his life whilst gaining first-hand experience of service as a Territorial

Army soldier, in the Front Line, he would insist. If he had been a member of the Regular Army, he would have been presumably in his own mind : a "Professional Soldier".

Reading between the lines it seems that in addition to the reasons given in the Foreword, he also wanted to give permanence to his memories of comrades regardless of rank, but all hall-marked as sterling characters. No doubt these were to be found in abundance throughout the Front in all regiments, but here refer particularly to: The 1st/4th (City of Bristol) Battalion the Gloucestershire Regiment; and the 16th (1st City) Battalion Manchester Regiment - their first Pals battalion.

In editing I did not feel that it was for me to alter his language, so it is as well to remember that some of the words used seventy-five years ago did not carry to-day's connotations. However, the change that I have been responsible for is when he has particularly castigated someone for thoughtlessly disregarding the health and general welfare of others, or neglecting to oversee matters of discipline and efficiency, I may have then slightly turned the thrust, as I am certain that although he would not have been in any sort of forgiveing mood, at the same time 'Pop' would not have wished to cause offence to relatives.

I have at last managed to devote sufficient time to do justice to this work and with the assistance of those mentioned in the Acknowledgements, now offer it to you to discover its special message.

The Author's .450 Webley and Scott Service Revolver No.173256
now exhibited in the Museum of the Manchesters.

Oct 10'

66, EVELYN GARDENS,
S.W. 7
KENSINGTON 4647.

My dear Mellsop.

I sent you off a pair of field glasses wh: I hope may be useful to you & wh: I hope have arrived safely.

I was so very interested to know that you are going out to Rhodesia I envy you. It is a grand

life. If you will let me know your address I will get some people to... about you. I hope too that you will let me know how you fare from time to time. Your father was the youngest Company Commander in my division in 1916-17. He led his men well because he tried to understand their need

2.

66, EVELYN GARDENS,
S.W. 7
KENSINGTON 4647.

and always listened to them with sympathy however trivial their fancies or complaints They knew this & so would follow him anywhere because they also knew that he never asked them to do a job he wouldn't do himself & would

never do anything wh: was mean or petty. I tell you this because he has given you a shining example. The best of good luck to you -

J H Shea

Letter from General Sir John Shea which may have
given the first impetus for this publication.

X

The Author marked 'X' as a Cadet,
of the University School Hastings, attached
to the 1st. Sussex Royal Engineer Volunteers.

ILLUSTRATIONS.

ABBREVIATIONS

Ammo (SAA)	Ammunition	Maj	Major
Bn	Battalion	MM	Military Medal
B	Bomber	OC	Officer Commanding
Capt	Captain	Pte	Private
CO	Commanding Officer	RG	Reserve Gunner
Col	Colonel	Rec'd	Recommended
Coy	Company	Sgt	Sergeant
Cpl	Corporal	Sgm	Signalman
DCM	Distinguished Conduct Medal	Sigs	Signals
Div	Division	SB	Stretcher Bearer
L/Cpl	Lance Corporal	Trans	Transport
2/Lt	2nd Lieutenant	TMB	Trench Mortar Bomber
LG	Lewis Gunner	VMG	Vickers Machine Gunner

A Soldier returning from the front
line as described on page 25.

Chapter One.

Our early training at Bristol and our departure from that city.
Great Totham. Billets at Colchester. Danbury.

> If men should ask, I would not have you say
> I went with ringing laughter in my eyes,
> Caught by the glamour of a high emprise
> And the imagined triumph of the day.

When the War broke out I was living in Bristol. By the end of August
it was clear that the time had come for every able-bodied man to offer
himself for military service and I tried to enlist. My first two attempts
were unsuccessful as the doctors discovered a weakness of the heart, not
entirely unsuspected on my part as I had only just returned from four months
sick leave on account of that same weakness. However, I had better luck on
my third attempt and on September 2nd. 1914 I was accepted for the 4th. Bn.
of the Gloucesters, a local Territorial Battalion of some renown.

My first two medical examinations were at the Colston Hall, and my third
at the Infirmary. It was a surprise to my family that I was accepted and
ultimately my old trouble was to prove my undoing, but in the meantime I had
the benefit of experiences not lightly to be valued.

I was sworn in at the Drill Hall on Thursday and told to report for duty
on the following Monday. Confident that I should be at the Front in a
fortnight's time I spent the intervening days in bidding a fond good-bye to
my relations.

On arriving at the Drill Hall on Monday I found that the Battalion proper
was stationed at Danbury in Essex, and that only a few officers and N.C.O.'s
had been left behind to deal with the recruits. Major Stotesbury and Lieut.
Holloway were the only officers and the latter impressed me as being a
very smart officer. For two, or three days chaos reigned supreme, and five
hundred men fought and struggled to get near the door of the Quartermaster's
Stores, which opened every half hour to admit one man for his uniform. Soon
however the small staff at the Depot succeeded in getting things under control
and we started work in earnest.

It is refreshing to remember our keeness in those early days; with what
respect we saluted the sergeants and the humble deference with which we
listened to those then splendid fellows, the trained soldiers of the Bn.
They condescended to accept drinks and cigarettes in return for their words
of wisdom, and I can well remember my eager questions and the unhesitating
belief accorded to the most preposterous replies.

Then there was the excitement of getting my uniform. Becoming impatient
at the delay I suggested to the Q.M.S. over a friendly cigarette that he
would probably want No. 2571 Pte. Nash to try on a uniform in the course of
the next few days. He saw my point of view and pocketed my half crown.
My friend made a small fortune in tips and in three weeks time I got my
uniform.

Now followed long days of drill and unaccustomed exercise, tiring,
but not wholly monotonous and so we gradually were licked into shape.
Many little coteries were formed; I had joined up without a pal but was
elected a member of a circle consisting of Best, Shepherd, Young, Dunsford
and Davies. After two months training at Bristol we were considered
sufficiently proficient to join the Bn. and after many false alarms the first
draft was sent off.

At a very early hour on October 30th. we paraded at the Drill Hall
with our kit-bags crammed with all sorts of useless rubbish and waited
to march for the station. Clustered about in little groups we made the
usual grim jokes about our chance of returning, and our spirits were
further enhanced by the arrival of a gun carriage and funeral party
bound for a military funeral. Few of us laughed at the Sergeant-Major's
sardonic announcement : "Gentlemen, your carriage awaits you."

On the way to the station I held up the entire column by slipping
on the wet and greasy tramlines. The Thermos flask in my haversac
broke and I was soon covered in coffee and mud. We caught the 9.10a.m.
for London and while my friends were saying good-bye to their wives and
sweethearts I busied myself in washing the coffee out of my hair.
We left Bristol with everyone hanging out of the windows to get a last
glimpse of their loved ones, and I congratulating myself heartily that
there was no one to weep over me.

And here I would take the opportunity of paying high tribute to
those men, of different stations in life and with little in common save
the desire to serve their country, who went forth so proudly to brave
hardship and danger. Many of them will never return; I have myself seen
many of them laid to rest in a foreign land. It is my earnest hope that
their memory may spur us on to further victory, and that their death may
forever stand between us and friendship with our enemies.

We had an hour's wait in London and arrived at Witham in Essex at
3.30 p.m. We then marched to Great Totham, whose sole greatness appeared
to consist of four small cottages and a public house. The memory of that
march will forever render odious to my mind the month of October. It was
a typical autumn afternoon, dull and dreary, the skies a leaden grey and
just beginning to rain. We were very tired and worn out with excitement,
and as we marched into Totham in the dark and found the Battalion under
canvas, our courage was at its lowest ebb.

Little groups of men stood around, looking curiously at the recruits;
men with tired eyes and hungry faces, uniforms caked with mud and collars
turned up to keep out the rain. Long lines of tents loomed ghostlike in the
darkness, shewing us our future quarters, and the clanking of tools as a
Company came in, wet and exhausted after digging trenches, warned us of
our future work.

We were issued with blankets, those Army blankets which serve so
many purposes, and so many men, before fulfilling their last use as a
shroud to the dead. Then tents were allotted to us, one tent to twelve
men, twelve tired hungry bad-tempered men. We had not fed since 6 a.m.,
that morning and we had no food that night. We soon realised that
hunger was to form one of the main features of our new life.

We bought a candle from one of the Corporals for a shilling and
spent the evening in settling down and giving away our idiotic possessions
to the trained soldiers of the Battalion who came to pull our legs and
to cadge all they could. They knew right enough that every recruit burdens
himself with all sorts of fancy kit far beyond his carrying powers, and
reckoned with justice that after our first route march we should be ripe
for plucking.

We listened to the weird camp noises, the buzz of conversation
from the tents around and the ceaseless bugle calls. At night the camp
presented a pretty enough spectacle when the tents were lit up, the

lights at the peaks of the tents looking for all the world like so many fairy lamps. From a distance only the points of light formed by the lanterns under the canvas are seen. We discovered later that one candle had been issued to each tent, but had been subsequently collected before our arrival by the N.C.O.'s in order that they might later be peddled at a profit.

As an indication of character it is interesting to note for what public institution men first ask when they find themselves in a strange neighbourhood. Some seek the station, others the local inn, a few the church. My first enquiry is usually for the post office. Four of my tent-mates went out to get their bearings; they found them in the public house and returned at Lights Out having regaled themselves all too well on onions and beer.

My previous experience of sleeping under canvas had been to have one of these tents to myself, with plenty of ventilation. It was a very different thing to share a tent with eleven others who were afraid of draughts and who did not appreciate the need of a daily, or even weekly tub. That night haunts me yet; the hot smell and human noises banished rest. Few of us were able to sleep while those who did made night hideous by snoring.

Reveille was at 6.15 a.m. and we washed in a muddy ditch at the bottom of the field. This was the sole washing place of the Battalion and in it we washed ourselves, our clothes and our feeding utensils. The approach to the ditch and its immediate surroundings were of liquid mud, like the much trodden watering place of cattle. I stole a bucket and washed in comfort but many of my comrades were too disheartened to wash at all.

After an hour's parade we had breakfast, our first meal for twentyfour hours. In the light of the present day comfortable camps of the New Armies it is inconceivable how we lived in those days. There was no cookhouse. Fires were lit in the centre of a field and over these were placed two dixies. These served in the morning and evening to boil our tea and at midday to cook the stew which invariably formed our dinner. The dixies were never washed between meals, so our tea was flavoured with onions, and the stew tasted of tannin. The lids of the dixies were used as frying pans for the bacon in the morning and at teatime in their capacity as lids allowed the congealed fat to melt and drop into the tea.

The unfortunate cooks were two of the roughest I have seen. They had not been selected for their culinary skill, but because of their physical unfitness. When the bugles sounded Cookhouse the men tumbled out of their tents, mess-tins in hand, and were marched by the Orderly Corporal to where the cooks were serving out breakfast. Each man received half a pint of tea, without milk, but flavoured with onions, and an undercooked piece of bacon two inches square handed to him in the cook's fingers. That together with a hunk of bread furnished our breakfast. All meals had to be eaten in the tent in which we lived and slept.

Having fed, each man took his mess-tin down to the same muddy ditch and tried to clean the greasy tin with cold mud. He then wiped the tin free from mud and the remaining grease with his handkerchief or face towel.

All this will sound preposterously exaggerated to the men of the New Armies and to civilians, but it is literally true. The Battalion was on active service from the time of mobilisation and everything was in a chaotic mess. The officers were wholly without experience and had no idea of looking after the troops under their charge. It may have done us good, but it should be understood that during the first months of War the Territorials underwent far greater hardship than the men of the New Armies in their training have been called upon to endure.

After breakfast on that first day our equipment was issued to us: the old bandolier and slung accoutrements, rolled overcoat and narrow leather belt. We dined in the same fashion as we had breakfasted; dinner consisted of half a pint of thin soup and a lump of fat, the whole being known as SHACKLES.

We had this dish every day for five months, the same old stew without vegetables, with uneatable meat and half an inch of floating fat on the top of the soup. Something was wrong there. Army rations are good and varied. Somebody must have been doing pretty well out of the grub issued to us.

All parades were carried out with absolute disregard of weather conditions. Although for a considerable time we only had one uniform apiece and had no chance of ever drying it, we were frequently kept doing rifle exercises in the pouring rain for three hours at a stretch; we have lain down on ground oozing rain, doing musketry drill by the hour. By every law of nature we should have died again and again, but while some did die, most of us survived.

Sir Ian Hamilton was commanding us in those days, while Colonel Butler was our C.O. While at Totham I walked into Maldon and had a really satisfactory tea. In those days there was serious fear of an invasion and that part of Essex was honeycombed with trenches which had to be manned at certain tides.

On November 3rd. we recruits left the Battalion and went to the ranges at Colchester to fire our musketry course. We had a six mile march to Hatfield Peverel where we entrained and reached Colchester at 6 p.m. The march to Hatfield was the first we had done in full equipment and we found it very tiring. The Bandolier with full complement of ammunition was a tremendous weight on the left shoulder and impeded the circulation. Our left arms and sides became quite numb. It was only sheer force of will that kept me going and if I who am a hulking great fellow felt the weight to that extent, how infinitely heavier it must have seemed to some of the smaller men.

We were at Colchester for five days, and were billetted in cottages, but it was a relief from the tents. My host was a plumber, with a large family of small children, and I washed in the scullery and fed in the kitchen. Mason was his name, Mason of 6 Beche Street, Colchester. He and his wife were very kind to Shepherd and myself. Our hours of parade were long, from seven in the morning till five at night and after that we had our rifles and equipment to clean. During the ten hours daily on the ranges we had only haversac rations of course. We were expecting to go to France on 6th. of December 1914.

One amusing thing happened on the ranges. We had just arrived one morning and were standing about in groups when one of the sergeants came up to us and told us to pick up some bits of paper and orange peel which were lying around. I suppose we none of us looked very enthusiastic, especially as the mess had been made by another battalion. Seeing that we were not jumping to it the sergeant said drily, "Come along now, hurry up, or I won't let you do it". He had a distinct and blessed sense of humour that chap.

On Sunday back we went to Hatfield Peverel and to Totham. On the following day the entire Battalion struck camp and marched twelve miles to Danbury. The officers lost their way and we went several miles out of our direct route.

Our life at Danbury deserves a chapter to itself. I am afraid it will not be much more interesting than this one, but the monotony of the recital is as nothing compared to the monotony and deadly discomfort of these early months of the War in the Territorial Army.

The Dog!

Before leaving for Great Totham 'Pop' took his dog to Plymouth to be left there with friends. Weeks later his Bristol landlady reported his return !

Commissioned   Commissioned   Commissioned   Commissioned
Med.Unfit   Killed   Killed   Killed

          Best   Dunsford   Penny
          Med.Unfit Commissioned Med.Unfit

Chapter Two.

Our life at Danbury and our departure from England.

> A piquet frozen on duty,
> A mother starved for her brood,
> Socrates drinking the hemlock,
> And Jesus on the rood;
> And thousands of others who nameless
> The path of duty trod-
> Some call it consecration
> And others call it God.

Danbury is a small village in Essex and is six miles from Chelmsford, the nearest town. It had in our days two shops, a church and a Common. Danbury Common was the Battalion Parade Ground. We were working upon the eight company system, and the various companies were scattered about the neighbourhood, a mile or two away from each other. I belonged to A Coy, commanded by a Captain Lewis.

On our arrival at Danbury we were first taken to an empty bungalow called the Grove and were preparing to spend the night there when plans were changed and we were marched further off to some stables and a loft. I was one of the lucky ones to sleep in the loft. There were forty three of us in there and there were two small windows and countless bats and other vermin. We went to bed by the light of one candle and when that was put out the fun began. Swarms of rats came out to play and chased round and over our recumbent forms. In the morning Dunsford wanted us to recommend him for the Albert Medal for saving life. In his own words, he woke up in the night just in time to find a dam' great rat carrying off poor little Joe Best down into its hole.

After a disturbed night we did an hour's drill before having breakfast which was at eight. We paraded again for a quarter to nine until half past twelve and again from two until five. When we reached the loft at the end of our labours we found it already occupied and discovered we had to move back to the Grove. This we did, and seven of us shared a room 12ft long by 10ft wide. We had very pleasant times in this tiny room, in which we had to eat, sleep and live. We had of course no furniture and not even straw to sleep on. Our washing place was a pond 200 yds away from the house and here we broke the ice every morning by moonlight in order to wash in time for seven o'clock parade.

We soon arrived at the conclusion that we should have to supplement our Army rations if we did not wish to starve, and our impromptu suppers were tremendous affairs. The purchase of an oil lamp and an orange box for a cupboard made a great difference to our comfort. The sight of men shaving in tea because they could not get hot water and of Joe Best airing his shirt over a candle, together with Dunsford's enquiry for the "naturalised milk", all provided us with much needed comic relief.

In spite of this , things were bad with us. We were always getting wet through and the atmosphere of many wet clothes in such a confined space was not pleasant. Added to which we were all thoroughly fed up with the treatment we were receiving and only indomitable determination and perseverance carried us on. We had been consistently exposed to totally unnecessary hardship ever since we had left Bristol.

There followed days of much hard work and too little to eat.
On November 12th. we had stew for dinner and went out at three in
the afternoon on night operations. We came back at nine to find the cooks
asleep and no tea, so went hungry to bed. After early morning parade
the next day we went to look for our breakfast, but the cooks had
overslept and we had nothing to eat until one, just twenty four hours
after our last meal. That sort of thing does not lead to efficiency
in a Battalion.

I have before me a note that I made at the time :"There are times
when I could positively cry with hunger. These are black days, days
when the men are hungry and angry, when we cannot laugh and dare not
joke; the men think things too dark to be uttered, mutiny and desertion.
The small things kill- however, when everything seems at its worst,
humour often forced, often hysterical, usually saves the situation".

The Winter dragged on; it was bitterly cold and the grates in the
bungalow had all been removed by a patriotic owner in order to prevent us
having fires. Needless to say the absence of grates did not prevent us
and we foraged for wood and fuel from the woods.

One day it was Dunsford's turn to provide the fuel and as it was
rather difficult to find wood we were surprised when he returned in
three minutes with a splendid load of wood. We asked him how he
managed it and his naive reply made us roar with laughter. "Oh, the
cook was chopping his wood on the doorstep, and when he was carrying
some into the kitchen I came in here with the rest". Our only regret
was that we could not go out and watch the cook's face when he returned
for the rest of the wood he had so diligently chopped .

One of our men who had rheumatic fever was lying in an outhouse
on a stone floor for a fortnight before he was taken to hospital,
and there were very many similar cases of neglect.

We had very long route marches followed by hours of trenching
several times a week. It was quite usual for us to marchfor some
seventeen miles in full kit, return to billets for a couple of hours
and then put in three solid hours of digging trenches in the dark.
There was very nearly a row one night. The Company had come back
after a particularly tiring day and we were told that we had to
parade at a barn two miles distant to attend a lecture by one of
the subalterns. The men were hungry and in a very bad temper and
the malcontents, the habitual grumblers who, like the poor, are
always with us, were very angry. The barn was a low roofed building
with a concrete floor, lit by the light of a single lantern placed
on the ground, casting long shadows about the dull interior. In the
centre of the floor forming a circle round the lantern stood the
little group of non-commissioned officers, like us dissatisfied
and with no confidence in themselves or their men. With his back
to the door stood the officer who had been ordered to lecture
upon "The Supply of Ammunition to the Firing Line"; a subject
of which he was ignorant and his listeners wholly indifferent.
An indistinct murmour was going on in the barn; three times the officer
shouted for silence, three times the hoarse voiced sergeants echoed
his order, and the murmour died away only to surge up again like an
angry tide. Then the more sober, more resigned men took the matter
into their own hands and let the roughs know that they hadn't it all
their own way, and the lecture went on in sullen silence. The trouble

was averted. It is however impossible to exaggerate the potential
danger of under-feeding and overworking men to whom a few months ago
discipline in any form was entirely foreign.

In the middle of November 1914, a severe fall of snow was not allowed
to interrupt our training, and the long columns of silent men marching
along in the snow were very picturesque, but found it develish
uncomfortable. We used to get the most glorious sunsets at Danbury,
which accentuated the homesickness of these Westcountrymen. At the end
of November we were given straw to lie upon, a distinct improvement
upon the bare boards, but we were still very cold and sleep was difficult
on this account.

Our training was going on apace and we did a lot of field work
At first we never took rations with us and after a long day's work I have
seen men eating raw turnips from the fields. At the end of any particularly
tiring day we usually did four or five hours digging to accustom ourselves
to active service conditions. We all looked forward to going to the Front
after these weary months of preparation.

I should like to mention my room-mates at Danbury. Young was the
best natured man I have ever met; he never said an unkind word about
anybody and was always the first to make excuses for other people's
shortcomings. He was a most untidy soldier and it took our united
efforts to get him ready for parade. If ever he wanted anything out
of his kit bag it was always at the bottom and the room was generally
strewed with his belongings. He applied for a commission before we
went out and was afterwards killed. Dunsford was his particular pal.

Shepherd was a very nice fellow, difficult to understand but a
really loyal friend. He had a very sarcastic manner and made an
excellent foil to Joe Best who was his own familiar friend. I met him
again later in the War and he was killed at Hebuterne.

Joe Best was the unconscious humourist of the party, always in
trouble, always deadly in earnest and childishly whimsical. He was a
little fat man with an enormous nose and a Cockney accent. He was
invalided out of the Army after many months of service abroad.

Sidney Davis was another good friend, fond of his food and hampered
by having to look after a cousin of his. He got a commission later on
in the War and was killed.

Dunsford was a delightful fellow with a great fund of humour;
he had a happy knack of getting out of unpleasant duties and was the
first amongst us to get a corporal's stripe. He too left the Battalion
before we went overseas and got a commission in the Worcesters.

On the 17th. of December 1914 I managed to get five days leave,
and was lucky to get it. On Christmas Eve we hoped to get into the
nearest town to do some shopping, but we had a route march until
two o'clock and then had to parade until seven o'clock for the
issue of new equipment.

I will pass over quickly the long dreary winter days, days when
we came HOME drenched to the skin to spend the evening in a tiny room
reeking with the odour of wet clothes and unwashed humanity.
Baths of course were never provided. If any of us were lucky enough
to be able to get into Chelmsford and could afford to go to an hotel
and ask for a bath once a month we considered fortunate indeed.

Our field operations were always conducted in a most realistic manner. We advanced across country over ploughed fields, through hedges and over fences, fording streams and climbing gates. Night work we made a speciality. One night early in March we were moved by compass across country. After many miles of getting over and through all sorts of obstacles we found ourselves up to the knees in mud and discovered that we were stranded in a sewage farm !

Scares of invasion were prevalent in Essex at this time. One night my Company and another had to attack a position held by six other companies. It was dark and wet and for two miles we crawled along ditches until we got within rushing distance of the cross-roads we had to attack. The order to charge was given and two hundred men with fixed bayonets flung themselves down the road. From all sides the defenders poured out rapid fire on us, with blank cartridges of course. The flashes and reports from the hedges, the cheers of the attackers, and the groans of the wounded and dying were most realistic.

The funniest part of the business was when two unsuspecting civilians passed on bicycles just when the attack took place. They thought that an invasion had really taken place. When they heard the reports of the rifles they leapt from their machines and took refuge under a hedge. Unhappily for them, that hedge screened more defenders who opened fire too, so the poor souls thought they were quite dead.

At the beginning of 1915 the snow storms were very heavy, and the roads blocked by fallen trees. Telegraph wires were down and the mails delayed. Four of us went to the Watchnight Service at Danbury; it seems centuries ago.

On January 2nd. 1915 I was on guard over 40,000 rounds of ammunition, fifty two horses, a deserter and a would-be suicide. The guardroom was a farm shed with one small window, the walls lined with cases of ammunition. A candle stuck in the neck of a bottle was our only light and the room was heated by a slow combustion stove. The fumes of the coke and the general atmosphere of the room, with five men sleeping in it formed an unwelcome contrast to the biting wind and frost of the night outside. The guards and the prisoners slept huddled together on the floor. Only Hogarth could have depicted the squalor of the guardroom, the flushed faces and contorted attitudes of the sleepers, while outside paced the sentry, a sleepy but picturesque figure in the moonlight.

On January 7th. I was inoculated; on the 11th. I marched in full kit twenty three miles in five and three quarter hours. This was supposed to be rather a record for a Territorial Battalion.

Major Baker had taken over command of the Company which had now become a double Company consisting of about two hundred and fifty men. It was about this time that Colonel Crawford of the Manchester Regiment offered to get me a commission in his Battalion and on the 12th. of January I went into Chelmsford to be medically examined.

On January 22nd. my great friend Cecil Reynolds, who was an officer in the Gloucestershire Regiment came down from Bedford in a heavy snowstorm to see me. He spent the night with us in our tiny billet and as the next day was Sunday I was able to go into Chelmsford with him after Church Parade.

On the 26th. we had a trial pack, loading transport and so on. In the evening we had a tin of lobster between us. Dunsford wanted a double share so remarked to Young that the only thing he had against lobsters was that they fed on dead bodies ! Then Best came in with a pathetic story of a man of seventy who had been sent to prison for a week for striking his grandfather : the peculiarity of Danbury natives was their longevity.

The eldest of our little party was addicted to strong waters. This was inconvenient as it not only meant that we had frequently to put him to bed, but that he would disturb us in the night as well by foraging for water to quench his overwhelming thirst. There was never water in our room, but often bottles of ginger beer would be lying about. On one famous night he awoke very dry indeed and by the light of a match espied to his delight a stone ginger beer bottle on the mantelpiece. He scrambled up, unscrewed the cork and took a long draught, and was promptly and violently sick. The bottle had been used out of its natural purpose to hold liniment for Young's sore throat.

About this time Colonel Butler who had commanded the Battalion from the time of mobilisation was found medically unfit for foreign service, and Colonel Davenport came to take over command. He was a Regular who laid great importance on looking after his men and from this time on conditions improved tremendously.

On March 6th. we moved to new billets at Woodham Mortimer; our abode there was a most palatial building with a delightful garden. The house itself was an old one with large spacious rooms, oak beams and a broad staircase. There was quite an air of mystery and romance.

We did night firing on the ranges and on the 7th. March we went to Goldhanger about 15 miles away to do field firing. Here we billeted one night and returned to Woodham Mortimer on the following day. We were nearing our billet late in the evening when we saw ahead of us in the dusk a figure we thought we knew. "Hullo there, is that the drunken Corporal ?", shouted Young. "No", replied an acid voice, "It is Captain Clarke".

Gradually our preparations for Overseas were being completed. Overseas boots and webbing equipment, field dressings and iron rations were issued. On the 18th. March I obtained leave to go and see Colonel Crawford. On the 21st. I was promoted Lance Corporal and was very proud of my first step.

We sent home our spare kit; we blackened our buttons and badges and from March 25th. we were marking time, ready to go off at any minute. There were many rumours as to our destination, but nothing definite was known and up to the minute of our embarkation everything was kept a profound secret.

The men for the most part were in a sober mood; wondering when they would see the hedgerows of England again. If not, what manner of death would be theirs. My own particular pal at that time was L.C. May who was about my own age. He poor soul was killed very early on.

Whilst waiting to leave there was much writing of letters, and I thought of the romance in most of those letters. My affection was for the sister of my best friend.

There is no greater purging power than pain, whether physical hurt, or heartache; and suffering alone can beget sympathy and

gentleness. Life is sweet but to the really noble minded, whatever
their age or station in_ life, there are things dearer than the mere
life which accident may extinguish, disease canker, or dishonour stain.
The men now fighting have chosen those better things: let us pray that
life may be added to them.

> And all through Life I see a Cross,
> Where sons of God yield up their breath;
> There is no gain except by loss,
> There is no life except by death.

On March 31st. we left Woodham Mortimer. We had been granted no
final leave of absence to make our adieux but in the field in front of
our billets many friends and relations had assembled to bid the Troops
God Speed. The Company fell in, piled arms, took off their packs and
those of them with friends there went to say goodbye. More harrowing
partings and more self congratulations on my part that there was no
one to weep on my shoulder. At last the order was given to fall in.
We put on our equipment and joined the ranks. Even then we imagined
we were going to Salisbury Plain for further training. We marched to
Maldon and entrained at 2.30 p.m. By seven o'clock we had arrived at
Folkestone where we embarked straightway.

In dead silence with not a light shewing we crossed the Channel.
On our backs we carried all our belongings. The weary days of
waiting and training were over; ahead of us lay France, Glory and
the Great Game. We landed at Boulogne that night, part of the
Expeditionary Force.

> What if the best of our wages be
> An empty sleeve or a stiff set knee,
> A crutch for the rest of Life,
> Who cares?

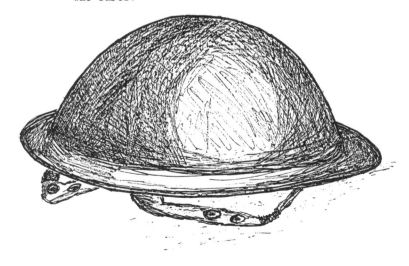

Chapter Three.

Our first weeks abroad. Doulieu. Armentieres. Trenches and Billets.

A month ago they marched to fight,
Away 'twixt' the woodland and the sown;
I walked that lonely road tonight
And yet I could not feel alone.

The voice of the wind called shrill and high,
Like a bugle band of ghosts;
And the restless leaves that shuffled by
Seemed the tread of the phantom hosts.

Mayhap when the shadows gather round
And the low skies lower with rain,
The dead that rot upon outland ground
March down the road again.

Our welcome in France was not the triumphal march our fancy had painted; gone were the cheering crowds, the waved bunting and the stirring mingled tunes of the Marseillaise and Tipperary. We landed silently in the dead of night, unheralded and unsung, save for a few dock loafers. Boulogne was asleep, and we marched over cobblestones between long rows of white houses shuttered and barred. Tired out and heavily laden we marched up an appalling hill to Oesterhove Camp on the heights above Boulogne, where a hundred years ago Napoleon's Army waited for so long in vain. Here we slept under canvas, sixteen men in a tent.

We were up at 5 a.m. the next morning and marched off to Pont de Briques where we entrained, forty six men to a cattle truck. For seven hours we journeyed in that wretched train and of course we had neither food nor water during that time. Many hospital trains had passed that way and our road was marked by white bandages with ominous red stains all along the track.

At length we detrained at Cassel, and after unloading the stores we marched off towards Winnezeele. As usual we were tired and hungry before we started our march and to the accompaniment of distant gunfire we crawled along the aching dusty road. When we halted for a rest we just fell in our tracks on the road, too exhausted to move to the side of the road. With every nerve and muscle strained beyond endurance we still moved forward. Long before the train journey was finished our water bottles had been emptied, and now we were parched and hungry. Our tempers too were strained and after a few miles we croaked curses at each other with parched lips and dried throats. Everything we did not actually need, the patent medicines, mufflers, enamel plates, and all the rubbish we had brought with us in addition to our regulation kit we threw away in order to lighten the load we were carrying.

After ten miles of this we reached our destination. Winnezeele is a little French village half a mile from the Belgian frontier and here we were billeted in farms and stables. My services were required as an interpreter and I had to accompany Major Baker to all the billets. I then returned to my own barn where seventy men were sleeping. I opened the door and stepped onto one man's face; he was far too tired to expostulate and went on sleeping. The floor was black with men. As the barns were full of straw all lights were out of the question.

We were still tired men who turned out next morning, but we were much refreshed. A peculiar feature of trained troops is their wonderful elasticity and the rapidity with which they can recover from dire fatigue. Within an hour of reaching billets absolutely tired out with marching I have seen the men playing football.

On that Good Friday's morning we washed and shaved round a little pond enclosed with willows and after a meagre breakfast we sallied out to inspect the village, fully armed. The firing sounds in the distance were incessant.

The inhabitants were hospitable folk and gave us coffee to drink. Unfortunately they had to live like pigs, and with them - their two-roomed hovels furnishing shelter for man and beast alike. Their bare feet and scanty rags told their own story. We were lucky to be lodged in their barns.

We all got very wet that day and of course had no change of clothes. We spent the night in the same barn but were aroused at 2 a.m. by something moving about in the darkness. It proved to be a large white pig which had broken in and was clambering over the recumbent figures of our men, and we had much trouble in persuading it to leave. On Saturday we marched five miles in pouring rain to be inspected by General Smith-Dorrien. On Sunday Major took Church Parade, a queer service for Easter Sunday. Afterwards we did four hours rapid loading practice, in case we became too religious I suppose.

Children pestered us for buttons, and the civilians were immensely surprised to find that we had come of our own free will and accord to fight the Germans. The French and Belgians could never understand that we were volunteers.

On Easter Monday we resumed our travels and leaving the village at 7 a.m. we marched seventeen miles, through Saint Sylvestre Capel, Cassel, Caester, Fletre and Meteren to Doulieu where we arrived at 3 p.m., pretty good going. The roads over which we passed had all been hotly contested and the way was marked by innumerable wooden crosses shewing the graves of English and French troops. We felt the march very much; seventeen miles of pouring rain with a heavy wind and over cobblestones and slush. Our longest halt was for the regulation ten minutes every hour, and when we did halt on these occasions we just fell down in our tracks.

At Doulieu the Company was billeted in crowded and draughty outbuildings. The farmers upon whom we were lodged seemed to resent our presence; troops had been in the neighbourhood since the start of hostilities and had done a certain amount of damage to crops. All the villages through which we passed had been wrested from the hands of the Germans and shewed their share of burnt-out houses and churches and bullet-riddled walls. Everywhere we heard the same record of savagery and wanton destruction, old men shot in the fields as they tilled the land, children murdered before their mothers' eyes, women outraged and mutilated. In this part of the World little brick shrines had been erected at frequent intervals along the main roads and these lit up by the candles placed there by the devout presented a queer spectacle at night.

There was a Canadian Ammunition Park at Doulieu, and on the afternoon of our arrival feeling very hungry and not knowing the town, I asked a Canadian Corporal where I could get some food. "Waal", said he, "I guess there is only one place in this muck-heap where you can get a square meal, and thet's our cookhouse. Go along there and say the Corporal sent you". I did so, and sure enough they gave me an upturned bucket to sit on, a panniken of delicious tea, some fried steak and potatoes and a huge slice of bread and marmalade. It was the best meal I have ever tasted, and I enjoyed their views of our American cousins almost as much as I liked my dinner. I have always felt particularly kindly to Canadians ever since I enjoyed their ready hospitality.

I went back to my billet and sat in the orchard. Around me I saw the typical red square-built farms of France; outlined against the sky rose the ruins of the church, burnt by the Germans, with the priest imprisoned inside. Two or three ruined homesteads bore witness to the hand of the invader. Picturesque French peasants in blue blouses and in sabots worked in the fields with prehistoric tools and drove to market carts that were old fashioned in Caesar's time. Occasionally patrols of Lancers clattered through the village and ever in the background was the rumbling of heavy guns.

It seemed to me that the stamina of the country lay in the women folk. The men for the most part seemed easy going and futile. Their enthusiasm was easily aroused but short lived. It was at Doulieu that German troops shot eleven French civilians without cause, after having made them dig their own graves. This happened on the 11th. of October 1914. Wherever we went we heard terrible stories of atrocities committed by the German soldiery.

On April 9th. we had a fall of snow, and on the 10th. we left Doulieu to take our place in the firing line. In warning us to acquit ourselves well in the sight of the Regular Army Major Baker added: "Take care of your small kit. These old soldiers are heroes, but they are - thieves".

We reached Armentieres at 6.30 p.m. and were warned to be ready to go up to the Trenches at 8.30 p.m. the same night. The whole Battalion was lodged in a large rambling building called the Hospice Civile. Armentieres too had suffered much during the occupation.

When the troops mustered in the Courtyard at the appointed time we were thrilled with excitement despite our fatigue. Each man carried in addition to his equipment a blanket, a waterproof sheet, two days rations, and a periscope or a sack of coke. We were reminded that the lives of our comrades depended upon our absolute silence and then we marched in the dark to Brigade Headquarters where guides met us, from the Battalion from whom we were going for instruction. Just before we marched off I was told unofficially that I had been granted a commission in the Gloucestershire Regiment, Special Reserve of Officers.

Our guide led us through the ruined streets, skilfully avoiding the huge shell craters which lay in our path. Passing through two barricades we got into a poorer neighbourhood where the houses had been shattered by the constant shelling. For the most part they had been abandoned but in rare cases a furtive gleam of light stealing under a door betrayed the presence of some poor soul who even then

refused to leave his home. Turning abruptly to the right our guide
then told us we were under rifle fire from the German trenches and
that relief parties suffered most heavily along this particular piece
of road. After advancing for ten minutes a barbed wire barricade
loomed in sight and our guide disappeared into a communication trench
on the left of the road.

This trench was deep and narrow and under water for most of the
way. We stumbled along blindly in single file, while stray bullets
whistled well over our heads. The guide was anxious to get some
sleep so hurried us along for half a mile or so until we reached
the actual fire trench. We filed along this, squeezing past the dark
and muffled figures of the night sentries until we were allotted to
our respective sections of the trench. We were then warned for certain
hours of duty during the night and until our turn came we were allowed
to sleep in empty berths in the dugouts under the parapet. I was soon
fast asleep beside a Regular who had not washed for six days and who
was correspondingly grimy.

The defences at Armentieres were breastworks, as opposed to trenches,
and the dugouts were constructed in the front face of the breastwork
and were designed each to hold two men. The frames were made of wood
and waterproof sheets hung on nails formed very good curtains. Three
feet high, three feet wide and six feet long, there was not much spare
room inside for a couple of men, but a niche scraped in the earth wall
held a candle and another niche served to hold food fragments.

Armchair critics tell us that dugouts are invariably built in the
support trenches and also that no fire trench is more than two feet
wide. At the time of which I write there were no support trenches in
Flanders, and a fire trench two feet wide was quite impracticable.
When afterwards I returned to England I found it difficult to reconcile
theory and practice to the satisfaction of my superior officers, and
after having seen the real thing for myself, to accept with becoming
deference the opinions of those who had not. It stands to reason that
as the Allied line extends some hundreds of miles conditions must vary
locally, and this accounted for the conflicting reports that we used
to hear, but nothing in Heaven or Hell can explain the theories our
Red capped and blue blooded General Staff at home try to force upon us.

.Our first night in the trenches passed uneventfully.
The Shropshire Light Infantry were splendid hosts and their trenches
were spick and span. I did duty with one of the Regular Corporals
and our job was to visit and change the sentries and relieve the
listening posts, making necessary reports to the Officer on Duty.

The night sentries stood on the fire step, their heads over the
parapet, watching for the slightest movement from the German lines
some two hundred yards away. It is anxious work and cold work, and
the men on duty presented a curious picture to the novice. They wore
their equipment over their greatcoats, and over that again long
mackintosh capes which came down to their feet. Round their necks
they wore two, or three mufflers and over their puteed legs straw
and sandbags. Weird and shapeless they strained every nerve while
on guard; upon them depended the lives of their comrades and the safety
of the line. Their loaded rifles rested on the parapet at each man's
appointed place.

Every man in the trench slept in full equipment ready at a moment's warning to take his place on the firestep. Sentries sometimes got jumpy and would alarm the garrison by seeing bushes move; the strain of watching by night is very severe. Later it was possible to post sentries in pairs, but in the early days there were not enough men to go round. The sentries have to be warned when any of our men are going out into No Man's Land, as the intervening ground between our trenches and those of the Germans is called. There are many things that have to be done in that eerie land of horrors, among the decaying corpses and hideous human remains, poaching snipers and whinnying ghosts. The barbed wire entanglements have to be kept in good repair, reports have to be obtained upon the state of the enemy wire and listening posts have to go out.

When the two lines of opposing trenches are some distance apart, both sides send out posts of three or four men each into No Man's Land whose job it is to listen for mining or sapping, and generally to keep the enemy under observation. Of course these men can only go out at night. At Armentieres the Bosche posts and our own were only a few yards apart but it was not considered etiquette to destroy each other.

Twice a day all through the year, before dawn and before dusk, every man in the British line prepares to meet an attack. While the dangerous half light lasts, every man stands to at his fighting place in the trenches. This period is called Stand-To, and that is the call of alarm if necessity arises to man the trenches at any other time.

During my first night in the trenches we visited the sentry posts and the listening posts, and an hour before dawn the order was passed down the line to stand to. After that the day sentries were posted and the rest of the troops stood down and began to clean their rifles and ammunition. Scrupulous care is always devoted to this, for a rifle that jambs in an attack spells disaster. After this the men cooked their breakfasts over trench fires lit in braziers, and here and there attempts were made to wash. In those days it was considered unprofessional to wash or shave in the trenches. After four or five days it can be imagined what the men looked like.

During the day watch was kept on the enemy lines by means of periscopes. To shew your head over the top of your trench was to court instant death at the hands of the German snipers.

After dinner, cooked in the same fashion, we saw our first air fight. Our machine guns opened fire on a German aeroplane which was flying over our trenches and after some time got his range. The machine heaved suddenly and burst into flames, coming down behind the German front line. Our Flying Corps was doing very well at this time, and the hero of the day was a pilot whom everyone called the Mad Major. He has since become quite a well known character.

We all felt very homesick on Sunday evening. We could hear from the trenches the church bells behind us in Armentieres and they with the sunset and our thoughts of home formed an incongruous contrast to the whistling bullets and bursting shrapnel. Suddenly with the last rays of the setting sun there fell a hush on the battlefield. For some reason all firing ceased and everything was still and beautiful. unconsciously reverent we attended the dying of another day and our thoughts turned to other sunsets we had known, with dear ones at our side; and so through the lychgate of memory we wandered into the

shadowland of retrospect, until a shriek of pain and a shout for stretcher
bearers reminded us that we had to deal with to-day and not with dead
yesterdays. We lived mostly in the past; the present was too unpleasant
and the future too uncertain.

The Yorks and Lancs Regiment relieved the Shropshires that night
but we stayed on in the line for another day. One thing was rather
amusing. We were in breastworks, and at the time there was a difference
of opinion between the two regiments as to the use of loopholes.
The Shropshires would have none of them and held that it was safer to
fire over the parapet. On the other hand, the Yorks and Lancs preferred
the use of loopholes, so loopholes were constructed but were filled-in
religiously when the Shropshires came in for their tour of duty.

I spent Sunday night in a machine gun emplacement with the machine
gun crew, five unshaven grubby fellows of sterling worth. Five of us
sat huddled over a charcoal brazier, nearly choked with the fumes,
whilst the figure of the sixth shewed up darkly behind us at the point
where he was on sentry duty. These men seemed hardly human as they
crouched over the fire, with tired eyes and fingers looked dead as they
stretched towards the dull glow of the fire. We talked in low whispers
to keep ourselves awake, and now and again we heard the whimper of a
man in pain and the ceaseless rustle of the ghosts in No Man's Land.

You don't believe in ghosts ? Nor do I, here at home in a well
lit room with a bright fire and a full tummy; but out there in the
darkness under the stars unimaginative men tell stories of trenches
manned by soldiers long since dead; of friends killed months ago who
keep them company on guard; and of brave foes who have rushed whispering
to our trenches at night, palsied with fright and with blanched faces,
surrendering to the nearest human beings in order to escape from the
horrors of No Man's Land. Such tales told over a charcoal brazier
seem likely enough.

On Monday Major Bailey D.S.O. of the Yorks and Lancs in a
lecture to the non-commissioned officers told us many things we ought
to know. He spoke of trenches too deep to be capable of defence and
of the danger in drinking untested water; he warned us against the
danger of firing machine guns from their battle positions and of
allowing our rifles to become dirty, and finally he finished by
telling us that we were fighting a foe who had no sporting instinct
and who could never be trusted to play fair.

In the evening we left our hospitable friends and, filing out
by the same waythat we came, returned to our billet in the town,
men who had been tested by fire.

By daylight the workhouse looked even more tumbled down than
before; the staircases were narrow and steep, and in all the rooms
there was an atmosphere of decay. Until recently these barren rooms
with their crazy floors had been occupied by little old people in
white caps and blue dresses, poor old souls whose only recreation
could have been the memory of other days. On the other side of the
cobbled square was a chapel and we were told that when any of the
inmates of the workhouse were dying, they were taken down and left
to die in the chapel.

Imagine the scene; some poor old soul about to slip its moorings;
the appearance of the attendants with the carrying chair; the pitying

glances of the other inmates, all destined to make the same journey sooner or later; the frail tired body propped up in the chair and strapped in, and the jolting of the journey down those steep stairs. Across the cold chill air to the chapel, and then the clang of the door behind the attendants as they go out and leave in that atmosphere of damp and death, in front of the cold repellent altar, the poor lingering spirit meeting death alone. Bumbledon survived longer in France than in our country.

We slept soundly on Monday night and vainly hoped for a rest on Tuesday. We paraded for physical drill at 6 a.m. and worked hard all day until 6 p.m. when we were marched off to do four hours trench digging. We were digging reserve trenches just behind the front line and the Hun had spotted the work upon which we were engaged and gave us a warm time with his machine guns. Every now and then a star shell would go up, illuminating the surrounding country for a good half minute. The only way then to escape being seen is to remain absolutely motionless.

I made my section work very hard, realising that therein lay their salvation. Again and again we had to drop flat while the machine gun bullets passed over us like a swarm of bees. Once while I was speaking to Sergeant Wilson a bullet passed between our faces so that we both actually felt the draught of it. When our task was ended we returned to billets.

On Wednesday we were allowed to go into the town for two hours and I bought some souvenirs and went to see The Follies, a troupe of soldier pierrots who were very good indeed. The town was being shelled, but not heavily.

On Friday we were told that we were to take over a section of the firing line for our own near Ploegsteert Wood at a place called Le Gheer. From our Company Commander we learnt that our new trenches became flooded at the slightest shower and that the parapets were continually falling in; also that all rations and supplies had to be carried a mile and a half in the open right up to the front line, owing to the complete absence of communication trenches. We were to relieve the Irish Rifles.

On Saturday, heavily laden with coke, wood, and all other accessories of trench warfare we left Armentieres at 4 p.m. for Plug Street. This place was just over the Belgian frontier and there was an ill-famed wood there which had been the scene of some particularly hard fighting. Plug Street was the troops' name for Ploegsteert, and was in itself reminiscent of battle, murder, and sudden death. But we were full of glee at the thought of taking over part of the Line for our very own.

It must be noticeable from my diary that we had ceased to grumble as we neared the front line; all soldiers grouse a bit of course, but we were more content now that we were doing the job for which we joined the Army. Gradually too our officers learnt the necessity of looking after their men.

It may not be out of place to say here that the morale of the troops is always better the nearer they are to the front line. The fellows behind the line and employed at the Base and on the lines of communication lacked in the main the same spirit.

The day is long and the day is hard,
We are tired of the march and of keeping guard,
Tired of the sense of a fight to be won,
Of days to live through and work to be done,
Tired of ourselves, and of being alone -

No.1 Platoon A Company 4th. Bn. Gloster Rgt. 31/3/15.
"Leaving Danbury this morning for Heaven knows where ".
(Pop in centre of centre row).

Chapter Four.

Plug Street. The Wood. Home again to the Manchesters.

Tommy.

The 'ireling soldier earns his bit of fame, poor blighter !
Takes 'ardish knocks and likewise gives the same;
Gets offered up on other blokes' behalf -
A bloomin' scapegoat, not no fatted calf -
No swank about 'im, but 'e's some fighter;
A ruddy shuttlecock - wot with the Staff
And critics on the 'earth (so 'ard to please)
Which always disagrees.

I often think 'e's like them Roman chaps,
Who'd file past Claudius (or it might be Nero),
Sayin' " 'ail Caesar !
My turn to-day to 'and 'em in pr'aps,
So cheeroh ! "
(The public being the Imperial geeser,
Wot did'nt care two raps.)

Ploegsteert is four miles north of Armentieres and is in Belgium.
As you enter the village from Armentieres you come to a row of red
brick houses on the right hand side, with an inn and a small shop.
Just past this is a small road which turns off to the right and at
the far corner is a large red brick Brewery. The tall chimney
stacks formed a good landmark, for the Germans as well as ourselves.
In this Brewery my company of two hundred and fifty men were quartered.
Following the road to the right you come to some more cottages on the
left and opposite these a concealed battery of Field Artillery.
This road led up to the trenches but became under direct observation
from the Bosche line after a certain point.

Opposite the Brasserie on the other side of the main road was
a pool where we used to wash until we found a bayonetted German in
there. He was a perfectly good dead German, but fell to pieces
when we pulled him out as he had been there for some months.
Straight on down the main road were more cottages and shops of small
importance where enterprising villagers advertised "Fish and Chips".

In the centre of the village were four cross roads. The ruined
church stood on one corner and cafes at the other three. We were
only concerned with the road down to the right which led us up to the
firing line, passing the workhouse on the right, a few small cottages
and the East Lancs cemetery. Opposite this was a cart track leading to
Hants Farm, where the Hampshire Regiment had met with disaster earlier in
the War and which now formed our Battalion Headquarters. From here onwards
stretched the Bois de Ploegsteert, the infamous Plug Street wood. I shall
have more to say about this later.

We had our dressing station, the Medical First Aid Post, at a little
cafe next to the cemetery and from here onwards the road was under direct
observationand therefore unsafe. Farther up it intersected our trenches,
and a Crucifix stood on the left of the road just behind our trenches.

On the other side stood a large ruined cafe, and every day men had to dash across from one side of the road to the other, in full view of the German trenches and at the mercy of their snipers. Often it happened that a man would be hit as he crossed, and would choke out his life at the very foot of the roadside Calvary.

The village was of course under constant shell fire. On the night of our arrival we took the first road to the right and went on until we came to a ruined farmhouse. Then we turned off to the left and crossed two fields, our only cover being the darkness. Our path was a rough one and led us through two more ruined farms and the garden of a Convent, which brought us practically to our trenches.

Here we were met by an indescribable odour which puzzled us all night. The solution was easy when the morning light came and we could see the heaps of dead Germans lying just in front of our parapet. These were the first Huns we had actually seen and there was a rush for the periscope. We had quite enough of them before we had done.

There was a field of decaying corpses behind our trenches and whenever we had to effect any structural alterations in the trench we invariably turned up dead bodies in varying stages of decay. In constructing a fresh dug-out, for example, we were almost sure to stick our spade into a corpse. The whole of this land had been very fiercely contested not once but many times.

The enemy's fire was much more active here than in the line at Armentieres, and we had to unlearn a lot of things we had been told about the Hun. He was a jolly good marksman and had reduced the study of war and lethal weapons to a fine art. The perfection of his engines of destruction bear evidence to years of energy devoted to the one purpose of slaughter. He took his job very seriously; we did not: just as well.

By Sunday night we were fairly at home in the Le Gheer line. The trenches were in a damnable condition. The last lot must have been an idle, dirty crew. They had been content with trenches half full of water and out of which they could not reach to fire. They had made no attempt to clear away the German corpses and had fouled our only drinking water supply.

The troops had been suffering from stomach pains and vomitting brought about mainly by the constant stench of dead and decomposing bodies. We were rarely hungry in the trenches and bully beef and dog biscuits left us quite cold.

Another thing we learnt too was that the flat top of the service cap, the old Broderick cap which the troops wear to this day, made an excellent reflector and an ideal mark for the Bosche snipers, so we used to wear our sleeping caps in the trenches, those shapeless knitted things. Owing as I thought then to the nervousness of our officers, it may have been due to other causes, we had to stand to arms all through the night, night after night, which meant that we could only snatch an hour or two of sleep during the day.

My knowledge of French stood me in good stead as I was often sent on little excursions to the village to buy food for the officers. On Monday I made my first excursion into Plug Street. In order to reach the village by day it was necessary to go along the whole length of the front line trenches until one came to the point where the road intersected it, just by the Crucifix I have already mentioned. One then hopped across this road as quickly as possible and gained the scanty cover of Plug Street Wood. Through this, a by no means safe path, led to the village.

The Wood itself was a place of horrors. The gruesome relics of the earlier hand-to-hand fighting were still in evidence, and broken fragments of rifles and bayonets, half buried bodies, swamped dug-outs and hastily built redoubts all told their story plainly. Who ran, might read; and it was not pleasant reading. The trees were snapped off short by the constant shell fire and the fantastic shapes they took accentuated the spirit of disaster which filled the whole place. In the midst of all this desolation, spring flowers were coming up and birds singing; and I heard the cuckoo there for the first time that year.

All the same it is difficult to imagine children playing there, in years to come and all the paraphernalia of picnic parties. One feels that it can never be clean again. Everywhere were scenes of terrific fighting, and the wood was oppressive with the spirits of men lain in passion, not honest healthy ghosts. Two large crosses marked the graves of German soldiers of the 104th. Saxon Infantry, in mass. Some of the dug-outs still bore the placards upon which their occupiers had written names. In one, Purity Villa, our men had been surprised by a German patrol and butchered in their sleep.

Crossing Hunter's Avenue I came to Hants Farm from which a path led me to the Dressing Station and so to the village along the road. Huge shell holes formed traps for the unwary, and at the sides of the road the ditches were filled with stagnant water in which could be seen German helmets and equipment and half submerged corpses. The village itself was much damaged. I made my purchases, buying bread, sugar, condensed milk and vegetables and then had some food myself before returning. It was hard work doubling across the machine gun swept road and harder still to get the rations past my comrades to their lawful owners as I passed along the trenches.

In the evening I climbed out on to the parados and tried to bury three Germans who were making their presence rather too well known in my own section of the trench. They had been there for many months and were falling to pieces; huge bloated corpses horribly swollen and partly devoured by rats. They were lying in full view of the Germans so that their funeral was not very popular. I mean to say that I was not overwhelmed by offers of assistance. Again and again I tried to get my spade into the ground. Every time I did so I only unearthed a fresh corpse. The place was one huge burial ground. Finally I had to give up in despair so I emptied a sack of chloride of lime on my three. There was a squelch like a heavy stone makes in a rotten cabbage, and oh the smell !

These Plug Street trenches were really trenches and not like the breastworks at Armentieres. Let me explain that a trench is a ditch of varying depth and width dug below the level of the ground, with just the parapet and parados shewing above the surface. On the other hand, breastworks are defences erected above the level of the ground, usually of sandbags. The Plug Street trenches at one time had been fairly deep. In places however they had been gradually filled in by the falling earth until it was no longer possible to stand upright in them. As against this there were certain stretches that were so deep that they were impossible to defend. It is no use having a trench out of which you cannot reach to fire.

When we started to deepen the parts which needed it we came across
evidence of former occupants. After clearing away several inches of
earth we came to a layer of straw and turned up bits of German equipment
and cartridge cases. On going down a few more inches we came to straw
and French equipment and cartridges, proving that the trenches had changed
hands several times.

In the evenings we used to crawl out into No Man's Land to snipe
the German sentries, a fascinating but dangerous game. A German sniper
had been levying a heavy toll upon the garrison of our trench and at
last we located him in a thick tree close to our lines. When he fired
again we let him have several rounds of machine gun fire. Just before dawn
three of us went out to see the result of our fire. There hanging by
his heels, head downwards, was our sniper. He had fallen from his
perch and had been caught by the foot in a forked branch. His poor
grey figure in the dawn remains in my mind's eye a perpetual monument
to all snipers.

It seems so curious to think that men like ourselves, who would
never be guilty of unkindness or ungentleness to the least of God's
creatures should consider it quite a matter of course to kill what
Germans we could. There was always an absolute absence of anger or
blood lust, of which some of our civilian novelists are so fond of
writing. We just did our job without animosity and accepted the same
fate without grousing. It was a rotten game seeing one's pals shot or
maimed, one after the other, and if it was possible to eliminate the
cause of their destruction one just did it; for my own part with less
compunction than setting a trap for the mouse who steals my cheese.
Bitterness only crept in when our friends the enemy disregarded the
rules of the game. It is not fair play to massacre the wounded and
we certainly did feel revengeful when we found in our exploration of a
ruined building in No Man's Land a Canadian soldier crucified on a door
with a bayonet through each hand and foot, nor were we inclined to remit
our toll when we found the mutilated bodies of five nuns in the cellars
of the convent just behind our lines.

On Wednesday April 21st. 1915 we left the trenches for a rest and
were relieved by the 6th. Gloucesters. We reached billets by 5a.m.
During the whole tour of duty I had had nine hours sleep. On the same
day we roused ourselves at 11a.m. and had breakfast, then dinner at
4.30p.m. In the interval we bathed in the pool near the Brasserie and
carried out a concerted attack on that minor horror of War, the louse.
I am aware that this insect is not regarded as being mentionable in
polite society and theorists will tell you that there is no need for
troops to become lousy. All I can suggest is that they try to live
under similar conditions themselves. Stripped to the buff and sitting
round the poplar girt pool, we ran our thumbs up and down all the seams
of our clothing with successful results. Occasionally an extra fine
specimen would be exhibited to one's neighbours and a mild rivalry
would ensue.

We had sixty men sleeping on the ground floor of the Brewery;
the windows were boarded up and the walls plentifully perforated
with shell holes. The floor was covered with dirty straw and mice
and spiders considered they had established a prior right to the
building and resented our presence, actively shewing their disapproval
of our invasion. The building was shelled on and off the whole time

we were there. The men slept and were still tired; they ate and were still hungry.

We thought that we had left the trenches for a rest but soon discovered our mistake when we left our billets at 6p.m. and marched 4 miles to dig trenches, returning after midnight. Our road took us through Plug Street, on our left as we went a particularly gorgeous sunset threw into vigorous relief trees and a windmill and a church spire; on our right one of our aeroplanes was being shelled, a graceful birdlike figure surrounded by puffs of smoke.

After two miles of the main road we turned off to the left and went through Bois de la Hutte, a beautiful wood where the troops had made themselves jolly log huts which looked like Swiss chalets in the glorious white blossom of the trees. The wood was thick with crosses and graves. We passed some lodge gates and went up a long drive which led us up a steep incline to a ruined chateau, outlined against the sunset. All but the outer walls had been destroyed. There were evidences of loving care about the gardens and I idly wondered whether they had once been the pride of some stately old French aristocrat, or the joy and delight of some young married couple; now it was only a symbol of this transitory life: tout casse, tout lasse, tout passe.

We passed along what had evidently been another drive and turning to the right went along a road literally torn with shell fire. Again we turned to the left and entered a field strewn with the wreckage of a past battle and here we had to dig support trenches. We were under direct fire from the German trenches but were hidden by the darkness. The stench of the soil and the unmistakeable odour of the battlefield made me violently sick. As we left on our return journey we noticed a glow in the sky to the north which grew redder and redder as we gazed. This was Ypres burning.

On the 23rd. April we went to Pont Nieppe for baths. Troops in the trenches suffer much from vermin, as has already been hinted, and in their periods of rest are given baths and clean linen in exchange for their underclothes. Their uniforms are baked whilst the men tub. Of course you did not get your own underclothes back again, and it was largely a matter of chance if those you got were the right size. After marching back to the Brasserie we learnt that we were digging trenches again that night. In a way I was lucky as I was warned for guard that night.

I was on duty with Mordy, Newman and Nicholls. It was bitterly cold and our guardroom was just an open archway. We had a busy time. All passers-by had to be halted and streams of Belgian peasants were passing along to dig trenches at La Hutte and Ypres. These civilians had a pass with their photograph signed by the Mayor and countersigned by a British officer. I was thankful when I was relieved at 2p.m., but my thankfulness abated somewhat when I learned that we had to parade again at 6p.m. for trench digging.

We returned at 1a.m. absolutely dead beat. The men were staggering along in full kit, reeling like the drunken men they were, drunk with exhaustion and want of sleep.

These men have earnt for themselves imperishable glory by their daily self-sacrifice. Heroism does not consist of the

throwing up of life's responsibilities in a gallant charge or in
the heat of battle, but in that wonderful daily giving of their
all, with the sure knowledge that the same will be required of
them each to-morrow as long as the war lasts. Under certain
conditions it is comparatively easy to behave gallantly. Most of
suffer occasionally from heroic impulses, but the daily task and
constant recurring hardship was not so easy to bear.

All honour to the men who stuck it; it was truly wonderful.
What was it that Kipling wrote ?

> If you can force your heart and nerve and sinew
> To serve your turn long after they have gone,
> And so hold on when there is nothing in you
> Except the will which says to them "Hold on".-

I have been so tired that every nerve in my body has been twitching;
I have fallen asleep when marching and have awakened to find myself
lying on the ground during a halt; I have marched until I could see
nothing but the head of the man in front of me going round and
round, until my throat was so dry that I thought it would have
cracked, when every vein in my hands and feet have swollen painfully
almost to bursting point, and often I have had to bite my lips and
my hands until they have bled in order to keep myself awake on duty.

On the 25th. of April we went up to our trenches again.
One of our chief troubles was the bringing up of supplies. Simple
folk at home tell you of the Army Service Corps who risk their lives
once a day to bring up rations to the troops who spend every minute
of the day perpetually under fire. The work is done by the Battalion
Transport Section who fetch the supplies from the Brigade Dump many
miles behind the danger zone. They bring the food up as near as they
can to the firing line and are there met by ration carrying parties
on foot, furnished from the men in the trenches. At Plug Street
timber, barbed wire, coke and food had to be carried a mile and a
half over open fields under machine gun fire to the firing trench.
Owing to the necessity of dropping to the ground whenever a star shell
or search light picked us out, our journey used to take us anything
from three to six hours. Search lights and machine guns work together
and the one follows the other as sure as night follows day.

At first all our water had to be carried - in petrol tins-
from the same place, the pump was at the Dressing Station, until one
day a man found a pump in the convent garden just behind our trenches.
High glee all round, but the Germans heard the squeaking of the pump
and we were met with a storm of bullets. This was the identical pump
immortalised by Bairnsfather. On the following night we fixed a
length of stolen hosepipe to lead from the pump to the trench itself
where we had made a reservoir so that only one man need expose himself
to the attentions of the Bosche machine guns. The orderly corporal
did the pumping, and for this tour of duty in the trenches I was the
orderly corporal. I have never really fancied water since !

It is interesting to note that the Germans first used gas at
this time and although we had only a slight whiff of it, highly
unpleasant it was. Of course gas masks, shrapnel helmets, and bombs
were quite unknown at that period.

I had a stiff attack of dysentery and was doubled up with pain.
I ascribed it to the natural revulsion of the stomach against the
eternal dead German. On the 29th. I felt really very bad and just
crawled about until Major Baker sent me to lie down. An hour later
he came along and sitting on the edge of my dugout said "It's a
shame to disturb you, Nash, but I have brought you some physic",
and he handed me a wire from Battalion Headquarters saying that I
had been granted a commission and was to report to them at once.
At the moment I was too ill to want anything but sleep, so asked
permission to go down on the following day. I slept until 9p.m.
when I had supper with Major Baker. The next morning after many
touching farewells with the men of my section I made my way out of
the trenches back to Headquarters, fully expecting a bullet to stop
my happy journey.

I have avoided all reference to our own casualties but will quote
just one day's entry from my diary.

"April 27th. Pounds was shot through the head at dawn and Voisey
later. Both are dead. I stumbled against Voisey wrapped up in a
blanket, waiting in a corner of C Company's Headquarters until the
body can be got back. More trouble this afternoon; a German shell
burst in Happy Valley wounding five men. Badman has since died and
Corporal Chapman and Granfield are in a critical condition."

Laden with my kit, I reported to Captain Rawson the Adjutant.
He was later appointed to the command of the 12th. Gloucesters and
did well. He told me that actually two Commissions had come for me.
In the one I had been appointed to the 3rd. Gloucesters and in the
other to the 16th. (1st. City) Battalion of the Manchester Regiment.
Colonel Davenport told me that he would like to keep me in the
Battalion as an officer and would do so if I accepted the commission
in the Gloucesters. I felt however that it would place me in an
invidious position to hold a commission in the same battalion as I
had served as a private, and chose to go to the Manchesters.

He told me then that I should have to return to England at once
and report there as my new Battalion had not yet gone overseas, but
as I was needed to give evidence in a court martial on the next day
I had luncheon with Captain Clarke, the Medical Officer, and then
paid my last visit to Plug Street wood in company with Sid Davis who
was the M.O.'s orderly. The Battalion came out of the trenches and
we all marched to Nieppe. We spent the night in an empty laundry.

The Court Martial assembled at 10 a.m. the next morning and I
gave my evidence after which I made my adieux and went to the railhead
at Bailleul which I left at 5 p.m. I reached the port of Boulogne
twelve hours later and got home at8 p.m. on the same night.

This is the end of my story as far as it concerns No. 2571
Lance Corporal Nash. I have never regretted the eight months I
spent in the ranks and I am prouder of having learnt my job as a
soldier before becoming an officer than of anything I have ever done.
I gained many friends and much experience. I enjoyed the fellowship
that hardship and danger created among men of very different stations
in life. Eight months' discomfort was a small price to pay for the
love and understanding of my fellow men that I gained during that
period.

Of my old room-mates at Danbury Young, Shepherd, Dunsford and Davies obtained commissions. All except Dunsford I know to have been killed. Best and Penny received their discharge as medically unfit.

Captain Rawson commanded Bristol's Own Battalion later on, after first going to the Argyll and Sutherland Highlanders. Major Baker was given a Staff appointment. Mansell transferred to the Flying Corps and Savile was killed. Requiescant in pace.

L ' E N V O I .

Under the lee of the little wood
I'm sitting in the sun;
What will be done in Flanders
Before the day be done ?

Under my feet the springing blades
Are green as green can be;
It's the bloody clay of Flanders
That keeps them green for me.

Above, beyond the larches
The sky is very blue;
It's the smoke of hell in Flanders
That leaves the sun for you.

By nests in the blossoming elm tree
The wise rooks caw on bough;
What blasts of hell in Flanders
Rive the bared branches now ?

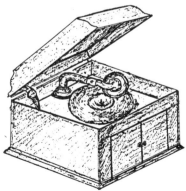

The Gramophone brought out to France and mentioned on page 43.

England again. Training at Grantham. Salisbury Plain. France.

A year ago were love and mirth,
And youth's gay careless flow;
For him flamed life in all its ardent worth,
A year ago.

Love came with her enchanting glow
And doubly blest his happy birth;
Yet those the gods love.........
Well we know !

Beneath a nameless mound of earth
He lies, where daisies grow,
Leaving a void in hearts that knew no dearth,
A year ago.

My first act on landing at Folkestone was to telegraph to the
Adjutant of my new Battalion for ten days leave. Then I made my way
home, arriving at Lapworth in the evening. I was still coated with
trench mud from Flanders and, as they told me later, smelt most
abominably of dead Germans. I put on my new uniform and on May 4th.
heard that my application for leave had been granted so went down to
Bristol and looked up the relatives of many of my comrades in the
Gloucesters.

On the 13th. of May I went up to Manchester to report for duty
at Heaton Park, and found that the Battalion itself had been moved to
Grantham but had left behind a large number of officers and men to
form the nucleus of a new Battalion under the command of Colonel
Ledward. I was received cordially by the officers; among these
were Sir William Geary, Cunliffe, Clayton, Prestwich MacDonnel,
Calvert and Dowling. I had shewn sufficient low cunning to report
without any kit, so had to get another weekend leave to collect
this from Warwickshire.

The troops were lodged in huts and were very well cared for;
they slept on paliasses and bed boards, and had separate rooms for
meals and recreation. They had hot and cold shower baths and
plenty of good food. The officers' quarters were most comfortable
and we each had a small room furnished with a bed and a stove,
an easy chair and a bookshelf. On the whole we had a most excellent
time. I was only at Heaton Park for two weeks; by that time I had
satisfied Colonel Ledward that I was competent to go on to my
Battalion as a Platoon Commander.

I found it an immense advantage to know my job without having
to submit to the indignity of learning it from an N.C.O. It had
always been a fad of mine to start from the bottom, and whereas

if I had been content to hang about in England a little longer
I could have got a commission from the start instead of joining
up in the ranks, I have never regretted the eight months I had in
the Army as a private soldier. The advantage of knowing my job
and of having actually seen active service gave me a good standing
with my men from the first.

I reported at Grantham and was given command of No. 16 Platoon
of D Company of the 16th. (1st. City) Battalion of the Manchester
Regiment. Colonel Crawford was commanding the Battalion at that
time, with General Westrop as Brigadier and Colonel Petrie as
Brigade Major. Major Comyns was the second in command of the Bn.
and Captain Sotham the Adjutant.

The Battalion was lodged in huts built in the grounds of
Belton Park, the estate of Lord Brownlow. I was delighted with my
men who were smart and intelligent and proved excellent material
to work upon. Sergeant Hawxby was my platoon sergeant and a sterling
fellow, most loyal and conscientious and ever my very good friend.
My batman was Private Hibbert G.F. and he remained with me in that
capacity until I was wounded. He was a delightfully sunny lad and
rendered me devoted service.

The troops had been training since the outbreak of war and were
desperately keen to get to France. They had been recruited mainly
from the offices and warehouses of Manchester and there was a tremendous
camaraderie amongst them. We were known as the First Pals Battalion.
Nearly all the officers were public school men and were a perfectly
ripping crowd of men.

During the summer of 1915 we went through very much the same
training as I had done before, but the conditions of life were very
much more comfortable for the men. We had a jolly good concert
party and had a merry time when the day's work was done. We knew too
that an officer's first care was to look after his men, and after a
long march or heavy field day no one of us thought of going to his
own quarters until the men were comfortably settled.

I spent my spare time cycling about the country with S.R.Allen,
who commanded 14 Platoon and who had come back from Ypres; and
motoring with Captain Johnson who was the second in command of my
Company. Allen and I had much in common, both having seen active
service, and Johnson kept a friendly eye on me and laid the foundation
of one of the deepest friendships I have ever formed.

The Mess formed the most delightful collection of fellows you
could find in a week's march. All the officers had been specially
selected by Colonel Crawford. He afterwards went out to command
the 1st. Manchesters and Colonel Petrie D.S.O. took on the Battalion
while Montgomery took his place as Brigade Major. They were very
pleasant days at Grantham.

On September 6th. 1915, the Battalion moved to Lark Hill Camp on
Salisbury Plain. I motored down with Johnson in his six cylinder
Sunbeam and he went through Kettering, Northampton and Oxford, where
we lunched at the Mitre. At Lark Hill we found ourselves in huts
similar to those at Grantham; the air was bracing but the Plain in
those days presented a depressing spectacle. The camps stretched as
far as eye could see and it was impossible to get out of the way of

khaki. From the camp we could see Stonehenge; the dawn and sunset
effects were very beautiful. While here I cycled to Bristol and also
through Savernake Forest.

In the way of work we did field operations ad lib and firing on
the ranges; this latter was a very tedious job. Major Comyns had been
posted to another Battalion and we suffered the loss with equanimity.
Major Kempster took his place, a nice old chap.Then came the forerunners
of our departure. Identity discs, first field dressings and iron
rations were issued and in the middle of October I was granted final
leave. Whilst away I sprained my ankle badly and was in agonies of
apprehension lest I should be left behind.

I had considerable difficulty in reducing my kit to the thirty five
pounds in weight allowed by regulation. I had still to learn that the
less baggage one has, the less one wants, and that a soldier's comfort
in the field is in converse proportion to the amount of kit he carries.

Before we left Lark Hill the officers of the Battalion were
photographed and I collected all their signatures on an autograph cloth
which I value immensely. I was awfully chaffed about this same cloth,
and must have had considerable courage to do needlework in Mess.

Colonel Petrie, Major Kempster (brother of General Kempster
commanding the 91st. Brigade), Captain Sotham the Adjutant, Captain
Fletcher, Medical Officer, Lieut. Morris Machine Gun Officer,
Lieut. Megson Signals, Lieut. Wilson Transport, Lieut. Ball Quartermaster
and the Revd. R.W. Balleine formed Battalion Headquarters Staff. We were
in the 90th. Infantry Brigade, commanded by General Stevenson.

In A Company :	Captain Worthington	B Company :	Captain Walker
	Captain Elstob		Captain Payne
	Lieuts. Mead		Lieuts. Oliver
	Phillips		Behrens
	Hook		Rhodes
	Slack		Percy
	Henriques		
C Company :	Captain Roberts	D Company :	Captain Greg
	Lieuts. Davidson		Captain Johnson
	Gibbons		Lieuts. Dalgleish
	Knowles		Allen
	Barber		Nash

On November 9th. 1915, we left Amesbury and embarked at Folkestone
at midday. My holiday in England was over and I went back to France
for the second time, very keen and happy in the command of a thoroughly
good platoon. I was the junior subaltern of my Battalion and promotion
would be a long time coming my way but my latest report from Bn. H.Q. to
the War Office had been that, "This officer is extremely capable, self-
dependant and conscientious", so I felt very bucked with life.

We were escorted across the Channel by a destroyer and an airship
and on the way over we saw a half submerged dirigible which had capsized.
And so on the 9th. day of November 1915 did the 16th. Manchesters
come to France.

The Author as the most junior subaltern of the
16th. Battalion Manchester Regiment, D Company,
16th. Platoon; but not the most inexperienced.

Chapter Six.

Boulogne to Hebuterne, and the Fourth Gloucesters again.

> For all we have and are,
> For all our childrens' fate,
> Stand up and meet the War,
> The Hun is at the Gate !
> Our world has passed away,
> In wantoness o'erthrown;
> There's nothing left to-day
> But steel and fire and stone.
>
> Once more we hear the word
> That sickened earth of old;
> No law except the sword,
> Unsheathed and uncontrolled.
> Once more it knits mankind,
> Once more the nations go,
> To meet and break and bind
> A crazed and driven foe.
>
> Comfort, content, delight -
> The ages' slow-bought gain,
> They shrivelled in a night,
> Only ourselves remain;
> To face the naked days
> In silent fortitude,
> Through perils and dismays
> Renewed and re-renewed.
>
> Though all we made depart
> The old commandments stand;
> In patience keep your heart;
> In strength lift up your hand.
>
> NO EASY HOPES OR LIES
> Shall bring us to our goal,
> But iron sacrifice
> Of body, will and soul.
> There is one task for all -
> For each one life to give -
> Who stands if Freedom fall ?
> Who dies if England live ?

We landed at Boulogne and I found myself climbing that same hill up to Oesterhove Camp. Remembering my previous experience I was not surprised at the number of men who fell out on the way up. It was still daylight and we received quite a cordial reception from the French people. No preparations had been made at the Camp for our arrival and we had to do the best we could towards feeding the men. After seeing them comfortably bedded down after some grub, we went to find something to eat for ourselves.

We all had a meal together in the Salvation Army Hut which was
the only place where we could get either tea or food. Here we had
sardines and biscuits and tea, after which we went to bed. I shared
a tent with Megson, Allen and Dalgleish, and I fear we were all
somewhat tired and cross.

Reveille was at 6a.m. and during the morning Johnson and I
got leave to go into town. We had luncheon at the Meurice and
drove back to camp in a fiacre. It rained nearly all day and at
7p.m. the Battalion set off for the Gare Centrale where we entrained.

After seven hours in cattle trucks we reached Pont Remy, not far
from Abbeville and from here we started at 2a.m. to march in the rain
to Saint Riquier where we arrived at 6.30 a.m., very cold and wet and
tired. Morris and the Interpreter had been sent forward to find billets
for us but had not expected us so soon. We had much difficulty in
waking up the inhabitants and finding our quarters. By 8.30 a.m.
however the troops were all in and I went off to my own billet with
a very nasty attack of asthma. I was lodged with M.Detuncq, the
village blacksmith. He was very nice to me while I remained at Saint
Riquier. I found my knowledge of French still very useful in getting
extra comforts both for my platoon and for myself.

The Colonel sent me into Abbeville to get English money changed
into francs and I had a very pleasant ride and a good meal into the
bargain. Abbeville was about six miles away. The Battle of Crecy
had been fought quite near St. Riquier. There was a good Expeditionary
Force Canteen also at Abbeville where I was able to buy tobacco and
cigarettes for the men. Barber rode in with me.

On the 12th. we went for a route march and saw a wonderful rainbow,
marching right through it as it happened to end just on the road
through which we passed. I remembered the title of a play I had seen
before the war, "Where the rainbow ends", and was rather pleased to
find myself actually where it did. You, my reader, whoever you may be,
will have found many sloppy and sentimental references in these pages;
I want you to realise how much a sense of romance helped one to carry
on and to preserve one's sanity under totally abnormal conditions.
To lose a friend by a natural death in the piping times of peace is no
light matter. To lose one's intimate associates one after the other
by every kind of painful violence, to witness their dying agony, and
to know that in every probability your only escape is to meet a similar
fate, well that is just hell - unless you can adapt your mind to
present circumstances, and take what comfort you can from foolish things
like the picturesque side of war. Half the poor gibbering maniacs who
came home with shell shock or nerves would never have got into that
state if they could have found relief in the small things that yet are
so big, a glorious sunset, the moonlight gleaming on the fixed bayonets
in the trenches, the unconquerable supremacy of mind over matter.

On the 13th. I was Orderly Officer and on Sunday I took Slack
into Abbeville to find a dentist. As he could not ride we drove
in the Mess-Cart, a painfully slow business.

In France we messed by Companies, that is to say that the
Battalion Mess was split up and the officers of each Company lived
together. At this place D Company had found a very poor place to
feed in, a disused cafe at the top of the village. Ordinary routine

work carried us on till November 17th. when we left St. Riquier in a heavy snowstorm on our way up to the firing line. My asthma was much worse and I had difficulty in getting along with a full pack. After a tiring march we halted at Brucamps, a very poor village where we spent the night. The next day we continued our march to Villiers Bocage; I travelled in a motor ambulance as I was too weak to march and therefore arrived before the Battalion. We had trouble with the Transport as the roads were very bad indeed.

Johnson had been sent on to do the billetting and I went round with him on his search for quarters.

Villers Bocage was a dirty little village and all the best billets had been bagged by the Army Service Corps and the Royal Army Medical Corps. We had the greatest difficulty in finding room for the Troops and the inhabitants made matters worse by meeting us with protests, complaints, and discourtesy. After infinite pains we found shelter for all the men and for all the officers except four. There still remained homeless Johnson, Greg, Fletcher and myself. Johnson as usual had left himself until last. It was already dark, and every mousehole had been commandeered.

In desperation we went to the one very dirty cafe the village possessed, where after a little persuasion they said we might all four sleep on the floor of the billiard room. We accepted with gratitude. We all had flea-bags, as we termed our sleeping bags and the continental bed with its damp sheets, musty hangings and feather mattresses upon which generations of people had died and thousands of living creatures still exist was a thing to be cheerfully dispensed with.

We climbed some very rickety stairs which were twisted as if in pain, and found ourselves in the billiard room. One large table was in the centre of the room, a bed in an alcove was covered with dirty red and white counterpanes, two more doors and two large windows which would not open, overlooking the market place, completed the scene. We sent for our valises and went downstairs to get some food. By this time we were all semi-hysterical with hunger and fatigue, it being twelve hours since we had had any food.

The cafe had only just been closed for the night and again only Hogarth could have done justice to the scene. The air was redolent of stale tobacco and drink; dirty plates and overturned glasses littered the disordered tables; the floor was dirtier than the street outside; the gas flared viciously as if delighting in the sordid spectacle it illumined and from the big fireplace came the fat greasy noisome smell of the family's evening meal. Behold la Patrone herself, a hugely fat figure tightly clad in a sort of black bombazine, with beady eyes that looked as if they could never sleep. Her feet were hidden by her dress but carried that immense bulk at a wonderfully quick rate. She seemed to move like a clockwork figure with no visible motive power.

Madame's daughter was there too, a black eyed damsel of eighteen, handsome enough but with every promise of developing exactly her mother's figure in a few years' time. She looked jaded and unwashed, and her laugh rang hard as she talked to an habitue of the place, a young civilian lounging at the bar counter. Two Belgian refugees, an old man and a boy, cowered over the fire and the waitress, a strong looking farm wench with untidy hair, dirty face and appalling boots cleared one of the long trestle tables for us, wiping off the more removable dirt with a filthy rag, and we sat down. Megson, Wilson and Allen came to join us.

The girl brought us some coffee, a little bread which reminded me vaguely of cider, and some butter that was frankly rancid. Ten minutes later she produced a tin of sardines and after another long pause some beans simply swimming in grease. We begged for some meat; we were hungry and would pay anything she liked but we wanted some food. In response to our entreaty she brought us a mottled slab of meat with a thick layer of solid grease on top. This she called galantine of pork. Fletcher was Medical Officer to the Battalion and after a rapid post mortem examination he said it resembled Nature's rejection of the chosen meal of a foul-feeding dog. (He did not spare our feelings and I do not see why I should spare yours !). This completed our uneaten, untouched dinner.

By this time we were uproarious with laughter. The family's meal was over - and Lord knows what they had been eating - and they began to prepare for bed. With utmost gravity the old man and boy took up the farthest trestle table and with solemn gait and mien stalked across the room with it past us and then disappeared through a door which we thought was a cupboard. They returned and repeated the performance with the next table. This time their slow pace and funereal bearing proved too much for our hysterical state of mind, and as the second long table was borne past us, we with one accord rose gravely and bowed our heads until the corpse had gone by !

We left the family to themselves and bidding them good-night we mounted the narrow stairs. So little had I liked the cut-throat appearance of our hosts that I loaded my revolver and slipped it under my pillow as I undressed and crawled into my flea-bag. The Doctor insisted on sleeping on the billiard table. I think he was wise; there were no flies on Fletcher, and I think he had determined that there should be nothing else alien on him if he could help it.

No sooner had we composed ourselves for slumber and put out our candle than we heard a creak on the staircase. I lifted myself upon one elbow and the hair slowly rose on the back of my head as I saw the door opening gradually. I clutched my revolver and waited. Very slowly the enormous figure of la Patrone heaved itself into the room and scurried across the floor and through a door on the other side, covered had she but known it by four lethal weapons, for I discovered to my amusement that my companions had taken the same precautions as myself. The four of us then sat up to await further developments. The doorway over the stairs opened again and four French soldiers in full regimentals marched across the room, followed by a bullet-headed youngster in a smock and noisy boots. By this time we realised that the entire household would pass through our room to get to their own quarters.

At intervals until far into the night appeared la Patrone's daughter, the two refugees, the waitress, a youth stupidly like Charlie Chaplin, the landlord, another very old woman who wheezed and grunted at every step, and finally an old man with a foolish and wobbly nose, bleary eyes and unsatisfactory grey hair, who came into the room like an arrow from the bow, collided with the billiard table, cannoned onto the wall, spun round twice and struck off through the other door. He was the last to pass and his gyrations were made the more amusing by the fact that he held firmly in his hand a certain article of toilet-ware that is not mentioned in polite society. We laughed ourselves to sleep and even then were disturbed by Greg's chortlings all through the night.

The bells ringing for Mass disturbed us next morning and we prepared to watch last night's procession re-pass before trying to dress. The fat old woman was the first to go down and was followed by the French poilus; then came the others, looking as if they had slept in their clothes. When we thought they had all gone through we stood on our beds and began to dress. The floor was so disgustingly filthy that had we seen it by daylight we should never have had the courage to sleep there. We dressed in safety except for Greg, who was put to confusion by the entrance of one damsel while he was still in short-drawers, those cellular things with a blue edge round the ends. He dived for his flea bag, but all too late as Mademoiselle said with a smile "Monsieur ne doit pas se gener, moi, je les porte aussi".

We managed to get a less exciting billet during the day and found quite a good room for Mess. Wilson and myself were lodged chez Madame Faucaert, a dear old soul who made excellent chocolate. We slept upon stone floors; but they were clean.

On the 20th. of November I paid my first visit to Amiens and had tea with Major Kempster at the Hotel du Rhin, a hostelry much frequented by A.S.C. officers.

We did bayonet fighting and bombing practice until the 28th. when we left the village and proceeded via Naours, Havernas and Canaples to Bonneville, a most inaptly named village twelve miles nearer the front. Here we found that the billets were even worse than those we had left behind. My first lodging was a little room which was simply streaming with moisture and only separated from a cowshed by a thin plaster wall. I moved to a slightly better one, which I shared with Wilson, at the other end of the village.

We continued work under Company arrangements and the men had quite a jolly stay here. I organised several concerts for my folk and Johnson and I were on a few wood-cutting fatigues together in the Bois de Canaples.

Rhodes and Henriques fell ill here and were sent home, without even seeing the German trenches. One I met in England later on when I was recovering from a wound. He was delighting a group with the story of his episodes in the trenches and collapsed when he saw me sitting at the other end of the room.

On December 7th. we left Bonneville and marched to Couin to spend the night there in a sea of mud. Here Major Kempster fell ill, and was sent to a job at the Base. After a year away from the Battalion he left the Army. He had been employed at Etaples. His brother was General Kempster, a fine old soldier with a good record.

At Couin we were within sound of the firing line. The tents were in poor condition and we all got very wet. We were going up to the trenches with another Brigade for instructional purposes and funnily enough my own old Battalion, the Fourth Gloucesters, formed part of that Brigade and I was to find them in the trenches.

On the 8th. of December we left Couin and marched through Sailly
le Bois to Hebuterne. This was popularly supposed to be a very quiet
spot, but whether through a blunder on the part of our guide or
mistaken instructions we marched up almost to the village in column
of route, and the Germans spotted us and started a vigorous bombardment
during which Lieutenant Behrens was our first casualty and lost his leg.
Mead was slightly hit and seven men of our Battalion badly wounded.
It was a bad beginning for a raw Battalion and after I had got my own
platoon under cover I went out to help with the wounded. In all thirty
five men were badly damaged during the shelling.

A First Field Dressing Station is worth a brief description.
The one at Hebuterne was slightly below the level of the ground,
being approached by seven steps down from the road outside.
It was a cellar in a demolished house. It was badly lit by a hurricane
lamp suspended from the ceiling. In the centre stood a rough deal table
under the flickering light; on this table were placed in turn the
wounded. Two doctors with their tunics off and shirt sleeves rolled up
were working with quick desperation on each case as it was placed on
the table. The perspiration was streaming from them. Whenever a shell
burst near the cellar outside the force of the concussion put the light
out. There were rows of stretcher cases awaiting attention, some were
brought in only to be covered with a blanket and carried out again to
await burial. Groups of walking wounded were also awaiting their turn.
The smell of mingled blood and anaesthetic pervaded the atmosphere.
On the whole there was not much noise beyond the exploding shells
outside, but just occasionally the pain would be too much for some
hard pressed soul in torment. A little of that atmosphere soon helped
me to realise that I was back at the Front once again. Curiously
enough the first two men of my old Gloucester pals I met were Corporal
Rex and Sid Davis who came to help me carry a wounded man to the
Dressing Station.

In the evening I went into the trenches to see Shepherd and
Captain Lewis, my old company commander. He had quite obviously
had enough of war and I was not surprised to hear later on that he
had got home. The next day I went round the front line trenches
with Balleine, our Padre, and very filthy we found them. We went up
by way of the Serre Road and turned in by the Fifth Barricade.
The mud and rain were waist deep. I called in to see Parkinson,
who had taken Rawson's place as Adjutant of the 4th.

My platoon was detailed to go in with D Company of the 8th.
Worcesters, commanded by Captain Clarke. He was very kind to my men
and when we got back to Bonneville I sent him a cheque with which to
buy some cigarettes for his men as a Christmas offering from mine.
He wrote back very appreciatively.

The men were provided with thigh boots from the Keep, and went
up to the trenches in the evening. These thigh boots would be very
comfortable if only they could be put on dry and if it were possible
to get a pair of the same size; generally speaking you had either to
have two right hand boots of the same size or a left and right of
different sizes. We found that there were no dugouts and the sentries
had to be posted on the parapet instead of in the trench as the trenches
were all waterlogged. It was not a cheerful night for my poor platoon,

but at 5p.m. on the 10th. we came out to our billets until 4.30p.m. on the following day when we went back to the same trenches.

During the night I was visiting sentries with my orderly Cummings and came across a man off duty sleeping on the firestep with a waterproof sheet thrown over him. Not wishing to disturb him I said jokingly to Cummings "Don't touch the corpse, old chap". Two hours later I discovered Sergeant Hawxby and a burying party looking for the body Cummings had said we had found, and which of course had come to life in the meantime and gone on duty !

On the 12th. we left the trenches again and I cleaned up and went to dinner with the Headquarters Mess of the 4th. Gloucesters. Curiously enough the sentry on duty outside Battalion Headquarters that night was my old friend Best. Colonel Davenport was still in command, Rawson had gone to command a battalion of the Argyll and Sutherland Highlanders. Major Thompson had bought some marrons glaces in Doullens which were very nice. He went home soon afterwards, but not on account of the marrons glaces.

On the 13th. we went into the trenches again. This in and out business was very trying but owing to the appallingly wet state of the line the troops had to be relieved frequently. While we were in this time Greg and Captain Clarke were sitting in the Company Headquarters dugout when one of our Manchester lads appeared at the top of the slippery steps leading into the dugout, proudly carrying an unexploded shell rather gingerly in his hands. Had he slipped and dropped it we should all have gone to perdition. It was explained to him in forcible language that dud shells like sleeping dogs are best left undisturbed.

Now was the time for Balleine the Padre to come into his own. In England he had seemed rather a wash-out but here we saw him in his true colours. Day after day he went round the front line sniped at and shelled like the rest of us but never turning a hair. His pockets bulged with packets of cigarettes for the troops and he had a cheery word for everyone. Again and again he was to prove himself to be one of the bravest men in the Battalion.

I dislike to hear anyone generalising on the subject of Army Chaplains. I have met many, some very good, others very bad. There was a fair example of the rotten sort in a chaplain who was attached to one Battalion in England; this priest because he was in khaki and wore three stars on the shoulder straps of his tunic adopted a thoroughly arrogant attitude, browbeating men if they failed to spring to attention when he spoke to them and while trying to exact the respect shewn to His Majesty's uniform behaved very little like an officer, was less of a gentleman and nothing at all of a priest. Others I met in France who lacked courage and others who in trying to acquit themselves like men fell to the level of beasts. On the other hand there were some really splendid chaplains who gained the respect and affection of all ranks. The greatest of the many handicaps we placed upon our ministers of religion was to put them in khaki and give them officer rank.

On December 14th. we left the trenches at dawn and marched through Jena trench to Authie-St-Leger. The new troops had stood the test well and won compliments from the high command for their morale.

We had suffered quite enough casualties to bring it home to us all
that we were no longer playing at soldiers. On the 15th. of December
we reached Bonneville again and were glad of the respite. It had
been delightful to see so many of my old pals again during our trial
trip in the trenches. We had not long to wait for the real thing.

Two of my Father's friends - Capt. R.E. Roberts
commanded 'C' Company and became 2 i/c of the
Battalion and C.O. briefly in October 1917.
He died of his wounds on 21/3/18 at Rouen.

Lt. R. Megson agreed to be godfather to my
Father's second born child. He died four
years before this - killed in action 23/4/17.

Ed.

Chapter Seven.

Christmas at Bonneville. From there to the Somme. Maricourt.

> They take my man and give me a dole
> That so I may be fed;
> But they do not pay for the heavy toll
> They take from the love and peace of my soul
> As I brood and pray he may not be dead.
>
> They take my son and add to the price
> That so I may be clad;
> But they do not pay for the grip of the vice
> That clamps my heart with a ring of ice
> As I brood and pray for my man and his lad.
>
> O bring them back, tho they both be blind
> And halt, and must be fed.
> Not a word I'll say that is not kind
> And till the end I will not mind
> How I work and pray if they be not dead.

On the march back from the trenches Captain Payne fell ill and was sent into hospital when we reached Bonneville. He was our sixth officer casualty. On the 17th. I borrowed a pony and rode over to Doullens to see Major Baker who was then on the Staff and very resplendent in red tabs and gold braid. He was very fit and jolly and gave me a good tea. On the next day I rode into Beauval to see Behrens but his father had just arrived from England and I felt I ought to leave him a clear field. Behrens lost his leg and had a succession of operations, each amputation higher than the one before.

Morris was attached to Brigade Headquarters as Lewis Gun Officer, and Gibbon took over the Battalion Lewis Guns. Knowles and myself were trained as understudies for him. It was rather fascinating work.

A Special Order of the Day was published on the 18th. of December by Sir John French in which he bade good-bye to the troops on returning to the Home Command. The text of the message will be found upon the following page.

On Christmas Eve we had a concert and the village cafes were allowed to keep open later than usual, with the result that some of the men became mildly hilarious. The concert went off very well and I still have the programme. Palmer sang "Shipmates o' Mine" and Hughes gave us "Two Eyes of Grey". The troops always liked sentimental songs the best. We had managed to smuggle out to France the Battalion Band instruments and so were able to keep the band going. For some stupid reason we were not supposed to have a Battalion band.

At about eleven o'clock we all went to bed feeling rather tired and wondering how many more Christmas Eves we should see.

SPECIAL ORDER OF THE DAY.

By Field Marshal Sir J.D.P. French, G.C.B., O.M., G.C.V.O., K.C.M.G.,
Commander-in-Chief, British Army in the Field.

In relinquishing the Command of the British Army in France
I wish to express to the Officers, Non-Commissioned Officers and
Men, with whom I have been so closely associated during the last
sixteen months, my heartfelt sorrow in parting with them before
the Campaign, in which we have been so long engaged together, has
been brought to a victorious conclusion.

I have however the firmest conviction that such a glorious
ending to their splendid and heroic efforts is not far distant,
and I shall watch their progress towards this final goal with
intense interest, but in the most confident hope.

The success so far attained has been due to the indomitable
spirit, dogged tenacity which knows no defeat, and the heroic
courage so abundantly displayed by the rank and file of the
splendid Army which it will ever remain the pride and glory of my
life to have commanded for over sixteen months of incessant
fighting. Regulars and Territorials, Old Army and New Army have
ever shewn these magnificent qualities in equal degree. From my
heart I thank them all.

At this sad moment of parting my heart goes out to those who
have received life-long injury from wounds, and I think with
sorrow of that great and glorious host of my beloved comrades who
have made the greatest sacrifice of all by laying down their lives
for their country. In saying Good-bye to the British Army in France
I ask them once again to accept this expression of my deepest
gratitude and heartfelt devotion towards them, and my earnest good
wishes for the glorious future which I feel to be assured.

(signed) J.D.P. French,

Field Marshal,

Commanding-in-Chief the British Army in France.

18th. December 1915.

At half past eleven on the night of Christmas Eve 1915, a fire
broke out at No. 15 Platoon's billet, and the Alarm was sounded.
The cause of the fire was never discovered but its effect was to
arouse the entire Battalion to put it out. There was only a very
old hand fire engine in the village and this had to be filled with
buckets of water passed up by a living chain from the nearest pond.

The inhabitants insisted on interfering and created a certain
amount of confusion during which someone wiped out a grudge against
the Battalion Interpreter by dropping a brick on his head and one
gay lad turned the hose on to the Mayor of the town, thereby giving
him the first bath he had had for a long time. Knowles did yeoman
work in getting the chickens and pigs out of harm's way. It was
not until noon that we had got the fire really in hand and by that
time we were all very tired and very dirty.

There were innumerable Courts of Enquiry afterwards and the general impression was that the blaze had been started by a match thrown into the straw. As all lights were strictly forbidden in these barns it seems unlikely, and my own idea remains that the fire was purposely started by the owner of the barn in order to secure excessive compensation. The resulting correspondence nearly drove poor old Greg off his head. As Company Commander he was held to be responsible. He was a very wealthy man and offered to pay the damages out of his own pocket, but nothing could stop the ceaseless official chits. I believe it is a fact that he offered to buy the whole damned village; this was to the Brigadier and his offer was not accepted in the spirit it was made.

Johnson, Greg, Megson and myself went to Holy Communion which Balleine celebrated in the village school. Our Christmas dinner was very late; we had ordered a turkey from England but it was too big to get into the funny little ovens beloved of the French so we decided to have a chicken instead. The landlady of our billet offered to sell us one and also to cook it. In due course it appeared on the table and Greg proceeded to carve. He had just started when he exclaimed "Hurray, it's stuffed". But it was not. The lady had omitted to clean the crop. We had sardines for our Christmas dinner instead. It was at Bonneville that we met our Waterloo at the hands of French peasant cuisine. Tiring of Army rations we thought that a rabbit might make a welcome change. The French tame rabbit makes a repulsive dish at the best of times but we thought we would try it. Again our landlady offered to cook it for us. When she set the dish upon the table, there was a large horrible grilled rabbit in the centre, surrounded by six baby rabbits, likewise grilled. She explained the little ones had been overlain and it seemed a pity to waste them. After this we depended on our mess-servant for what food he could provide.

The troops had an extra large meal for Christmas and Greg was in great form. We had quite a cheery day and in spite of the fire thought ourselves very lucky to be out of the trenches.

We now thought it would be a good scheme to buy a gramophone for the Mess, so sent home for a H.M.V. Table Grand machine and seven of us each chose two pounds worth of records. We therefore had a pretty catholic assortment and it was a great boon to us. A few of the records I still have but they naturally suffered from damp and constant packing. Greg, Johnson, Dalgleish, Megson, Allen, Wilson and myself formed the syndicate. Allen chose all grand opera records, Johnson's taste lay with Gilbert and Sullivan, Megson went in for Revues, so that altogether we managed to provide a varied programme.

CHRISTMAS DAY 1915.

O Christ who came when all the world was still,
Dim with the silence of a winter's night,
While through the darkness, hushing weald and hill,
Only your star shone bright.

How can we greet You, whom we count our king
But sweat of death and anguish manifold,
Where princes knelt in lowliness to bring
Myrrh, frankincense and gold?

How can we greet You, save with roar of guns,
Hotmouthed as hell, the sword's tumultous clang,
Screaming of shell that tortures ere it stuns,
You, for whom angels sang ?

But yet we know You will not turn aside
Before our little strife and agony,
Who came, Yourself, that far December-tide
To fight Your fight, - and die.

    Until the end of the month the Battalion was employed in
fatigue work, and Johnson and I spent most of our time
superintending woodcutting parties in the Bois de Canaples. On
January 2nd. we both went to Holy Communion and at 12.40 p.m. the
Battalion marched out of Bonneville on a four days journey. The
men's shoeleather was in a shocking condition and we could not get boots
for love or money. At the end of the first day's trek we reached Talmas.
The next day we got as far as La Houssoye where we all slept in a school
and on January 4th. we reached Etinehem, a little village on the banks
of the Somme. On the following day we marched through Bray and Suzanne
to Maricourt where we took refuge in cellars.

    The village of Maricourt was only three hundred yards from the
front line trenches and was under constant machine gun and shell fire.
Machine guns played down the streets at night and stray rifle shots
inflicted many casualties. We did not go up to the trenches on our
first night there and in the morning I explored the village more
thoroughly.

    The chateau and church were completely destroyed but shewed signs
of having been extremely beautiful. The mosaic floors and wide marble
staircases, the stables with wonderfully ornate state coaches still in
them, all bore token to the prosperity that the chateau had once enjoyed.
Maricourt had been entirely spared by the German guns during its occupation
by the French and there were current well authenticated stories of French
and German officers dining together at the chateau. When the English
took over in August of 1915 those friendly relations came to an end and
business commenced in earnest.

    The Germans shelled the village to bits and when we got there only
the cellars afforded any degree of safe shelter. The Germans had developed
the objectionable habit of opening rapid bursts of concentrated artillery
fire when they were least expected.

    We were now the southernmost English troops and the Divisional
boundary was the north bank of the Somme River. On the right of my
Brigade was the French army. The arrangement in existence for the defence
of the village and trenches was as follows. A Battalion did two days in
the fire trenches, two days in the Maricourt defences, and another two
days in the firing line and then two days rest in Suzanne, a village two
miles back where were our transport lines and Quartermaster Stores.

The main road from Albert to Peronne ran due south of the village.
At the junction with the road from Suzanna stood the Brewery Yard which
served as a dressing station and ration dump. Farther west along the
Albert road was the Napier Redoubt which was used as an engineers' dump.
Opposite the Brewery Yard was an old cafe which served us as Battalion
Headquarters. In School St. was another building which also served as
Battalion Headquarters. The streets of an occupied village were always
renamed for the benefit of the troops; School Street, Church Street,
East Street and so on. On the night of the 6th. of January my Company
took over the trenches immediately north of the Peronne Road.

These trenches seemed even worse than the ones we had left at
Hebuterne. We were still up to our waists in mud and water, and
it was very difficult to get along the trenches at all. Men got stuck
at every step and had to be dragged out by their pals. In two instances
in the 19th. Bn. men were reported as being missing, believed killed,
and no trace of them was found until in a spell of dry weather the
trenches were cleared and the missing men were found drowned in mud.
They had fallen into sump holes from which the trench boards had floated
away and had sunk below the level of the mud. There were one or two
dugouts in fairly good condition and one of these I shared with my
platoon. Rats were all over the place, huge beasts as large as cats
and almost as tame. The Germans were only sixty yards away at the
nearest point and were quite active.

No one at home can conceive the horror of living in mud. In no place
in the trenches was the mud beneath our knees; in most places it was
up to our waists, cold foul liquid mud which trickled over the tops of
our high gum boots, worn up to the thigh, and remained inside chilling
us to the bone. When we sat down in the dugout we sat on mud and had
our feet in a perpetual bath of mud; when we ate our food became covered
with mud, until at the end of two days our clothes and boots and gloves
were full of the foul stuff. It may be imagined how difficult it was to
make one's way down the trench through this thick heavy treacly mud.
We could not pump it out because it was too thick, we could not shovel
it out because it was too liquid, we could not bale it out because it
was too heavy. There was nothing to do but endure it and swear, both
of which we did rather well.

Our greatest difficulty under these conditions was to get the
rations up and to evacuate the wounded. For instance if a man were hit
by a sniper there would be an instant cry for "Stretcher Bearers".
In the ordinary way a wounded man could be carried by one man out of
danger, placed on a stretcher and two stretcher bearers could get him
back to the Dressing Station. With trenches in this condition stretchers
were out of the question, and the mud made the injured man about ten times
the normal weight. I have myself with five other big fellows toiled until
we were soaked with perspiration in pulling in a weedy little fellow that
normally I could have carried under one arm.

We were able to send up hot food at frequent intervals by day and
by night, cooked in the Brewery Yard and carried up to the trenches
in dixies by the platoon ration carriers, three men whose sole duty was
to get hot food up to their mates in the trenches, and this they did
however deep the mud or heavy the firing. We had made wooden yokes
which supported a dixie or camp kettle and were carried each by two men,
resting on the shoulders. The remaining man carried dry rations, bread

or bully beef. These ration carriers were the bravest men in the Battalion. They were consistently shelled but never failed to feed their platoons. Wallace and Bell carried rations for my own platoon.

The way to the trenches from the Brewery Yard was along the Peronne Road for two hundred yards until you came to the Crucifix when you turned off into a communication trench to the right. The road went on and intersected both our front line trenches and those of the Germans. The trees along the roadside had been shelled until few remained. The rest sprawled over the roadway. The road formed the dividing line between two Battalions.

It was a cheerful walk along to the Crucifix on a dark night, with the German machine guns searching the road for relief parties and ration carriers.

It was on this road that I nearly broke my toe by kicking it against something very hard. I bent down and shoved the obstacle into my pocket; I subsequently found it to be the base of a whizz bang shell which now serves me as an ashtray. I was taking up the rum ration to an advanced machine gun post at the time. It was one of our strictest regulations that the rum ration should be issued by an officer.

After two days of this awful mud we were relieved. It took us exactly six hours to get along four hundred yards of trench, so you can imagine what the mud was like.

We eventually got back to the village where we took over the Maricourt Defences. The village was held as a fortified redoubt in case the Bosches broke through.

On the 9th. the Colonel sent me into Amiens to buy food for the various Messes, another instance of the usefulness of being able to speak French. I got up at 4.30 a.m. the next morning, walked into Suzanne where an orderly was awaiting me with two horses. We rode eleven miles to the railhead at Mericourt Ribemont where I caught a train for Amiens reaching there at 9 a.m.

My first care on getting there was to go to the Hotel du Rhin and have a jolly good bath and coffee, rolls, fresh butter, some ham and a glorious omelette. Then I set out to do my shopping. This proved a big job as every officer in the Battalion had given me certain commissions I had luncheon at the Grand Hotel de l'Univers and engaged my room for the night. I went to bed at 8.30 p.m. and slept until 8 a.m. when I rolled lazily over and rang for a cup of chocolate and my bath. I did some more shopping and caught the 3.42 back to the railhead where I found my pony and the Mess Cart to bring back all my purchases. I arrived at Maricourt at 10 p.m. The next day I was sent into Suzanne to find billets for the Battalion. S.R. Allen got leave to go home as his father was very ill and the Colonel told me to take over his job as Intelligence Officer and Officer Commanding the Snipers. From that time onwards I remained on the Staff of Battalion Headquarters until I got my Company and never again comanded a platoon. It was rather a distinction for the most junior subaltern of the regiment, and while I regretted the loss of my platoon I rejoiced in the greater measure of freedom and experience. It meant that my activities were extended to the whole length of the Battalion front and no longer to the fifty or sixty yards held by my particular platoon.

At Maricourt there were many graves scattered about all over the place. Four French soldiers were buried in the garden of our Mess. The inscription over their grave was one which we usually found - "Enfants de la France, morts pour la Patrie". On the night of the 12th. of January the Battalion was relieved and we marched back to Suzanne, shelled most of the way. The road from Maricourt to Suzanne was fully open to the German gunners and they never failed to shell it when they suspected the movement of troops either carrying rations or on relief.

Suzanne was at this time still occupied by civilians. There was a very handsome chateau in which lived the Marquis of something or other. This was used as Brigade Headquarters. The marshes round the chateau and the paths leading through them to the Somme Canal and river were very pretty. There was an abundance of wildfowl and fish.

Until we came Suzanne and Maricourt had the reputation of being two of the quietest spots in the line, but within a week of our arrival all the civilians were shelled out of Suzanne, our nice billets had to be forsaken for damp cellars and henceforward not a day passed without the village being shelled. Soon there was not one undamaged house in the village and our casualties during our periods of rest were infinitely heavier than those we suffered in the trenches themselves.

On January 13th. the fun began. As the officers of D Company and myself were sitting at dinner in our modest quarters a 5.9 shell went right through the wall of the house and burst in the room above our heads. Mercifully only one man was hit; I went up to the room for the nose-cap, or timefuse, of the shell. This I still have. I have rather a large collection of these trophies and I may explain that it was in no morbid souvenir hunt that I gathered them but in the course of my duties. A shell fuse can yield much information as to the size of the shell, the distance of the battery from which it was fired and more or less accurately the direction and position of that battery.

On 14/1/16, the Bosches started in earnest and at 10.30 a.m. whilst Colonel Petrie was taking Battalion Orderly Room, one shell burst in the yard and another at the very door of the room. The C.O. was taking the case of a Private on a serious charge and although the room was full of officers, only the prisoner was hit and his was not a severe wound. It was really rather lucky for him as the case against him was dropped.

This was the beginning of a four hours intensive bombardment during which the Germans systematically shelled every part of the town. One shell alone accounted for twelve casualties in B Company. As I was crossing an open field I heard another shell coming towards me; its tone altered to that peculiar note it makes when about to burst and I flung myself down on my face. It landed with a shriek just eight paces away; I measured out the distance afterwards. It was my nearness to the point of impact that saved me. Had I been twenty yards away I must surely have been hit. That sounds a paradox but is not, as a shell-burst is conical in effect.

It is an unpleasant thing to hear a shell coming towards you. When a bullet sings past your ear you know that the danger is over or you would not have heard it - of course it is always possible that the next one will find its mark but you don't worry about that - but a shell comes with a gentle soughing of the wind and then gets louder and louder

until with the roar of an express train coming straight for you, it
bursts because it cannot roar any louder - and then in comparative
silence you hear as you crouch on the ground the fragments of shrapnel
and case come swishing down through the air to fall with a soft thud
into the earth all around you.

For a few days the merits of our respective cellars formed the
only topic of conversation. Do not attribute this to cowardice.
If there was work to be done or a fight to be won, well we were on
the job, but as we had to husband our resources for the trenches it
was just as well to findwhat legitimate measure of comfort and
security we could find while we were supposed to be resting.
Of course when we were shelled we did not get in a panic, but just
naturally took shelter for a minute and then continued on our way.

After this not a day passed without Suzanne being heavily shelled
at intervals from one direction or another, and as we walked about on
our business we kept a weather eye lifting for shelter if a shell should
happen to come along. The existing shell holes and craters were regarded
with much favour as it was unlikely that a shell would burst in exactly
the same spot as before. In time we became contemptuous and if the Huns
were shelling any particular stretch of road we had to pass we would
time the burst of the shells, drop down for a minute just as they landed
a few yards away and then continue our journey until the next batch was
due. Occasionally we made an error of judgement. There was one particular
Bosche battery that for no logical reason seemed to be usually firing
when I was about on my lawful occasions and the commander of this particular
battery was a most unmethodical Hun. Instead of firing all four guns
simultaneously he would fire perhaps one, two and three, and then after
a short pause and you had assumed that number four had fired a shell
which had failed to explode - in other words a dud - along it came.
This chap caught me napping for a long time until I had tumbled to his
little tricks.

As Intelligence Officer my duties were many and varied. Chief
amongst them was the maintenance of a system of observation that did
not permit any movement of the enemy to escape notice. By means of a
small body of Scouts and trained observers I had to gather as much
information about the habits and movements of the opposing troops as
possible. The arrival of their ration parties, the hours at which the
sentries were relieved, distant noises of their trains and transport,
all were carefully noted. Any fresh work on their trenches was duly
logged and in time we had most of their sniping posts and machine gun
positions located. Fresh erections of wire entanglements, new sandbags
on their parapet, extra loopholes, smoke from their trench fires - all
these things had their own special significance and had to be reported
daily to Brigade H.Q.

In time we learnt how often the enemy troops were relieved and
at what hours they had their meals; we knew where they cooked their food
and at what hours they were most alert. We knew the position of their
sentry posts and where their various Company headquarters were.
Any new weapons of offence such as liquid fire or the installation of
gas cylinders in their trenches were within the range of our activities.
Patrol work every night in No Man's Land was a necessary corollary of
our observation. In addition I commanded the Battalion snipers, who

exacted a steady daily toll on our friends the enemy, and lastly I had
to keep in touch with our neighbours the French. It was a busy life
and an exciting one.

Capt. Morton Johnson, a big manufacturer
in civil life, had a Sunbeam 6 car and
chose Gilbert and Sullivan's opera music,
for the Mess syndicate's gramophone.

The Author with the satisfying prospect
before him of luncheon at the Godbert,
Amiens, with Colonel Petrie and Maj.Knox.
5th. June, 1916.

Chapter Eight.

The last days of January. The Fall of Frise. An Air engagement.

> And the high gods took in hand
> Fire and the falling of tears,
> And a measure of sliding sand
> From under the feet of the years;
>
> And froth and drift of the sea,
> And dust of the labouring earth,
> And bodies of things that be
> In the houses of death and birth:
>
> And wrought with weeping and laughter,
> And fashioned with loathing and love,
> With life before and after,
> And death beneath and above:
>
> For a day, a night and a morrow,
> That his strength may endure for a span,
> With travail and heavy sorrow
> The holy spirit of man.

On January 16th. 1916, we returned to the trenches in the evening. The Germans shelled the roads and valley viciously but failed to do much material harm. The arrangements were altered so that we were to do four day shifts instead of two. On the 18th. poor young Barrett was shot through the head. His death would have been prevented if we had then been in possession of shrapnel helmets. He was on sentry duty and had straightened his back for a second, but a German sniper got him at once. He was buried the next day in the little Maricourt cemetery. The C.O. and the Adjutant and myself went to his funeral and the Bosches shelled the cemetery the whole time.

On the 20th. we went back to Suzanne and we were lodged in the Petit Chateau. Spies were known to be at work among the civilian population and upon our earnest representations all the civilians were evacuated. I will refer briefly to two men we caught red-handed. There was in Suzanne a church with a tower which was visible from the German lines. There was a clock in the tower. Although the clock had stopped it was noticed that the hands of the clock had changed their position. The gentleman who had altered the position of the hands had used them to semaphore information to the Huns as to our movements. He was eliminated, not by us but by the French authorities to whom we handed him over. There was also a farm on the top of the hill with a ploughed field and pigeon loft. The farmer excited our suspicion by his erratic ploughing. He did not follow a straight furrow; sometimes too he worked 2 brown horses : occasionally he worked one brown horse and a white one. The white horse seemed to have an easy life of it but it was remarked that it was usually at work when we were due to return to the trenches. This gentleman was also called to account; I have no doubt that his rather overdue account was settled in full.

I had a long talk with M.le Lieutenant Bernard of the French Army on various matters not unconnected with espionage and general intelligence work, and on the 22nd. at his invitation visited the

French troops on the South Bank of the Somme. On Sunday after going to Holy Communion with Johnson I took the Colonel and Major Knox over to see the French batteries in action. We had a very cordial reception and a pleasant walk back across the marshes.

I have not referred to Knox before. He had been in the 2nd. Manchesters and had been wounded severely at the battle of Le Cateau after which he had been invalided home and then given a soft job on the lines of communication. He was far too good a fellow to stick that and had wrangled a transfer to us, taking Kempster's place as Second in Command. He was a most charming man, very capable and a delightful companion. We saw a great deal of each other when I joined the Battalion Headquarters Mess and I think our liking was mutual.

On the 25th. we went back to Maricourt. On this visit I met a Lieutenant Evans of the Chestnut Battery of the Royal Horse Guns. He used to live at Henbury Court, which I knew very well. We were still short of artillery in those days and had a battery of Horse Gunners to cover our front. A curious thing happened with Evans. We were sitting at Mess in a house in School Street at Maricourt at about 7 p.m. when we heard the German machine guns popping away and the whizz of bullets sweeping the street outside. We were all seated at table, and Fletcher the Medical Officer and myself had our backs to the lath and plaster wall nearest the street. Evans sat just opposite us in a chair with a very high back. Suddenly the Doctor and I felt something whizz between our two faces and a machine gun bullet embedded itself in the high back of Evans's chair, just missing him by half an inch. We chopped the bullet out and gave it to him as a souvenir.

On the 25th. a heavy mist gave me a chance of going over the top and exploring the ground behind our front line trenches. I saw a large number of German corpses and discovered a good deal of Hun equipment. On the 26th. all was fairly quiet. We expected a strafe on the following day as it was as we thought the Kaiser's birthday. However all was quiet, but at 11 p.m.(which was midnight by German time) three green flares went up from the German trenches which were followed by cheering and a burst of rapid rifle fire which lasted a quarter of an hour.

On the 27th. Colonel Weber, the Chief of our Divisional Staff, came up to have a look round the front line and I was deputed to show him round. He was immaculately dressed, nicely cleaned and polished, and I thought of the conditions under which the men in the line were living. So I thought that I would show him all that there was to be seen. I took him through the muddiest of trenches and nearly drowned him; I led him past every dangerous corner there was pointing out the German sniping posts after we had passed each one; I finally got him back to Battalion Headquarters simply smothered with mud and with all the curiosity sweated out of him. I will say that he bore no malice and frequently during our journey expressed anxiety for my safety, not entirely disinterested in his own perhaps however, he never forgot me or his remarkably hectic outing and we were always very good friends although he never asked me to take him round those trenches again. Few lads of twenty had such an opportunity of making their mark on the Chief of Divisional Staff.

Private Lee was killed in Fire Trench No. 20 at the same spot where poor Barrett lost his life. We got the sniper who shot him but that was poor consolation; Lee was an awfully nice kid.

Except for a rumoured gas attack in the evening the Kaiser's birthday had passed peacefully and we started to congratulate ourselves - all too soon. At dawn on the following day the Germans began to shell our batteries in terrific fashion and also all the approaches to Maricourt and Suzanne. At 10 a.m. they shortened their range and hammered the villages very heavily until 2 p.m. when they again shortened range and turned their full attention on our front line trenches. The bombardment lasted until 6 p.m. and was thought by us all to be the preparation for an attack. The Bosches used a good number of lachrymatory gas shells and many of our troops were badly gassed.

While this circus was going on the Germans launched an attack on the French and captured the village of Frise, just across the river from us. Half a battalion of the 17th. Manchesters went up as support but by that time the Bosches had got the village and our Allies had given up the ghost for the time being. For twelve consecutive hours we were completely cut off; the wires had all been destroyed by shell fire and we could not get into touch with either Brigade Headquarters or our covering batteries. Maricourt was an inferno of shell fire and Colonel Petrie transferred his Headquarters to Round Point, in the trench system. Sotham the Adjutant had to hold on at the old Headquarters in School Street and I remained with him in case he were knocked out. During the twelve hour bombardment we had over twenty thousand Bosche shells on the Battalion frontage; the noise was of course terrific and there was hardly left one brick upon another in the village. Maricourt was in a salient which meant that we were shelled from several directions at once. Even our indefatigable transport section was not able to get up with the rations until 2 a.m. the next morning. I was with Sotham nearly all day, except for my journeys to the Colonel in the trenches, and we really did have a hectic time. The ramshackle cellar which served us as Headquarters was directly hit again and again. The house above it was brought down in ruins; one shell burst in the entrance to the cellar and another rolled down the small flight of steps almost to our feet - and failed to explode. Sotham and I had to stay there as it was the recognised Headquarters of the Battalion to which messages from Brigade were delivered and as the wires were cut we could not notify them of our proposed change of address. After the fuss was over on the following day we went to Round Point which being in the trenches afforded us a greater measure of security.

At 4 a.m. the following morning we were aroused by the report of a gas attack on our left. As it was misty I walked over to see the barbed wire entanglements in front of Greg's trenches which he had reported as being badly cut by the previous day's shell fire. I took Slack with me - he was then Bombing Officer - in order to shew him the nearest way up for his bomb supply in case of attack. While we were out in the open the mist lifted suddenly and we had an exciting time getting back to cover.

Suzanne was still being heavily shelled and the French were launching counter attack after counter attack in the effort to get Frise back. Their colonial troops won forward as far as the Bois de Vaches, but beyond that they could not penetrate. Colonel Petrie told me to understudy the Adjutant in case he should be knocked out. I was very pleased about this as I was still the junior subaltern of the Battalion. Captain Sotham was a Regular and was most cordially disliked by nearly every officer in the Battalion.

He had been Adjutant from the very first and had always been a strict disciplinarian, seldom relaxing even off duty. The troops were devoted to him and there is little doubt that it was to him that we owed our extreme efficiency as a fighting unit, but he had no time for soft soap and could not see the necessity of handling his officers tactfully.

Sotham was rather a saturnine figure; he was six foot six in height; very thin and very dark. His manner was unconciliatory and he rarely smiled. He had been on the African coast for many years and was really a sick man. Incompetence and failure he could not stand at any price. He was a stickler for etiquette and woe betide any officer of the Battalion who departed from the regimental code. To wear a safety pin in the collar of your khaki shirt was a most heinous offence. "Officers of the Manchester Regiment do not wear jewellery", I heard him tell one of our captains on parade. When we were in England he and I had many a row, in which naturally I always came off worse. I admired him tremendously and imagined he hated me like poison; I was therefore immensely flattered when we got out to the Front and I discovered that he really liked me and trusted me implicitly. I have rather enlarged on the subject of Sotham because he was such a splendid fellow and yet was so wholeheartedly disliked by most of my brother officers, who were in their turn such excellent fellows. I think perhaps that the true explanation of their differences of opinion was that these men were conscious of the fact that they were temporary officers and expected to receive, if not constant praise and recognition of the fact that they had given up very responsible positions in civilian life, at any rate a tolerant acceptance of any little irregularity of discipline; while Sotham's attitude was that they had become soldiers voluntarily - and all praise to them for it - but that by doing so they had not placed him under a perpetual debt of gratitude to them, and since they were soldiers they should be damned good ones. When one of the Company Commanders wanted him to recommend a stretcher-bearer for rescuing a man under fire he replied in astonishment "But that is his job". While the other Battalions of the Division were getting decorations galore, and priding themselves on the number of Military Crosses they were being awarded, we took pride in the fact that we had none, but had done more to deserve them.

At 2 a.m. on the 30th. of January we heard a Zepplin cross overhead and could just distinguish it faintly. I believe it was afterwards fetched down in England. Again the morning was misty and one of my Scouts, Thompson, spotted three Germans repairing their wire. Casson got one man and the other two Huns picked him up and took him back to their trenches. We marked the spot and when a wiring party came out that night we had them on toast.

On the 31st. January 1916 came the welcome news that an attempt would be made to relieve us that night. We had been in the front line trenches for eight days without a break but the troops were wonderfully cheerful. Headquarters and D Company got back to Suzanne on the 1st. at 3 a.m. A Company and two platoons of B and C Company were placed in the Maricourt Defences. C Company were sixteen days in the trenches without a rest.

On February 2nd. Colonel Petrie and I went up to a place of vantage called Royal Dragons to watch the French troops attacking Bois de Vaches. They advanced to the attack again and again only to

be blotted out under the murderous artillery barrage of the Germans.
At the close of the day the Bois de Vaches consisted of just seven tree
stumps instead of a three acre wood. We went up again on the 3rd. to
the redoubt at Vaux School to watch the battle.

All this time Suzanne was being heavily shelled by day and night
to distract our attention from the Frenchmen's troubles. On the 5th. I
walked up to Maricourt with the Padre. Birds were singing and the
skies were blue, but the German artillery were searching for some gun
positions of ours in the valley and made the day hideous. My old quarters
at School Street Maricourt had been completely wrecked.

The night before three Huns had approached a sentry post of ours
from a disused sap. They tried to bolt when challenged so the sentry
fired and killed one man. He had three German grenades tucked into
his belt and was dressed in the usual grey uniform. He looked a very
decent young fellow.

There is a good story about Fletcher our Medical Officer. He was
a wonderful fellow in looking after the wounded and as brave as could
be; he had an idea that he was the best known and (because he was Doc),
the most popular officer in the Brigade. He was attending some of our
lads who had been gassed with lachrymatory shells. The effect of the
gas was to make them very sleepy and Fletcher wanted to assure them
that they were in no danger. There were about forty of them in the
Dressing Station, propped up against the walls or lying on the floor
all very drowsy. Fletcher went from man to man, shook each in turn
and repeated the same formula. "Now, my man, you know me, and when
I say you are in no danger, you know that I am telling you the truth".
The men dutifully replied "Yes Sir", until he came to an alien soul.
Fletcher began in the same way. "Now, my man, you know me, don't
you - " The man opened one eye and looked at him. "No, I'm damned
if I do, and I don't want to" he interrupted and went to sleep again.

Another rather amusing thing happened on January 28th. when the
shelling was at its worst. Now it is a point of honour that if a
wounded man is capable of walking he should walk to the Dressing
Station. Those who are stretcher cases are supposed to be incapable
of movement. Two stretcher bearers of another Bn. were coming down
the road with a case on a stretcher. The shells were falling thick and
fast and as the wounded man was strapped to the stretcher they were able
to swing along at a good pace.But finally in a hurricane of shells their
courage gave out and they made for the ditch whereupon the wounded man
sat up, undid the straps and also bolted for cover !

On the 6th. of February we moved to our old trenches, this time
with Battalion Headquarters at Round Point. On the 7th. I fixed up
several surprises for the gentle Hun and on the 9th. I went over to
look at the trenches. On the 11th. we went back to Suzanne and took
up quarters in the cellars of le Petit Chateau. The shelling was as
bad as ever. The French were still counter attacking, and the
Germans wanted to ensure that no troops of ours were moved to their
support. Heavy shelling continued all through the night of the 12th.
The Colonel was walking down East Street when suddenly whiz-z-z came
a big shell. He dropped on his tummy in the middle of the road and
rolled over and over until he got into the ditch. When he got there
a soldier passing by said "It's all right, Sir, that's one of ours".

On the 13th. the shelling still continued. The German guns
scored three direct hits on our Headquarters and D Company's mess
was absolutely destroyed. The shelling was most intense from 6 p.m.
to 7.30 p.m., just when people were at church. As we sat eating our
tinned apricots word came that some men had been buried in a cellar
which had been blown in on them. I hurried out with Fletcher and
found some volunteers to dig them out. The cellar was one which we
had used as a Battalion post office, and at first we were told that
there were three men inside. It was hard work getting to them as the
shell had exploded at the entrance to the stairs and the fallen masonry
and timber were pinning them under. We got the first man out by drag
ropes. This was poor Eckersley; the shell had burst on him and he was
blown inside out. He was on top of two men who were still living.
Somebody handed me his foot with his ankle completely severed. It was
only after an hour's heavy work that we got him clear. The whole time
the shelling was pretty fierce and the Colonel came along just as we
got Eckersley clear. He was promptly very sick. It was rather awful.
The two men were left under heavy stones. We got one out after another
hour and a half. He was alive but both legs were broken. The third we
got out at 10 p.m. He had a broken leg and a fractured skull. Although
we could see his brain pulsing up and down as it was exposed through the
hole in his head, he was able to tell us that there were yet two more
men to get out. These we got clear at midnight, in pieces. Their faces
were completely black and totally unrecognisable. The cellar had been
quite a good one, but the shell had detonated on the top of the steps
and the men inside had no chance of escape. We had worked from 7.30
until midnight under heavy fire. The stretcher bearers did excellent
work and Fletcher's splendid courage commanded my eternal admiration.
When all was done I placed a guard over the cellar during the night to
keep the dogs away until the stretcher bearers should have an opportunity
of collecting any remaining human fragments in daylight. The three men
were buried in Suzanne Cemetery on St. Valentine's Day - pathetic
enough to see the one whole man carried to his grave - worse to see the
two other stretchers with their load of sandbags containing all that
was left of the other two. When I have sat through Evensong in some
quiet English church I have often thought of that particular Sunday evening.

On the 15th. I was in charge of a fatigue party for Fargny Mill,
and was not pleased about it either. On the 16th. we went back to our
old trenches. Up to this time we had suffered seventy seven casualties,
rather heavy considering we had not been in battle. We had a jolly
good squadron of airmen attached to the Corps and an engagement in which
two of our planes were engaged against heavy odds deserves description
in detail.

One of our machines to which the second was acting as escort was
engaged in reconnaissance work over Cambrai. They were attacked by six
German Fokker machines, firing through the propeller.

It should be explained that the Fokker machines are monoplanes,
expressly built and contrived for fighting and pursuit of the enemy,
to which duties its activities are by strict order confined, and for
which it is essentially adapted on account of its high speed. It is
not allowed to expose itself by venturing across our lines on reconnaissance
work. It must be added that in contrast to the arrangements on our
aeroplanes, the machine gun on the Fokker is immovably fixed in front of
the pilot, with the barrel straight to the front - the correct aim of the

gun being ensured by the manipulation of the whole machine, just as the correct aim of a torpedo is contrived only by the manipulation of the submarine itself.

The Fokker's machine gun being fixed on the same plane as the body of the machine fires through the propeller. Such bullets as miss the propeller carry straight to their front, while such as are intercepted by its blades are dispelled by angled and bullet proof deviators attached to the back face of the blades. The Fokker when in action seeks by the exercise of its superior speed and climbing powers to attain a position above its adversary and then, by diving at a steep angle, to bring the machine gun to bear upon him by correct alignment.

As a result of the machine gun fire of the six Fokkers our escorting machine was immediately shot down; its occupants seemed to reach the ground safely so landing as to effect intentionally the destruction of their machine without injury to themselves. This was of course in Bosche territory. It was followed to the ground by two of the Fokkers.

Our remaining machine succeeded in driving off and seriously injuring the Fokker first to attack it. It was out of control when last seen and was nose diving with every prospect of injury or death to its occupants. Our machine was then attacked by the three other Fokkers which we fought for fifteen minutes, and then our machine guns being temporarily out of action, the pilot decided that escape could only be sought by a very risky dive to within twenty feet of the ground. It was risky in that it entailed a descent by very steep spiral at a speed of quite a hundred miles an hour, with little room to recover. Only very delicate and confident handling could ensure the success of this manoeuvre, which only the absence of other means of escape could justify.

The manoeuvre was prompted by two considerations. In the first place a Fokker, being less handy, would not dare to pursue within twenty feet of the ground, the margin for recovery after the nose diving being so very restricted, and secondly if our machine was once more to reach friendly territory in safety, it was desirable we should conceal from armed enemies to be surmounted its nationality as displayed by the rings painted on the lower surface of its planes, and this it could only do by skimming over the enemy ground at as low an elevation as possible.

Skimming along just above the ground, as skims a grouse under a hawk, our machine hard pressed turned westward for home, whereupon one of the German machines, all of which had maintained an elevation of a thousand feet, swooped towards it but was promptly driven off by rapid fire, one of our guns by that time having been repaired. Making westward still, every experience was momentary, but certain impressions remained. An armed German party ran out of a farm house close at hand was treated to half a drum of the Lewis gun. Enthusiastic cheers came from French peasants working in the fields - still behind the German lines. A mounted German staff officer in spick and span uniform was passed within a few yards and gave a target that could hardly be missed, but the temptation was discreetly resisted in view of the most dangerous risk of capture yet to run when crossing the German trenches.

The fight continued half way to the British trenches when the two Fokkers gave it up. The British pilot at once started climbing to

attack the single remaining Fokker, but this brought back its two
companions and our machine resumed its original elevation. The three
German machines ultimately turned back, giving up the chase when about
a mile from the German line before crossing which our pilot naturally
sought to climb. Our aeroplane was unable however to attain a greater
height than eight hundred feet owing to the engine having been hit in
the fight and we were subjected to heavy rifle fire, machine gun fire
and artillery fire which the machine fortunately survived. Its planes
and spars were much damaged and more than one of its stays nearly severed.

The anxieties of the position had for long been greatly increased
by the knowledge that only sufficient petrol remained to bring the
machine just within friendly lines if a direct course was pursued.
To be driven out of the course in any degree would be fatal. Early in
the engagement the oil feed had been shot away and with an engine
injured by rifle fire the chances of ever reaching home seemed remote,
but an expiring effort landed the machine just within the French lines
south west of Arras. The pilot and observer alike were congratulated
on fine performance.

On the 17th. we had the welcome news that we were to be relieved
by a fresh Brigade and on the next day I reconnoitred our route back
to Bray through Bronfay Farm. · In the afternoon I took the Intelligence
Officer of the 1/6 Black Watch round the line. We went overland as it
was misty. Everything was ready to hand over, the stores had been moved
out of the trenches and we sat down to await the incoming troops.
At 6 p.m. orders came to cancel their arrival. On the 19th. the
Gordons turned up, and said they were to relieve us in the evening.
I took their Colonel round the line. Knox and Megson went off on leave -
the first to go from the Battalion.

On the 20th. I went to meet the Gordons at Bronfay Farm
and brought them up. The relief was not over until 1.30 a.m. by
which time I was very tired. We went back to East Street Suzanne
and for three days did fatigue work in heavy snow. On the 23rd.
we took over a fresh line of trenches south of the Peronne Road,
just separated from our previous ones by the road, and we had
much trouble with the transport as it was still snowing hard.

Instead of our long promised rest out of shell fire, we had
been hustled back into the firing line after three days. We
cursed and swore in our disappointment, not knowing the reason
thereof. The bursting of the thunder-clouds at Verdun soon
provided the reason of our postponed rest.

1907 Pattern Bayonet found
among his memorabilia. Ed

Chapter Nine.

Trenches South of the road. Verdun. Leave. Divisional Rest.

> He was a babe so short a while ago,
> My little son -
> To-day his race is run.
>
> But yesterday he was an eager boy
> Of gay and tireless heart -
> Now he has played his part.
>
> He fell ! The rest marched on to victory;
> The hard fought day was won -
> Ah God, my little son !
>
> He is not dead, my son ! There is no death.
> His strong and tireless soul
> Marches to some great goal.

I explored our new line of trenches on the morning of the 24th. of February, accompanied for part of the way by two French artillery officers who wanted to find a good observation post. Coming back along the Peronne Road I saw some fragments of German equipment lying at the foot of a shell shattered tree. I looked up and saw a German field boot caught in a forked branch, with the leg bone showing white inside it. Remembering my experience at Plug Street earlier in the war I looked on the ground again and discovered a few whitened bones and many empty German cartridge cases. From the withered branch a bird was singing beautifully. It seemed in a nutshell the life story and epitome of a sniper.

In the evening Captain Walker commanding B Company wanted to post a listening patrol between our lines and the German trenches. He detailed Sergeant Fairbank and three men for the job. At the appointed time Fairbank went out, got through our own wire and then through some more. He and his men were then challenged in a guttural tongue which the Sergeant took to be Scotch - the Scots Fusiliers were our neighbours at the time. He replied gaily to the challenge "16th. Manchesters". Again came the challenge "Halt - Wer da ?" This time he again said "16th. Manchesters. What the devil is up with you ?" To his surprise he was immediately met with rapid fire; he had meandered over to a German listening post. All the men got back safe so there must have been some rotten shooting

On the 25th. we had another heavy fall of snow and could hear the Germans stamping their feet to keep them warm and coughing and spitting. It was curious to be able to hear them so clearly, like living in a jerry built flat. Luckily all neighbours have not the same murderous propensities.

Our orders were brief and to the point. The 16th. Battalion would capture Trones Wood and hold it until relieved. It was true that about three battalions of about four times our numerical strength had failed, but they were not the 16th. Manchesters.

There was no time for elaborate plans. The Colonel extended the Battalion into two lines, placed the Lewis gunners on the flanks, and himself at the head, re-took Trones Wood.

The Wood was already a shambles; nearly every tree hid a German sniper and a net work of trenches ran through the wood. But the Battalion had taken the Wood and although the German artillery pounded it with all the violence of which they were capable and in face of all the counter attacks, the Battalion held the Wood until relieved thirty hours after. Then they marched back - sixty five men strong, and many of these wounded.

Of the officers, Venner, Oliver and Smithers were killed. Payne, Davidson, Megson, Jackson, Harvey and one other were wounded. My own dear Platoon Sergeant Hawxby was killed, also C.S.M. Reddy and C.S.M. Adamson, also Sergeant Acheson.

Sotham had come home with appendicitis, at least that was what I was told at the time. Actually he had had a row with a gilded Staff Officer, who had come along to ask him for a copy of the Colonel's recommendations for decorations in the Montauban show. Sotham had just come out of the Trones Wood show, was fagged to the world and had just got to sleep when this popinjay rolled up and roused him. Sotham's temper was never particularly sweet and he just damned this man to all eternity. The original list of recommendations had been submitted. If the Corps Commander had to employ bl...y office boys in red tabs, why couldn't he employ bl...y efficient ones, and more in the same strain. Unfortunately the gilded and be-sanguined one was a relative of the Corps Commander and the result was that Sotham was sent home and not one single decoration did the Battalion get for the Montauban show.

When the Battalion went back to rest, the Corps Commander again congratulated them, and said that we had earned the soldiers' high privilege of fighting again. So although there were only about sixty of us left, he made the Battalion up to strength with drafts from the Sherwood Foresters, the Border Regiment and the Royal Warwickshires. Ordinarily our poor remnants might have gone to make up another Battalion, but the 16th. Manchesters were too good to lose their identity.

On the morning of the 29th. of July the Battalion attacked for the third time in a month at Guillemont, in a thick mist. Here once again we suffered severely. After this the Battalion was sent north for a rest, but attacked again at Flers in October, when the tanks first went into action. By that time the Division had gained the nickname of Shea's Tigers, Shea being our Divisional General.

Colonel Peterie was invalided home in July and came to see me in hospital. He told me that he had recommended me for the D.S.O. for the Montauban affair, and I was very thrilled. For months after I scanned the Honours List with eager eyes, but not only did my D.S.O. fail to materialise, but also any other decoration for any man of the 16th. Manchesters. It was only when I got back to the Battalion that I heard about the Sotham episode and then of course I understood. I went home from hospital on the 27th. of July, my twenty-second birthday. I travelled in a certain amount of discomfort as my arm was still painful, but I was tremendously glad to be home again for a bit.

I was still very much in love with my job. It was fine to have
a roving commission, answerable to no one but the Colonel, and not
tied down to one small section of the trenches. I used to set out
in the morning in my little cut down Burberry, the tails cut off to
be out of the mud, thigh gum boots, a gas helmet over one shoulder
and binoculars over the other, pockets stuffed with maps and notebook
and a stray piece of chocolate for lunch, a long trench stick,
revolver, trench gloves and shrapnel helmet. I used to feel like
a country squire going round my estate. There they were, my trenches,
mine because I knew them as no one else had a chance of knowing them.
Every sandbag and loophole had its own history and I used to feel the
pride of proprietorship as I gaily went on my rounds. Going up and
down the Battalion front and in and out of the trenches was of course
slightly more risky than staying put in one place, but it was vastly
more interesting and at twenty-one danger was the spice that enabled
one to bear the monotony of trench warfare.

I know nothing whatever about psychology but I do know that
life was very full of zest in those days. There was a thrill in
walking with death at one's elbow. There was immense satisfaction
in taking what was perhaps a totally unjustifiable risk and getting
away with it. It was rather fun to be sniped at, and just missed,
and when a shell burst very near or overhead and you listened to the
bits of shrapnel coming down it was distinctly exhilarating.
There is a phrase about the "joy of battle". I have appreciated this
to the full, but I wonder whether I shall be believed when I say that
this feeling of joy and lightheartedness does not come from any pleasure
in killing - that's the rotten part - but in the risk of being killed.
My days in the trenches were days of utter content; I cannot explain
why, even to myself. It is not a case of looking back when everything
in the past is wonderful and nothing is so depressing as the present
and future; my actual notes of the time are full of happiness and joy.
The natural sadness of losing one's dear friends was mitigated by
knowing that one shared the same risks and would probably meet a
similar fate to-morrow.

Since the War a lot of books have been written about life in
France during the war. It appears from these that the troops
when out of the trenches gave themselves wholeheartedly to every
form of licientiousness. I do not doubt that soldiers on the
lines of communication and at the Bases behaved very much as they
do when they are at home; but the fighting troops were of very
different calibre. If there were cases of immorality as it seems
evident there were, at places like Havre and Rouen and Boulogne,
these were confined solely to the "safety first" soldiers. As a
matter of sober fact throughout the whole of my experience with
the fighting troops, both in the ranks and as an officer, I have
not come across a single case of immorality. WE didn't have
W.A.A.C.'s and V.A.D. nurses and all sorts of stray females running
round. What went on at the Base and in the occupied areas, I do not
know, but I do know that the farther back from the firing line the
worse was the morale of the troops and probably that also applied
to their morals.

We were relieved in the evening of the 26th. and went back to
East Street Suzanne. At 3.15p.m. on the 27th. the Germans scored

another direct hit on the Mess. At 5.30p.m. we were shelled heavily
and again at 7.30p.m. At 8.15p.m.they started again and again at 9.
I went to bed in disgust and in a cellar ! The next day being Sunday
I went to Holy Communion and in the evening we returned to our trenches.
It was still abominably cold. We were heavily shelled on leaving the
village and the Bosches made a tentative attack on Knowles Point, which
was driven off.

A short account of the commencement of the struggle at Verdun
may be of interest. During the winter the sector of the attack from
the Meuse - Etain Warcq, thirty four thousand yards, was held by the
9th. and 10th. Reserve Divisions of the 5th. German Reserve Corps.
From Warcq south to Fresenes, seventeen thousand yards, the line was
held by the 5th. Landwehr Division. From Les Eparges south to Saint
Mihiel lay the 33rd. Reserve Division and the 3rd. Bavarian Corps,
but these two units did not take part in the attack.

During the fortnight between February 6th. and 20th. eighty five
battalions were concentrated in the area immediately north of the
sector of attack, so that three divisions held from the Meuse to
Fresnes with nine divisions in reserve.

Just before the attack the 7th. Reserve Corps, 18th. Corps, and
15th. Corps relieved the 5th. Reserve Corps and from each regiment
of the latter attack Battalions (shock troops) were formed and put
at the disposal of the three other Corps.

The attacking Corps were given the following sectors of attack
from west to east.

7th. Reserve Corps	Meuse to Bois de Cannes	7500 yards
18th. Corps	Bois de Cannes to Herbebois	5500 yards
3rd. Corps	Herbebois to Maucourt	7000 yards
15th. Corps	Maucourt to Warcq	14000 yards
5th. Landwehr Div &		
Bavarian Ersatz Div	Warcq toFresnes	17000 yards

Each Corps had both its Divs in line side by side; each Div had 2 Regts
in front and 1 in reserve.

Here follow the various stages of the attack:
On February 21st. the Germans opened an intensive bombardment
on the front opposite the 18th. and 3rd. Corps, that is from Bois
de Cannes to Maucourt. During the night these two Corps sent
forward strong patrols, each consisting of two officers and fifty
other ranks to discover result of the bombardment.

On February 22nd. the attack developed on the whole front
from the Meuse to Herbebois. The assault was preceded by a very
intense but comparatively short bombardment on the whole of the
sector of attack; the area subjected to the bombardment had a
depth of a thousand yards. Again strong patrols were pushed forward
to ascertain the results of the bombardment.

The assault was carried out by successive waves which followed
each other at a hundred yards distance. Some regiments were
echeloned in depth by battalions, the leading being in two lines.
Each unit had a definitely assigned objective, beyond which it was
not to advance, further advance to be carried out by the troops in
reserve. The infantry was ordered not to persist in efforts to

overcome any resistance which had not been broken down by the
artillery fire, and each unit was to await artillery support
before continuing the attack. The leading principle seems to have
been to obtain the maximum of artillery effect with the minimum of
loss to the infantry.

February 23rd. was spent in endeavouring to re-organise the
units which had become hopelessly mixed and in relieving regiments
which had suffered most severely. In the course of this latter
operation all the available reserves were used up.

On the 24th. the attack was resumed but met with heavy losses.
The 13th. Reserve Division and the 18th. Corps and the 3rd. Corps
were worn out by this time. On the morning of the 24th. the 15th.
Corps attempted an assault en masse on the Maucourt - Warcq front
but was driven back into its trenches by the French barrage fire.
In smaller groups at 2p.m. the 15th. Corps renewed the attack and
in the evening they succeeded in carrying the French front line.
The 15th. Corps had been ordered not to attack until the road had
been opened by the advance of the 3rd. and 18th. Corps.

On February 25th. the French withdrew their right flank from
Warcq to the foot of the Cotes de la Meuse at Fresnes.
The 5th. Landwehr Division followed up this movement but did not
attempt to attack until the following day.

On the 26th. there was heavy fighting about Douamont in the
centre but very little in either the Meuse area or on the eastern
flank. On the 27th. the fighting in the Douamont - Louvemont
section became more intense, and the German units in this area
suffered very heavy losses.

On the 28th. of February a lull took place in the fighting.
The French consolidated themselves in their new line and the
Germans tried again to re-organise.

On the eastern flank the 5th. Landwehr Division re-inforced
by the Bavarian Ersatz Division delivered a series of attacks
on the front from Rouvaux to Mauheuilles without success, and
during the following days the 15th. Corps, the 5th. Landwehr
Division and the Bavarian Ersatz Division attacked the
Cotes de la Meuse.

I am afraid this account has been rather tedious, but
Verdun was destined to be to the French what Ypres was to the
British and I want to record what facts I have about the
beginning of the struggle.

On March 1st. 1916 we went down to the Suzanne billets and on
the 3rd. a dug-out collapsed under shell-fire, killing three men of
D Company - amongst them Corporal Brown. They were buried in the
cemetery in Suzanne in pouring rain.

It may be interesting to hear a little more about these war funerals.
During the more or less stationary period of trench warfare small military
cemeteries were consecrated near each sector of trenches and in every
village. Sometimes these were entirely apart from the old French
civilian cemeteries, occasionally they adjoined them. Whenever possible
men who were killed in the front line trenches were conveyed by stretcher

bearers to the rear in order to be buried in one of these cemeteries.
It was considered a disgraceful thing to leave one's dead behind one
and every effort was made to bring them out.

The grave would be dug by the Battalion Pioneer section and the
body would be sewn in a blanket and carried by bearers on a stretcher
draped with a Union Jack to the graveside. The Padre then read a
shortened form of the Burial Service, which was usually attended by
the man's own officers or particular pals. The service was always
reverently carried out, although frequently shells would be dropping
around us, and everything was done decently and in order while a note
was made of the exact map reference of the place of burial. A bottle
containing a slip of paper with the man's name, regiment and rank was
usually placed in the grave, and a wooden cross erected straightaway.
Most regiments affected their own particular style of cross which of
course bore the particulars of the buried man. In the Manchesters
we had a cross with an arc of a circle in each right angle. Very
rarely when it was not possible to get the Padre, the service would
be read by the Company Captain.

On the 4th. we were back again in the trenches and I was told
to investigate some new work in the German trenches. It was a bad
night for this as the ground was covered with frozen snow which
crackled at every step and the air was very still. However the
Brigadier wanted information at once and I was told to take a strong
patrol with me. As it was only for reconnaisance work I did not feel
inclined to jeopardize the lives of my scouts, and I sallied forth
alone.

After three hours of ticklish work I got back all right but
just as I had clambered down into A Company's trenches Captain
Worthington, commanding that company, came up in a great state
of mind and threatened to put me under arrest for going out
alone ! Hubert Worthington was an awfully nice fellow and
we were great chums, but he had been badly worried by my
prolonged absence and before I set forth on the jaunt had said
that it was suicidal to attempt to get into the Bosches lines
on a night like that. So it would have been with a dozen of us.
He was really upset about it but I told him to mind his own
damned business and give me a drink, before I went to make out
my report for the Brigadier.

Snipers were very busy opposite No. 15 sap.
Poor Keeling was killed. A triangular shaped piece of shrapnel
had cracked the skull and chipped a large bit off, without
lacerating the brain. Death was due to the exposure of the
nerve centres. On the 6th. I was busy setting up some fixed
rifles and preparing fresh sniping posts. At night we went out
to find a new German sap-head near Fire Trench 14. We found it
heavily wired and strongly held, so chucked in a couple of Mills
bombs just for luck.

Rest again on the 7th. and on the 8th. Slack and I went
into Amiens to buy some duck pies and marrons glaces.
On the 11th. we went back to the trenches, and on the 12th.
Colonel Petrie risked his life and mine on a mad excursion across
an open tract of country from the Ravine to Fargny Mill under fire
from the German lines for a full half hour. The weather had changed

and was very pleasant.

On March 14th. we had a very heavy bombardment and suffered many casualties. More rumours of a relief were followed by the advance party of the 7th. Buffs and on the 17th. we went back to Bray. Johnson was billetting again. My snipers were specially mentioned in Routine Orders for excellent work.

Now came another split in the Battalion. Captain Greg went home. No reason was vouchsafed but it was certain that it was not by his wish. His courage was of the highest and he was an excellent tonic as he was never depressed or in low spirits. He had probably never been forgiven for the episode of the Bonneville fire and he was never particularly amenable to discipline. Johnson was the second in command and obviously the man to have the Company, but he too was under a temporary cloud; he had been given leave for Amiens and thought he would like to go on to Paris. So Elstob was given command of D Company.

Percy and I rode over to Heilly. He had taken over Wilson's job as Transport Officer; Wilson being one of the senior subalterns wanted to get his captaincy. On Sunday we had a very picturesque open air service on the marshes and were shelled by the Huns. The Colonel went home on leave. On the 21st. I took temporary charge of the Lewis Gun section as Kerry was going on leave. He was a newly attached officer from the Devons; Gibbon had been attached to Brigade as Lewis Gun Officer.

On the 26th. Major Knox and I rode into Froissy where we met the French Colonial troops who had re-captured the Bois-de-vaches. Whilst at Bray we were busily employed on fatigue work. On the 28th. we went back further to Corbie. This was a delightful old town and the troops were glad to be out of shell fire for the first time since we had taken over the Maricourt trenches. It was a blessed relief not to be continually listening for a shell and to go to bed without gum boots and a candle by your side.

At the end of March I went to an Anti-Gas School at Saint Gratien where I learnt a bit about German gas. While I was there I managed to get into Amiens for luncheon at the Cafe Godbert. This was a very exclusive restaurant frequented almost solely by French officers of high rank. The English usually went to feed at the Hotel du Rhin, where the food was not of the best, charges very high and service poor. At the Godbert the cooking was wonderful and every meal a work of art. It was not cheap, but it was jolly good. This particular day I met Papa Joffre having lunch there and mine was the only British uniform in the place. He returned my salutation very graciously and gave me his left hand to shake !!

On the 4th. of April I rode back to Corbie where we were engaged in making railways and quarrying stone. I was billetted over a pork butcher's shop. Whether it was this or missing the excitement of the trenches I don't know, but I contracted a bad attack of asthma which lasted from the 8th. to the 12th.

On the 12th. of April it was my turn for home leave and off I started, taking with me as trophies a German cavalry sword and a German rifle. The journey was appalling. After hours of train, a terrible crossing from Havre to Southampton, twelve hours in a crowded

- 65 -

railway carriage and an eight hour crossing with all the troops eating
oranges and chocolates and being very sick after. From Southampton I
went straight to Bristol. Two days after my arrival I had a telegram
from the War Office telling me to go back on the 18th. I hurried up
to Warwickshire for a couple of days and on the 17th. caught the 4pm.
train from Waterloo and landed in France the same night after another
bad crossing.

Everyone on the boat had also been recalled from leave and
rumour was busy as to the Big Push. We were all very excited, but
rather fed up that our long expected leave should have been cut short.
It afterwards transpired that all we poor wretches had been recalled
by a stupid blunder on the part of the War Office.

As usual at holiday time the Railway companies had written to ask
that as little leave as possible should be granted on the 18th. so as
not to interfere with the Easter traffic. This of course was never
meant to interrupt the leave of the men from overseas. When I got
back to my Battalion I found them peacefully at rest at Breilly -
near Amiens.

On the 19th. and 21st. I had to go into Amiens to buy things
that we wanted for the Brigade Horse Show, which was being held at
Picquigny, and where my Battalion carried off the bulk of the prizes.
All this time we were doing Brigade training. We had very comfortable
quarters at the Printanerie and after a hard day's work it was pleasant
to sit in the garden for an hour.

At about this time experienced officers were wanted for the
Machine Gun Corps, and as promotion seemed very slow in the infantry
I put in an application for transfer. Major Knox asked me on the
following day to withdraw it, as Sotham was not likely to be with the
Battalion much longer as he was in very bad health and then I should
have the job of Adjutant. I was not at all anxious to leave the
Battalion so withdrew my application.

On the 28th. of April Sotham went on leave and I took his place
for the time being. On the 29th. we began to make our way back to
the line. We left Breilly at 5 a.m. and marched in the cool of the
morning through Amiens to Corbie where we spent the night. The next
day we continued our journey to the Bois de Celestins, a beautiful
camping ground above Chipilly. Here we were joined by two new officers,
Swain and Hanscombe. On the 1st. we marched into Suzanne where we
arrived at 9.20 p.m. after a very fatiguing journey.

On May 2nd. we relieved the 7th. Queens in Y3 subsector, our
old part of the line. During the morning the Colonel and I made
a hazardous journey up to the trenches. During our absence from
the line the Germans had contracted a bad habit of subjecting the
fire trenches to heavy bursts of rapid fire from their field guns
at frequent intervals during the day and night.

On May 3rd. they opened a vigorous bombardment on No. 15 sap
at the evening stand-to. The parapets and wire entanglements were
all blown in and destroyed; the sap itself was very badly knocked
about; four men were killed and five wounded. Percy had shell shock.
While the bombardment lasted the sap was an inferno of smoke and noise.
The Germans left their trenches with the evident intention of making
a raid but by rapid fire they were beaten back and by daybreak our

parapets were repaired.

On May 4th. the Battalion stood to arms at 2 a.m. as a gas attack was expected. Ordinarily all troops in the firing line stand to arms for one hour before dawn and one hour after sunset; but when the wind was favourable for the use of gas by the Huns we had to be up betimes.

On the 5th. of May a heavy bombardment started on our right at 1.50 a.m. and at 2.12 a.m. Brigade Headquarters wired us to stand to arms as they thought an attack was pending. However things quietened down again and at 3.20 a.m. we had orders to resume normal conditions. At 11 p.m. the Germans celebrated the Crown Prince's birthday by opening rapid fire all along our trenches. One unlucky shell knocked out a Lewis Gun team and a sentry group. Lance Corporal Pickering, one of my best scouts and a jolly good singer, was killed and three others besides; six men were wounded.

On the 6th. very heavy shelling started on our left at 2 a.m. and during the day hostile artillery registered Deansgate and shelled S Works in reverse. We buried four more men. By the way, I forgot to mention when describing a military funeral that the blanket in which the man was buried used to be charged to his account and stopped from their arrears of pay. This shameful practice was afterwards stopped.

On the 8th. we were relieved and went back to Suzanne and on the 10th. Sotham returned from leave and took over his job again. As my first leave had been so rudely interrupted I was lucky enough to get away again on the 11th. and travelled home with Payne. We drove to Heilly where we billetted for the night and had a good dinner and a decent breakfast. Another long rail journey followed by the usual bad crossing brought us home.

On May 13th. an interesting little raid took place and I am going to record it here, although I was safely at home, as it so intimately concerned my own Battalion. At 1 a.m. a bombardment was opened upon the full length of our trenches from Fargny Mill to the Peronne Road and at the same time a barrage was formed round Suzanne. An attack was made upon our trenches west of Y Wood out of which the attacking party issued. The fire from our artillery and machine guns was most effective and the attack nowhere reached our lines. Several dead Germans were left lying on our wire and two wounded soldiers of the 63rd. Regiment were captured. The attack was made partly with the object of getting prisoners. It consisted of several parties over an extended front. One of these came upon a wiring party of ours in front of our trenches. A bombing fight took place. The Germans were being driven back by our men when more Germans who had worked round a flank took our men in the rear and carried off three prisoners, all of whom were reported to be wounded.

From information received we learned that the attack was made by men of the 63rd. Regiment to the number of one hundred and twenty with three officers. They were picked men and distinct from the garrison of the trenches. They had been billetted in Combles and had arrived on the night of the 11th. For the attacks on our sap

heads sections of twelve men were told off with two non-commissioned
officers to each section. Each man's duties and objective were
clearly defined. The raid had been practised beforehand and the
men had been shewn a map of our trenches made from aeroplane photos.
A prisoner stated that two machine guns were to have supported the
raiding party but failed to advance.

The attack was prepared for by bombardment by artillery and
minnenwerfer which had considerable effect on our wire for two days.
Artillery was quieter on the 12. instant but towsrds the evening
sniping and rifle grenade firing were active, no doubt in order to keep
down our observers. An enemy wiring party was seen at 1030 p.m.,
presumably opening paths through their own wire and later machine gun
fire swept the sector.

An intense bombardment was preceded by four reddish lights
and five minnenwerfer bombs into fire trench A 29/4. The intense
bombardment of our entire front line, support and communication
trenches and Battalion Headquarters started at 1 a.m. The parties
which attacked the sap-heads tied white rags to our wire to mark
their way back.

All telephone wires were cut, but red rockets were sent up and
promptly answered by barrage fire from the artillery. The cross fire
of our machine guns was useful. By 3 a.m. the action was over. From
one of the prisoners we obtained useful information. Here is the result
of his examination:-

Faskar Johann.

Musketier of the 4th. Coy. 1st. Bn. 63rd. Regiment.

Captured at Y Wood on May 13th. 1916.

The prisoner is intelligent and talked freely. According to
him Major von Weller commands the 63rd. Regiment and Hauptmann von
Kupfer the 1st. Battalion. The 4th. Company is commanded by an
acting Lieutenant. The prisoner has a poor idea of the German
regimental officers in general. Many of them are very young with
no experience. His own company was up to strength and consisted of
men from 21 to 28 years of age.

The prisoner admitted the presence of gas chambers and cylinders
built in strongrecesses on the parapet of the fire trenches. He said
they were put in in December. The men have been issued with the
new gas mask.

Every regiment has a telephone listening apparatus; they are
used by special personnel and are kept very secret. An instrument
in front of Frise proved very useful in January. Telephone wires
lead up to the front trenches. Dug-outs are built in the front and
support lines under the parapet. There are twenty or thirty steps
leading down to them and they are dry and comfortable.

Food has deteriorated in quality lately. The only drink has
been coffee or water, but beer can be bought in the canteens. The
prisoner says the men are mildly dissatisfied as there appear to
be no chances of an early finish to the war. Two months ago metal
cases were installed in the front line intended to produce a gas
cloud. These cases are rectangular and are painted grey. They are

called GETESCHRANKS. They stand four feet high and the top measures
fifteen inches by eighteen inches. The prisoner maintains that no
pipe or nozzle projected from the case. On one face however were
four gauge dials and the case had wheels and at the sides were
lugs for carrying bars. The case was heavy - 250 lbs, but 2 men could
carry it by means of the carrying bars.

Several days before his capture the prisoner had been served
out with a new type of gasmask. This had a larger container than
the previous pattern.

My leave had commenced on May 13th. came to an end on the
24th. and I had the usual rotten journey back. Traffic was much
congested but I got a berth on the S.S. Archangel and on my
arrival at Havre snaffled a corner seat in a first class carriage.
I was met at the railhead at Mericourt Ribemont by the Mess Cart
and we jogged along the nine miles to Suzanne. When we got there
I found my Battalion was in the trenches, so slipped and swore my
way over three miles of fields to the Colonel's dugout where I
arrived at 11.30 p.m. on the 25th.

Requiescant.

The anguish and the pain have passed,
And peace has come to them at last;
But in the stern looks linger still
The iron purpose and the will.

Dear Christ, who reigns above the flood
Of human tears and human blood,
A weary road these men have trod;
O house them in the house of God.

Capt. Megson (bareheaded) and Adjutant Gibbon (?)

General Sir John Shea, G.C.B., K.C.M.G., D.S.O.
Commander, 30th. Division.

Changes in Command. The French take over Maricourt. The Assembly.

> Sing me to sleep where bullets fall,
> Let me forget the War and all;
> Damp is my dugout, cold my feet,
> Nothing but biscuits and bully to eat:
>
> Sing me to sleep in some old shed,
> A dozen rats about my head;
> Stretched out upon my waterproof,
> Dodging the raindrops from the roof.
>
> Far far from Wipers I long to be,
> Where German snipers can't snipe at me;
> Think of me crouching where the worms creep,
> Waiting for Sergeant to sing me to sleep.

France was looking her best in this month of May, 1916.
The poppies and the sanfoin were beautiful and even the trenches
looked better in their spring garments. What was more to the point
was that they were dry. France and our Armies in France had not
yet adopted the advanced time.

I found that General Fry had been removed from the command of
the Division: Old Chocolate, as he was disrespectfully known. He was
replaced by General John Shea, who had been on Haig's staff. He was a
very live wire. He was a fiery little Irishman and before the war
had been a major in the Deccan Horse. Montgomery the Brigade Major
had also gone and Captain Ramsden had taken his job over.

The Battalion was still holding the sector of trenches south
of the road and the Colonel had shifted his headquarters to S Works
as the hill dugouts were no longer habitable. It was through the
wall of one of these dugouts which I occupied when acting as Adjutant
that our own Artillery fired an 18 pounder shell. Luckily it failed to
explode. On the 27th. I took over my duties from Mead who had been
acting for me and helped the C.O. to write up the War Diary. The
German guns registered on our communication trenches.

I wonder if you know what is meant by registering. Our Hun
friends had very accurate maps of our trench country. Whenever a
new trench was dug, or a new machine gun position located, or new
company headquarters spotted, the German batteries covering that
sector would proceed to find the correct aim to hit that particular
mark.When they had found by practise the correct distance, and the
right direction they just made a note of the map reference and the
elevation until it should become desirable to shell that spot again.

All our battery positions and ammunition dumps and cross roads
and trenches were systematically registered and then when need arose
the gunners could just open fire and be sure of hitting their mark.

It was quite instructive to watch this going on. They would
discover by means of their aeroplanes some new work on our trenches.
A German battery responsible for that section would estimate the
distance and send a shell over. Probably it would fall short or to

the left; another shell would come over, this time too far and a little
to the right, a third gun would try and perhaps land a shell just where
it was wanted. The observer, either in the Hun trenches or in an
aeroplane would signal O.K. and they would then shut up shop, having
got the right range.

We learnt that the French were to take over our trenches up to
a point north of Maricourt, the Powers that Were having rightly
decided that the actual river Somme formed a bad dividing line between
the French armies and our own, more particularly so in view of the
intended offensive. For though nothing was known definitely, it was
common knowledge that the Big Push was coming at last.

The roads were full of troops and the whole countryside just
crawling with guns and howitzers of every calibre. The dumps were
crowded with trench ladders and all the other stage properties of
a general attack. We were very excited and the famous Iron Division
of the French army, which had so distinguished itself at Verdun had
been selected for our neighbours. The 30th. Division of which my
Battalion formed part was the extreme right of the British Line,
a place of honour for which we were to pay dearly.

An aeroplane was brought down by our machine guns and at night
the body of the aviator was recovered. The machine crashed in
No Man's Land by Fargny Mill. The German proved to be a second
lieutenant of the 87th. Regiment. He had no papers and no means of
personal identification upon him but was wearing the ribbon of the
Iron Cross. The body was that of a well built man and well-dressed.
He was buried in the cemetery near fargny Mill.

Portion of the machine was brought in and also the machine gun.
This was crushed under the machine, the muzzle being driven into the
ground and the barrel bent so far that the recoiling portions were
jambed to the rear. The barrel was stripped and oiled and the following
observations made :-

On the fusee spring box were stamped the words
MSCH. GEW. 08. GEWEHRFABRIK. SPANDAU. 1915.
There was also on the fusee spring box a scale graduated from zero
to seventy, indicating the tension of the spring. The gun appeared
to be a combination of the Vickers and Maxim types, having the Vickers
roller action and the Maxim inverted crank action. The lock mechanism
resembled that of the Vickers guns. Battle sights were fitted.
In place of the thumb piece there was a Bowden wire entering the
breech-casing for firing the gun.

On the crank handle was a small grooved pulley round which passed
another wire whereby the crank handles could be rotated, and a third
wire lifted the safety catch which engages with the crank handle.
These two latter wires were both actuated by the same lever to which they
were still attached. Evidently the gun was placed beyond the reach of the
operator, and was the standard type of gun as the barrel casing not being
required had been cut away for lightness. Every part was plainly
numbered 6806.

An aluminium camera with a large bulls eye behind which were
two shutters marked YELLOW and WHITE was also brought in, and a
metal slide. The engine itself was of a very heavy type with six
stationary cylinders. Being too heavy to move whole, it was dragged

into a trench for safety and the three magnetos brought away. I have at home now a small piece of this machine as a souvenir of rather an exciting night.

Rain came again and the trenches were flooded. The rats at this time were getting really beyond all bearing. They used to parade regularly for rations and if the ration party were late in getting up for supplies, these fat monsters would get terribly angry and run about making the most indignant noises. Let me be sure you have got this right because it was really rather interesting. Every evening at more or less the same time the Battalion transport section would bring up the next days rations, sacks of bread, bacon, butter and cheese and so forth. These would be put down at Battalion Headquarters or any other convenient dump and would be collected by the ration carriers from each platoon, who would take their respective shares up to the trenches. It was the job of the Quartermaster Sergeant to apportion these rations and naturally there would be crumbs spilt and little bits of fat bacon occasionally. Hordes of rats would appear as punctually as the platoon ration carriers and await the arrival of the Battalion transport and the subsequent division of food. The ground around would be just one moving mass of rats, not the pleasant homely and domestic creatures to which we are accustomed here in England, but great fat fellows the size of small cats, with red tusks and very vicious habits, beasts which battened on the corpses and which would attack without fear even the wounded if they were isolated.

On June 1st. I went down to Suzanne to meet the Colonel of the French troops who were to relieve us. I took him round the trenches and in the evening again went down to guide the French troops up to the trenches. There had been shocking bad management somewhere as they had succeeded in crowding three thousand troops into Suzanne in the small space between the chateau and the church and if the gentle Bosches had opened fire at that moment they would have suffered terribly. However we got clear at last, after much very bad language on my part - I had necer realised how useful it would prove to be able to swear fluently in French - and finally I marshalled that sanguinary crew into the trenches without the loss of a solitary man.

By the time I had got them installed I had had quite enough of them but I had to remain with their Colonel for several days until they had settled down comfortably. I felt more like a prisoner than a Liaison Officer, surrounded as I was by foreigners and with the exception of Hibbert the only Englishman in the sector.

I lived with the French Colonel and they were most hospitable, but they quickly made our spotless trenches an awful mess and the characteristic smell of French troops soon pervaded the entire neighbourhood. I really was very glad however of the opportunity of studying their methods and weapons of war.

Some of their little ways were very funny. I remembered with difficulty to retain my knife between courses, and that only after I had been reduced to eating with my fingers once or twice. Dinner was an elaborate affair even in the trenches and consisted of one sardine, half a boiled egg chopped in vinegar, a scrap of boiled liver then saute potatoes as a separate course, followed by jam eaten with a spoon as a sweet and cheese. The Colonel's way of paying me a compliment was to offer me tit-bits from his own plate on his own fork.

I watched the famous Soixante Quinze batteries in action and sent home several of the empty shell cases. The French were far more economical of officers than ourselves. Their regiments consist of three battalions and are commanded by a Colonel. Each Battalion is commanded by a Major. The Battalion consists of four double companies with three officers apiece, instead of our six. The adjutant of a French Battalion is a non-commissioned officer. Altogether they employ about a third of the number of officers we do per division.

The French troops have all the dash for which they are noted, but possess also a terrible calm. We used to think they were very good in attack but restless under punishment. Of course these were the flower of the French Army, but they certainly were steady enough under bombardment. I have been in the trenches with them when all the fury of the German batteries have been concentrated on one small stretch of trench. I have seen them blown off the firing step by the concussion of the bursting shells again and again, only to immediately resume their firing positions. I have seen a French sentry lifted thirty yards by the explosion of a trench mortar bomb, pick himself up and shake the dust off and return to his post.

On the 4th. I was able to return to my own Battalion which had gone to Etinehem under canvas. On the 5th. Colonel Petrie went on leave and Major Knox and I went as far as Amiens with him and we all had luncheon at the Godbert. Incidentally the French C.O. told me that he had asked for a Cross of the Legion of Honour for me in token of my usefulness to him in handing over the line. It arrived in due time at Divisional Headquarters, but I imagine that one of the Divisional Staff was short of that particular decoration so the label became unstuck ! Anyhow I never got it. I was rather sorry as I should have liked to wear that little bit of red riband in my buttonhole when I revisit France.

Now followed long days of fatigue work. We were busily engaged in burying telephone cable up to the front line from the heavy batteries behind. Several miles of narrow trench seven feet deep had to be cut in the unyielding chalk and it was tough going. After the day's work we used to return to Etinehem, bathe in the Somme and then settle down to an evening's gramophone recital.

Captain Sotham's eyesight was giving him a great deal of pain and he made many excursions into Amiens. I was President of the Headquarters Mess and as such had to order meals for the H.Q. staff and buy extra grub and so on. Sotham was difficult enough to feed at any time but just now he was really rather trying. In evacuated areas it is difficult to secure a constant supply of fresh eggs, butter and green vegetables; however we managed very well on the whole. The Headquarters Mess consisted of the Colonel, Major Knox, Sotham and myself. Actually the Padre and Doctor, and a Signalling Officer and Lewis Gun Officer and Bombing Officer should have been with us but the Colonel got bored with them and they always had a separate Mess. Probably they were very thankful as the atmosphere of Headquarters was rather oppressive at times.

On June 8th. we heard of Kitchener's death, which affected us profoundly. We felt that the one man whom we could trust had gone.

Among the liars and schemers at home he had seemed to be our one
mainstay and support. The following was the Special Order of the
Day which brought us the news:

"It is with deep regret that the Commander-in-Chief
communicates to the Armies in France the following telegram
received from the War Office:

'By His Majesty's Command the following Order has been
issued to the Army:-

The King has learnt with profound regret of the disaster
by which the Secretary of State for War lost his life while
proceeding on a special mission to the Emperor of Russia.

Field Marshal Lord Kitchener gave forty five years of
distinguishing service to this State, and it is largely
due to his administrative genius and un-wearying energy
that the Country has been able to create and place in the
field the Armies which are to-day upholding the traditional
glories of our Empire.

Lord Kitchener will be mourned by the Army as a great
soldier who under conditions of unexampled difficulties
rendered supreme and devoted service both to the Army and
the State '. "

Kitchener was the one man whom the troops could trust to
stand firm, unshaken by popular clamour and unswayed by desire
of personal gain or aggrandizement. Once again we were at the mercy
of political mountebanks. When the news reached us we could hardly
believe it, and then as men do we wondered who would be his successor.
One waggish cynic suggested a name and was met with howls of
delighted laughter.

This for Remembrance.

Thor's hammer he ! He took the British Race
Raw metal, full of flaws but veined with gold,
And laid it on an anvil - smote it hard,
Till it became a blade of tempered steel,
Inlaid with magic scrolls of sacrifice.

Five million willing soldiers, think of it !
Called from the ruts of easy life and love
By one man's quiet voice, by one man's name,
That made their souls ashamed to stand aloof
While blows were struck for England's liberty.

Great Captains have led armies - he did more;
He made an army grow on sterile soil
Of peaceful use and custom, millions strong;
Quicker than Cadmus with his dragon's teeth
His simple magic, "England wants you, men".

On the 9th. I rode with Major Knox to Bronfay Farm and Billon
Wood and went over the new line of trenches we were to hold. These
stretched west from Maricourt Wood to Machine Gun Wood and were
directly opposite the Brickworks and Montauban. The idea was to
give us all a good look at the ground over which we were to attack
later. All the approaches were crawling with troops and guns and
the valleys were alive with movement, huge howitzers and batteries
of heavy guns.

Sotham was nearly mad with neuralgia and I did his job for
him. It was difficult to keep the peace as he was usually at
loggerheads with the Company Commanders at the best of times and
just at present he was raelly insufferably rude to them.

On the 10th. we relieved the 18th. Liverpools, commanded by
Colonel Trotter. We took up our Headquarters under the chateau at
Maricourt. The trenches were bad and the relief not completed until
4 a.m. On the 11th. we received the following letter from our
French neighbours :

        146th. Reg. d'Infanterie.   11th. Juin 1916.
                        Note !

    On me communique le renseignement suivant. "Les troupes
sur la Somme ont surptis une communication telephonique
allemande disant 'Les anglais recevront notre visite ce soir'
C'est du moins ce qu'on croit avoir compris.
                    Le Lieut. Colonel

                        R. Jeanpierre.

Actually on the night of June 13th. after 4 days heavy shell fire the
Germans essayed an attack and penetrated the French trenches on the right
of the line but were driven back.

On the 12th. Colonel Jeanpierre came to luncheon. The 146th.
Regiment was on our immediate right. The bombardment was extremely
heavy, the Germans turning on all the available trench mortars and
heavy guns as well. They were searching for the point of junction
between the French and ourselves and subjected us to pitiless fire.

On the 13th. Machine Gun Wood was practically destroyed by
the German shell fire. At noon the mortars were still very busy
and I warned Brigade Headquarters that I considered a raid likely
to take place that night. For days the Germans had been registering
our communication trenches and our wire entanglements had been
systematically cut and there was suspicious activity among the
garrison of the Hun trenches. At 9.30 p.m. I turned in for an hour
of sleep. The Brigade had pooh-poohed my idea of an imminent raid
and had instructed working parties to go out as usual. I was not
satisfied about the situation and wanted to snatch a little sleep
while I could.

For the last two days we had been engaged in digging a new
trench from Machine Gun Wood across the Battalion frontage in No
Man's Land, about 150 yards in advance of our own line. A party of
170 men were engaged on the work of deepening this trench while in
front of them again we had a covering party of thirty men under the
charge of Lieutenant Fowler. The working party was found by the 18th.

Manchesters and not from our Battalion. The covering party were our own men. In addition to the garrison of the fire trench there were numerous parties at work on the surface saps so that the trenches were unusually full of men. The digging party of the 18th. Battalion of course had their rifles with them. Although it was not my turn for duty I was feeling uneasy and went along to the fire trenches to see what was going on. For a short space all was quiet.

Then at 11.35 p.m. a light went up from the German trenches; this was the signal for the opening of a very intensive shelling of the right of our line where we joined the French, the fire and support and communication trenches and Maricourt itself.

We sent up the S.O.S. rocket signal, five red lights in quick succession, and repeated it over the telephone to our covering batteries. For once in a way the line held good and our artillery replied with exemplary promptitude on the German front line and support trenches. The line to the artillery was cut after we had got our S.O.S. through, and lamps were used for visual signalling quite successfully. Communication with the French on our right, the Scots Fusiliers on our left and Brigade Headquarters was maintained by telephone throughout the engagement.

Two platoons of the reserve company assembled with the Battalion bombers in the cellars of the Headquarters in case of need. The front line was very heavily shelled; the parapet was blown in in twenty different places and in many cases the men were literally blown off the firing platform by shells bursting near them.

The communication trenches were effectually blocked by the German guns and in every respect the enemy's marksmanship was excellent. The Bosches left their trenches in large numbers but in no single instance succeeded in penetrating our lines. The French were not so fortunate and lost several prisoners.

The working party from the other battalion were out in front of our trenches when the row began. They suffered no losses but in their haste to get back into cover had left many of their rifles behind them; consequently those were more of an embarrassment than assistance when they reached our trenches. Our covering party naturally did not attempt to get back until all the digging party were safely in. Fowler was badly wounded; Norris was killed, and four other men wounded. Fowler was hit over a hundred yards from the trench, but faint with loss of blood nevertheless managed to crawl back.

In the front line we only had six casualties. Phillips was severely wounded. Throughout our men behaved with exemplary calm and perfect self control. The Lewis Gun sections held their fire until a really good target presented itself and the men's rifles worked freely and easily. From the commencement the situation was perfectly in hand and remained so until normal conditions were resumed at 3 a.m.

Of our two officer casualties, Phillips had been with the Battalion since its start, and Fowler had only lately joined us. I helped to get Fowler back through our own wire. He was fearfully heavy as he was covered with mud. Onthe 14th. we repaired the damage to our trenches and buried our dead.

On the 16th. of June we were relieved by the 2nd. Bedfords at dawn and marched by platoons to the Bois de Tailles where we had brekker but no sleep. We continued our march to Heilly where we entrained for Ailly-sur-Somme. Here we detrained again and marched to the village of Le Mesge, arriving there at 11.30 p.m. We were dead tired after seven days incessant shelling followed by an exciting raid and a twenty five mile march.

At Le Mesge we had good billets and were able to get plenty of strawberries and cream. We took up our Headquarters at a very pretty little villa. On the 19th. we started to rehearse the part we were to play in the Big Push, namely the capture of Montauban, a strongly held and fortified village three thousand yards beyond the German front line trenches.

A facsimile of the German trenches and of the village itself, roads and church and houses all complete, had been cut out in turf at Briquesmesnil, and here we went through all the stages of the attack, day by day, explaining carefully to the troops what was happening at each stage and making sure that every man knew his own job.

On the 21st. we changed billets and moved to Oissy where the Battalion Headquarters were billetted in a magnificent chateau with beautiful grounds and artificial lakes by whose borders frogs croaked all night and most of the day. My bedroom was a sumptuously furnished apartment. On the 22nd. the Padre and I rode into Amiens and had a ripping lunch at the Godbert, thinking that it might well be our last, and two days later we had a battalion concert in the grounds of the chateau.

The officers sat on the terrace outside the chateau and the men lay at their ease on the green sward that sloped away towards the lake. The flowers were in their full splendour and it was a perfect June evening. The scent of bean blossom was reaching us from a near-by field, and the busy hum of the bees was very sweet to our ears. In the old days in England our concert parties were rather noted, and as we listened to Pickering singing "Where my Caravan has Rested" and to Healey's favourite song "I hear you calling me", we all felt that the concert was almost sacramental. We all knew what was before us, what a welter of mud and slaughter, and it was a heavenly respite to lounge at ease in the sunlight, listening to the silly sentimental songs we loved, and absorbing the sheer beauty of our surroundings.

On the 25th. I had to go on to Bray to make a reconnaissance forward to the assembly trenches which we were to occupy on the night prior to the attack. The Colonel told me to take any officer I liked with me, so I chose Allen.

We billetted at Etinehem for the night and on the 26th. the Brigade Major showed us the route we were to follow in taking the Battalion up to its assembly trenches.

We were surprised by the tremendous activity we found as we crossed the valleys of Billon Wood and Bronfay Farm. Enormous howitzers - huge squat monsters - trench mortars, heavy naval guns and cannon of every calibre were firing all the time; the noise was deafening and the huge stacks of shells proved that here at any rate was no shortage of

ammunition. Our route was a very devious and involved one, but we
made ourselves sure of the six miles we would have to traverse and
returned to Etinehem again for the night.

The Battalion having finished the rehearsal arrived at 11 p.m.
at Etinehem on the night of the 26th. On the following day Allen and
I took a party of N.C.O.'s from each Company over the route and again
had the opportunity of watching the tremendous artillery preparation
in progress. Our original orders were to move the Battalion into
the assembly trenches on the night of the 28th. ready for the attack
early on the 29th. but just as we were getting ready to leave Etinehem
at 2 p.m. on the 28th. we received orders to remain where we were.
I do not know whether it was ever intended to attack on the 29th. but
think it more than likely that the date was advertised to put the
Bosches off the scent, while the true intention was to attack on July 1st.

My part in the performance was to lead over a small party of
Headquarters despatch runners and my snipers and scouts, and on our
arrival at Montauban to carefully search all German dugouts for
artillery maps and regimental papers and send them back at once to
Corps Headquarters. I detailed Corporal Kelly and L/Cpl. Stevens
to help me in this job, while naturally Thompson, my own runner,
and Hibbert, my batman, would accompany me. Thompson was a dear
fellow, and had been my very devoted companion in most of my work.
Ever since my appointment to Battalion Headquarters Staff he had
acted as my personal despatch runner and bodyguard. He was a man
of singular courage and intelligence. Hibbert had been my personal
servant during the whole time we had been in France and my very
good friend.

On the 29th. Johnson and I went to evening service together
and received Holy Communion. Morton Johnson and I had been very
close friends since the day I joined the Battalion. He was much
older than myself but we got on exceedingly well together. Actually
he was not fit to go into action as he had been a sick man for the
previous fortnight, but he was determined to be with his company
in our first big battle.

At 7p.m. on June 30th. we left Etinehem, and I successfully
guided the Battalion into its assembly trenches which we reached
at 12.45 midnight. It was an intricate business as our allotted
path lay across country, and any deviation might well have brought
us in the line of fire of our own artillery. The assembly trenches
lay north of the Peronne Road and east of the Talus Boise, just in
front of Oxford Copse. Our right flank rested on Cambridge Copse
and our left on the Talus Boise.

The roar of the guns shook the earth and continued without
ceasing all throughout the night. The noise was appalling and there
was no chance of sleep. The hour of attack, in military terms zero
hour, was fixed for 7.30 a.m. on July 1st. We were on the right of
the line, and the French were to attack at the same time. It was
a curious night, and I spent much of the time talking to the troops,
although such was the noise of the guns that conversation had to be
carried on at the tops of our voices.

The Germans opposing us were the 6th. Army Corps and particular
details of its organisation are given in the appendix to this diary.

Montauban was a fortified village three thousand yards behind the German front line. It was used as a rest billet for the 62nd. Infantry Regiment who also had supply and ammunition dumps there. No civillians were allowed in the village. There were several batteries of 77mm. field guns west of the village. According to the statement of Paul Schaffgrezyt, a prisoner of the 2nd. Bn. of the 62nd. Regiment captured at Carnoy on January 28th. 1916, the kitchens of the Regiment were at Montauban where there were also hot baths for the troops and a canteen. The water supply also came from there.

The following notes from our own Corps Intelligence Summaries are worth recording:-

21.1.16. Traffic in and near Montauban at night seems to be on the increase; during the night of 20/21st. a train was heard from the direction of the village at 10.45 p.m., light transport from 11.15 until midnight and a heavy traction engine entering and leaving the village at about 12.45 a.m.

22.6.16. At 2 p.m. a lorry was seen going from Longueval to Flers and ten vehicles were seen in Longueval. There appeared to be considerable activity behind Caterpillar Wood about the same time. The barbed wire has been considerably strengthened along the Carnoy - Montauban road at S.27.c.6.2. Fifteen trucks were seen in the valley east of Caterpillar Wood about S.21.d.80.68. and three dumps on the south side of the valley at the same point. The two large sheds in the quarry at S.21.d.95.55. were very visible.

23.6.16. The number of dumps in Caterpillar Wood valley has increased from three to five since yesterday. Since June 1st. an average of about three trucks a day have been seen on the Caterpillar Wood - Trones Wood railway; by far the largest number were observed on June 22nd; the position at which these trucks were seen makes it appear probable that they are almost entirely employed in connection with the dump in the quarries at S.21.d.80.50. to S.22.c.0.5. and at S.22.d.9.4. Reports on the station at Guillemont give an average of six trucks a day and at Combles of twenty three trucks a day.

24.6.16. Between 6.45 and 8 p.m. one of our heavy batteries firing with aeroplane observation scored seven direct hits on a hostile emplacement. During the 24th. and night of 24/25th. our artillery and trench mortars bombarded the hostile trenches intermittently. There was practically no retaliation. The 15 cm. long range guns of the enemy fired occasional rounds on to the Bray-Corbir Road during the afternoon. A movable anti-aircraft battery was observed on the railway east of Guillemont between 7 p.m. and 8 p.m.

26.6.16. The bombardment proceeds with satisfactory results. The enemy's retaliation is feeble against the 30th. Division and is apparently carried out by single guns firing rapid, and consists almost entirely of 10.5 cm. shells on Machine Gun Wood, Maricourt and Oxford Copse. During the afternoon hostile artillery was much more active against the left division, mostly near the assembly trenches north of Carnoy and the communication trenches where they cross the Peronne Road. The shells were of 77 mm. and 105 cm. calibre and come from Caterpillar Wood.

A few 10.5 cm. shells were fired into Bray and airmen report
that the 66th. Siege Battery yesterday blew one gun completely
up in the air at S.19.b.44.40.

Observation Posts at Maltz Horn Farm and Montauban Mill were
bombarded. A house in Longueval was burning at 10.30 a.m. In front
of the 30th. Division the German wire is reported very much damaged
and in many places completely cleared. The enemy's defences are
much damaged. One of our patrols found two concrete machine gun
emplacements destroyed. No machine guns were firing from their
front line. There are fifteen trucks in the station at Combles
and a large dump of pioneer stores.

In Caterpillar Wood there is no activity apparent to-day. The
valley behind the wood has been heavily shelled. There are five trucks
on the railway and four dumps at S.21.d.80.68. and these do not
appear to have been damaged by shell fire to any extent.

So much for the intelligence reports. The bombardment lasted
without ceasing to July 1st. Allthe German observation balloons
were brought down in flames. My Battalion was not allowed to take
all its officers into action as it was desired to retain a nucleus.
Knox, Payne, Oliver, Mead and Davidson were left behind, also some
new officers who had only just arrived - Jackson, Stafford Badger,
Smithers, Hoskins, Scudamore, Venner and two whose names I have
forgotten. Those of us who did go into action wore Tommy's tunics
in order to baffle the German snipers. This was a Brigade order.

The general idea for attack for the 30th. Division was as here
follows:-

Zero had been fixed for 7.30 a.m. on July 1st. and for one hour
before zero every gun and trench mortar were firing as rapidly as
they could. At 7.30 the 89th. Brigade who were holding the front
line trenches were to capture what was left of the German front line,
while the 21st. Brigade were to follow through and take the Glatz
Redoubt. At 8.30 the 90th. Brigade were to push through and capture
and hold Montauban. This Brigade consisted of the 16th., 17th.,
and 18th. Battalions of the Manchester Regiment and the 2nd. Battalion
of the Royal Scots Fusiliers. The 16th. and 17th. Bns. were to capture
Montauban and consolidate, the 18th. Bn. was given the job of carrying
material and the Royal Scots Fusiliers were in support. We had been
told that having captured Montauban we were to occupy a ridge along
the northern perimeter of the village and consolidate an old German
communication trench known as Montauban Alley, and that we should be
relieved in the early afternoon and under no circumstances were we
to press on farther.

An extract from Brigade Operation Order No. 23 para. 30 gave me
my instructions.

It is the especial duty of all Intelligence Officers to
obtain information as regards the enemy and to pass it on as soon
as possible. Battalion and Company Headquarters and indeed all
dugouts in Montauban should be searched. The information and documents
it is particularly desired to obtain are :-

(a) Enemy artillery maps   (b) Telephone message books
(c) Ammunition states   (d) Maps and sketches.

- 81 -

The non-commissioned officers will be detailed by each Battalion as Intelligence men. They will wear a white, or yellow armband marked Intelligence. Their duty is to collect documents from dugouts, off dead Germans, et cetera and to send them back with the prisoners' escorts to be handed over to the Divisional Parties at A.14.b.9.5. It is the duty of every officer to see that if the Intelligence Men become casualties, some other man is told off to carry on.

Now we come to the hour of attack. The troops had been in the assembly trenches all night but had got little rest in the inferno of noise and smoke from our own guns. We had suffered some loss during the night but on the whole the German artillery had not been very active. They were saving their ammunition for the time of our attack. This was to be our first pitched battle. We were confident that the end of the War was in sight, and if we were afraid we managed to conceal it. How we should acquit ourselves is matter for another chapter.

Through learned and laborious years,
They set themselves to find
Fresh terrors and undreamed of fears
To heap upon mankind.

When all was ready to their hand
They loosed their hidden sword,
And utterly laid waste a land
Their oath was pledged to guard.

They paid the price to reach their goal
Across a world in flame,
But their own hate slew their own soul
Before that victory came.

The German Occupation of Belgium.

A German Time Fuse made into a Bell by the Author.

MARICOURT. JUNE 1916

GERMAN TIME FUSE.

Chapter Eleven.

The Glorious First. Montauban captured and held. Happy Valley.

Deserted Temples.

These are the newly dead
Who lie
So stiff, so strangely still;
Their last look frozen on their pallid mask
And their dull eyes so pale -
Like china, staring pale -
The shattered dead:
Poor tortured wrecks
Of once such lovely form;
How can I write of them
Who are so hideous as to be obscene !
My eyes burn hot with sad and angry tears;
Poor Horrors !
What can expiate the crime
Of all these ruined shrines ?
Fair temples of the Gods.
Oh, then the piteous little ones
Whose breath
Has passed full many days....
Ah God,
Pity the unburied Dead.

At last the morning of advance came. All night long our guns had thundered and roared, culminating in a furiously intense bombardment for the final hour before zero. At 7.30 a.m. we saw the first wave of the 18th. Division who were on our left going into the barrage. We were not due to start until 8.30 a.m. We issued the usual rum ration to the troops; they needed it after their sleepless night in the cold unsheltered assembly trenches. He who says that British troops went into action drunk lies in his throat. In spite of the intolerant teetotal cranks a very small rum ration was issued to all the troops in the trenches every morning at stand-to. At times like the present, before going into action, the usual ration was never exceeded; if ever men needed all their wits about them, it was now in time of battle.

At 8.10 a.m. came the news of French successes on our right and the Colonel told me to tell the troops. I went slowly up the line shouting at the top of my voice "The French have taken Hardecourt and Faviere Wood; Germans are surrendering along the line". Only the two or three men nearest me in each spot could hear on account of the gunfire, but the news spread from man to man until such a cheer went up as drowned for the moment even the hideous row of the guns. All the troops were very cheery and we all felt extraordinarily light-hearted. Our souls seemed divorced from our earth-bound bodies. I do not think that anyone of us was afraid then; that came afterwards.

At 8.20 a.m. we got out of our assembly trenches and the troops
lay down in little columns of artillery formation, ready to move
off sharply to time. By now we were being very heavily shelled and
some of the men climbed out of the trench, only to slide back at once -
dead. I was standing by the Colonel, counting the minutes on my
wrist watch; 8.27 - 8.28 - 8.29 - each minute an eternity of waiting -
8.30 and off we went.

We had to work most carefully to a timetable. We were to follow
a creeping barrage put down by our own guns, and to press forward
too fast would be just as fatal to our success, as getting to our
objective too late. Our objective was Montauban and we had three
thousand yards to go before reaching it. A mad short charge is rather
fun and soon over, but a steady advance of a mile and three quarters
over broken ground and under a hellish barrage was a good test for
staediness.

Through the fire we advanced in little columns in file, about
a dozen men in each; no rubbing shoulders for company and so presenting
a good target for the enemy. We had to cross our own front line
trenches and those of the Germans, and their support lines and
countless communication trenches. These trenches were full of dead
and wounded, ours and the Germans. Small isolated parties of the
enemy remained active and we had to clear a few machine gun nests.
German medical officers and our own were attending to the wounded.
To cross the trenches each section carried a trench ladder which
could be laid as a bridge from side to side.

Over these ladders the little columns would file, one by one,
forming up again as they got across. There was no confusion, no
hurry or bustle. On we went at a steady walking pace while the
German barrage fire punished us severely. Occasionally a shell
would drop right in the midst of one of our columns, totally
obliterating it.

My own little party consisted of Pennington, Kelly, Stevens,
Palmer, Thompson, Hibbert, Blears, Smith, and Carroll. When any shell
came uncomfortably close I shouted "Steady, men, steady", as one
would speak to children crossing the road, and steady they were.
I felt quite curiously detached as if I were merely a spectator.
My heart thumped a bit sometimes. When we were going across the
German second line, the trench ladder slipped and another had to be
put into position; we were held up for a minute. In sheer bravado I
lit a cigarette, conscious of a hand that did not shake.

On we went at our steady pace, paying no heed to the high explosives
all around and the shrapnel bursting overhead. Every man had his eyes
fixed on Montauban, making always for our goal. It was cruelly hard
for men to see their best pals drop mortally wounded and not be able
to stop and succour them, but our orders were of the strictest.
No man was to check for any reason save sheer inability to go on, so
steadily onward we went, cries of comrades disturbing us more than the
German messengers of death.

At one point we had to wait a while for our own barrage to go
forward. The advancing troops halted and lay down until the barrage
should lift. Sotham was just in advance of me and I went along to
pass the time of day. At 9.56 a.m. our barrage moved forward and on

went we. Now we came under heavy machine gun fire and our little files
extended into line, keeping distance just as if they had been on the
Battalion parade ground.

Matters were made worse when the 18th. Division on our left were
held up at Pommiers Ridge. Our job was still to go forward and we
were subjected to murderous fire which simply mowed our men down.
I saw Sotham drop and feared they had got him, but he had only caught
his foot in some wire and was up at once.

As we approached Train Alley, I took a snapshot of our men
crossing it and later I took a photograph of Montauban itself as we
were advancing on it. I had carried for long a small V.P.K. camera
in my hip pocket. The snaps are unique, but not very good as I could
not ask the troops to stand still and look pleasant ! We left poor
Horley in Train Alley, his shoulder smashed by a bullet and cursing
horribly because he could no longer go on. Train Alley was a very
deep and very wide trench where our ladders were no use, but we
scrambled in and out of it all right.

Now we swept up the last long slope into the village. We had arrived
so far without undue exhaustion and into Montauban we poured, breaking
down all resistance. Hardly one brick had been left upon another,
but the Germans had sheltered in their deep dugouts during the
bombardment and were ready for us with bombs and machine guns.

However, in ten minutes all the Bosches in the village had been
captured or killed, and Montauban was ours. By 10.30 a.m. our troops
had reached Montauban Alley which was beyond the village and was our
furthest objective.

Our orders were to consolidate and hold this trench with three
companies, thereby defending the village against any counter attack,
whilst the fourth company remained in reserve along the northern
perimeter of the village. Battalion Headquarters were established in
Montauban and got into touch with Brigade H.Q. by means of visual
signalling.

In Montauban were many dugouts containing equipment and stores.
In one dugout we found forty Germans whilst in another we surprised
a German artillery General having breakfast with his Staff !

We also captured a battery of field guns, and Aldous and Price
chalked the name of the Battalion on the barrels. I collected many
very valuable maps and documents and orderly room papers and sent
them back without delay. By 11.30 a.m. my own job was done and I
went along to Battalion Headquarters to report. By this time the
re-action had set in, and I was feeling rather exhausted and sick.
However I had no time for re-actions as Sotham told me that all
A Company's officers had been knocked out during the advance and the
Colonel wanted me to go up to Montauban Alley and take charge.

I found there all that was left of A, B, and C Company, about
250 in all, and Johnson, commanding C Company, the only officer.
Johnson decided to take the right of the line and I took the left.
The men were terribly tired, and suffering from that same re-action
that I had experienced momentarily, the inevitable re-action which
follows mental exaltation, hard fighting and bodily fatigue.

Through having had a roving commission along the Battalion front for so many months, I knew most of these men personally and by name and this helped me tremendously in the task before me. It was vitally necessary to set to work at once and convert the old German communication trench into a fire trench for our own defence. In its present state, it was very deep; the men could not see over the top, and of course there was no parapet. For one short hour we should be free of shelling as the German artillery would not open fire on the village whilst there was any doubt as to their own people being still in occupation, and we had to make the best of our chances and prepare for the inevitable counter-attack.

The men worked like Trojans and cut fire steps and platforms and reversed the parapet of the trench, until at last we had made it capable of defence. After their work they felt better and set to cleaning their rifles and ammunition.

We had a frontage of eight hundred yards to hold. On our left we had an exposed flank until late in the afternoon as the 55th. Brigade could not attain its objective to time. On our right flank the 17th. Bn., whose business it was to guard the east side of the village, had established a bombing post and strong point or redoubt.

When I visited this post in order to assure myself that our right flank was secure, I ascertained from the officer in charge that his orders were to fall back in case of attack. This was hardly according to plan and would have rendered our own position well-nigh untenable, so I sent an urgent message back to Sotham asking him to see the Colonel of the 17th. Battalion and get these instructions modified. This was done and when I went along later in the day, I found that this contingent of the 17th. Battalion had received fresh instructions to hold its ground in face of all opposition.

As quickly as could be I organised my own sentry groups and placed the Lewis guns at my disposal in the best positions. I then sent back to Montauban for ammunition, bombs, rocket signals and Verey lights, none of which I ever received. I could not spare men from the firing garrison to carry stores and it was the job of the support company and the 18th. Manchesters to get them up to us.

Having consolidated as well as we could I mounted a few sentries along the line, and made everyone else get some sleep. There was no sign of the 9th. Division which was supposed to be coming up to relieve us and carry on the advance and our only hope preparing for the counter-attacks was to get the troops back to more or less normal conditions of trench warfare.

The troops were tired out; they had not slept at all during the night and had fought hard in the morning. At noon the German guns started to shell us like blazes, and put down a barrage on the ground intervening between Montauban Alley, which we were holding, and the village itself. This they maintained continually and the two hundred yards which separated us remained a sheet of fire from now onwards. All the telephone wires we had run out were destroyed by shell fire as quickly as we put them out, and after eight wiremen had been killed in succession trying to repair the line, I abandoned any attempt to communicate with Headquarters other than by despatch runners. As the evening drew on I sent message after message for ammunition and water and above all for the rocket signals which would enable us to communicate with the artillery. Every message was acknowledged but no supplies reached me. Sotham afterwards told me that he had sent up what he could, but it never got to the firing line.

From midday on July 1st. until we were finally relieved at 3 a.m. on July 2nd. I had no help or support of any description whatever from Battalion Headquarters. When we were relieved, Elstob commanding the support Company, told me that he did not even know we were out in front of him ! There was something radically wrong with the staff work in Montauban Village.

At 1 p.m. Johnson came along to say that he had found an old German dugout which he intended to use as Company Headquarters for himself. I preferred to establish my Headquarters in the open trench, as being less likely to be known to the German artillery. His dugout was a long shelter with many compartments, one of these was full of wounded and another contained a carpenter's bench.

The ground in front of Montauban Alley fell away into the Caterpillar Wood Valley, and we could thus only command a field of vision and fire for three hundred yards. In this valley the Germans massed and at 9.30 p.m. they launched their first real counter attack. We were able to beat this off with comparative ease and by 10.15 p.m. we had resumed more or less normal trench life, except for the continued furious bombardment of the ground between ourselves and the village, and the unusually heavy shell fire directed upon our trench.

No word of relief had been received and the situation was far too precarious to admit of any man sleeping during the night. They were dead tired in spite of the rest I had given them earlier in the day, and I spent the entire night walking up and down the line watching and talking to the men to keep them awake.

We were all very thirsty as we had no chance of refilling our water-bottles since 5 p.m. on June 30th. One dear fellow, Poynton who afterwards became one of my signallers, gave me a spoonful of marmalade which was the nearest approach to a drink that I had for twenty four hours.

Sergeant Haslam asked permission to send one man from each section back to the well in front of the village to fill the water bottles of his comrades. We could ill spare them from the defence of the trench, but I consented. The village was being heavily bombarded and when the party neared the well, they found it a centre of bursting shells and under direct machine gun fire. They were forced to give it up as a bad job, except Lance Corporal Bowie. He was determined to carry out his job, and with especial heroism penetrated the circle of fire and filled his bottles, one by one. For ten minutes he was in that inferno of fire and yet he lived. He brought back ten bottles of water, and I recommended him for the Military Medal.

That night was very trying and the responsibility weighed heavily upon me. I sent a note to Johnson asking him to come down himself or to send Elstob, as I felt further attack was imminent and I could get no satisfaction from Battalion Headquarters. He wrote back on a grubby slip of paper "I am sure you will do all possible. I am remaining on the right because I judge it to be the most dangerous. Good luck".

All through the night the men stood at their firing positions
with the remains of their ammunition laid out on the parapet ready
to their hand. The night passed quietly except for a good many
casualties from shell fire. At 3 a.m. I was standing on the fire step
with Haslam who was acting as Sergeant Major; it was almost day and
I said to him "I think it will be light enough for the troops to stand
down in a few minutes. They must be worn out".

Hardly were the words out of my mouth when I saw advancing over the
ridge, shoulder to shoulder, long lines of grey uniformed figures in
great coats and helmets. The second counter attack had begun. On they
came, wave after wave. No need to issue fire orders, no need to tell
the troops what to do. As soon as the Germans topped the ridge every
man of my garrison was firing rapidly and with deadly accuracy.

Our machine guns and Lewis guns got to work at once; now I
wanted those red artillery rockets for which I had asked so repeatedly.
Without them the only way to send an S.O.S. to our covering batteries
was through the telephone of the brigade on our left, which had
escaped the punishing fire to which we had been subjected. I raced up
there and put through the S.O.S. but it took valuable time.

The rifle fire as well was wonderful in its effect; there was no
undue excitement and in many cases the men climbed out on to the
parapet so that they might get a slightly better field of fire. The
attack was broken up simply and solely by rifle fire and by the help
of the Lewis guns. After four waves of the enemy had been dispersed,
our artillery came into action and put down a barrage. In a few
solitary instances the German infantry reached our lines and were
driven back by the bayonet.

We then proceeded to straighten things up, attend to the wounded
and count our losses. A despatch runner reported that Morton Johnson
had been killed while handing up ammunition to a machine gunner when
the rest of the team had been knocked out. This was a bitter blow to
me and I was just going along to his body when Corporal Waldron, one
of my best scouts, came running down the trench in spite of a severe
wound in his leg. He had been in charge of our extreme right post
and reported that the redoubt of the 17th. Manchesters had retired at
the beginning of the fuss and had let the Germans in our right flank.
These were then bombing their way down the trench in the hope and
with the intention of clearing Montauban Alley.

We had no bombs at all so I sent along to borrow some from the
55th. Brigade on our left and then took a bombing party along the
trench and sent another along the top to deal with the Huns. We drove
them out of our own frontage and established a block where the 17th.
Battalion's post should have been. Beyond this we could not go as
it was vitally important to preserve intact our own frontage and
our small garrison was already sadly depleted.

By this time the troops were thoroughly exhausted and I mounted
sentries and allowed the remainder of the garrison to rest.

I was the only officer left in the front line and I myself
presented a curious sight; my tunic and puttees had gone long ago,
the latter to put a tourniquet on Waldron's leg, and bare headed and
in my shirt sleeves, my face and arms covered with sweat and blood
and grime, I looked anything but the conventional officer in command

of a beleagured garrison; but I was in command and not by virtue of
any badges of rank which had long since disappeared.

At 9.10 a.m. I saw a Colonel coming down the trench. He was asking
for the officer in command and when he was directed to me his face was
a picture. This was Colonel Gilson of the 2nd. Wilts and he told me
that my Battalion Headquarters and the support company had been
relieved, but that he could not get his men into the firing line
until after midday. I cursed, but said we could hold on until then
provided our ammunition lasted.

Actually beyond the shelling we had no further trouble and
the relieveing troops turned up at 2.30 p.m. There were crowds of
them and they had not been in the battle, but still showed
considerable strain. We gathered up what wounded had not been
already evacuated, and one by one my men filed along the trench.
They had done wonders, achieved the impossible: for sixty hours
they had been practically without sleep, for thirty hours they had
battled against overwhelming odds. Without water or provisions,
short of ammunition and small in numbers, worn out in body and
mind, they had captured Montauban and had held it against all the
counter-attacks the Germans had been able to launch.

But as they passed by no light of triumph shone in their faces;
they were not radiant with success as the newspaper men like to say.
They had done their job, and that was the end of it. For the rest -
they were whacked; sick of the whole business, sick with the sense
of loss of comrades, overwhelmingly tired. Even so they would have
turned and fought had the necessity arisen. They were just splendid.

Sending Haslam at their head with orders to avoid the village
which was still being heavily shelled, I waited until they had all
filed by and then looked my last upon Montauban Alley. One hundred
and sixty five of us were left, many of these wounded badly but
carrying on, and we had between us one Mills bomb and less than
three hundred rounds of ammunition. Ordinarily each man carries
two hundred and fifty rounds, so you can see we were almost down
to our last shot.

By my orders Haslam led the way past the western end of the
village and into a deep communication trench called SLAG ALLEY which
led down to the German front line system. It was rather a longer way
round, but I had no mind to lose more of my men by the German shelling
than I could help. Slag Alley was very deep and as we filed along we
had to clamber over the dead bodies of Germans. These already looked
waxen and yellow; it was a hot July.

It reminded me of the Chamber of Horrors at Madame Tussaud's,
with the awful difference that these scenes were real. Here was a
German machine gun; still seated at the gun was the German who had
been killed whilst firing it, and around him lay the remainder of his
gun team. There was a trench mortar emplacement, the gun and crew
together destroyed by a direct hit of one of our shells. Here was a
bombing post, still strewn with the bodies of its garrison, some killed
in the position of throwing their bombs. It was pretty ghastly and as
soon as we could we left the trench and struck across the open.

When we crossed the German second line we found it full of corpses;
no need here of trench ladders, we were able to walk over the bodies.

Our own dead littered the battlefield. Some of my poor remnants recognised the bodies of their friends. Sick at heart we stumbled on through the wreckage of barbed wire and shell holes. When we reached the German front line I headed for the Talus Boise where I knew there were water tanks. At long last we reached there and the parched troops drank their fill; how good it was.

We learnt that the remainder of the Battalion had gathered at our old assembly trenches and there we made our weary way. Sotham, undemonstrative fellow that he was, started to blub when he saw me. He had been told that I had been killed in the second counter attack. The men fell into the trenches and so to sleep. Sotham made me lie down but I could not sleep, so he and I and Petrie went into the Brigade dugout for tea.

At 9 p.m. when the troops had rested a little, we were told to make our way back to Bronfay Farm where guides would meet us and conduct us to a camp in Happy Valley. Very slowly we moved back to the Peronne Road and then through trenches to Billon Wood. The trenches were congested with troops going up to the firing line and it was over midnight when we reached Bronfay Farm. Oliver met us with the guides and we went on and on for miles until we reached camp at 3 a.m. on the 3rd. of July. Here we found Knox waiting with hot food ready for the troops and after I had seen my crowd fed, I turned into a tent and slept. There were five tents for the officers but the men were in the open, covered with their mackintosh sheets.

The Colonel, Adjutant, Elstob of the reserve company, Harvey also of D Company, Megson the signalling officer and myself were the only surviving officers. Battalion Headquarters and the reserve Company (D) had escaped fairly well, but of all the officer ranks of the three companies in the line only I had survived. Since then I have sometimes wondered why.

My batman Hibbert and Thompson, my runner, had both come through unscathed and I had got my poor remnants back from Montauban Alley without a single casualty. I had the supreme consolation of knowing that I had not needlessly sacrificed any lives. Lots of people at Home imagine that an officer's job is an easy one. To be responsible for the lives of men is no light burden; to know that an error of judgement will result in needless deaths has a somewhat ageing effect upon one: to deliberately send men to certain death when imperative occasion demands is not an office to be lightly assumed.

So ended our first big battle. We all felt that so far as we were concerned the war was over. What we had actually done on the first and second of July and at what cost shall be told in the next chapter.

A Mk ix Periscope with magnification
designed to see above a trench.

Chapter Twelve.

The cost of victory. Burying our Dead. Trones Wood. Blighty.

> The trails of the world are countless,
> And most of the trails be tried;
> You tread on the heels of the many
> Till you come where the ways divide:
> And one lies safe in the sunlight,
> And the other is dreary and wan,
> Yet you look aslant at the lone trail,
> And the lone trail lures you on.
>
> And somehow you're sick of the highway
> With the noise and its easy needs,
> And you long for the risk of the bye-way
> And reck not where it leads:
> Often it leads to the dead-pit,
> Always it leads to pain,
> By the bones of your brothers you know it,
> But oh, to follow you're fain.
> By your bones they shall follow after
> Till the ways of the world be made plain.

For this first battle of the Somme the 30th. Division had been given the place of honour as the Right of the Line. The 90th. Infantry Brigade had as its right hand neighbours the famous Iron Division of the French Army. The 16th. Manchesters as the senior Battalion in the Brigade had been allotted the task of the capture and defence of Montauban. The holding of this key position was reckoned to be one of the most glorious incidents of the whole war. Had Montauban been recaptured by the Hun, the whole British and French line would have had to retire. Of all the Brigades in the attack on that first day of July, ours was the only one to fully and successfully carry out its allotted programme.

Now a word as to the cost; from my Battalion eight hundred and fifty men and twenty two officers went into action. Five hundred and sixty five men were killed and wounded; those who were wounded had continued in the attack until they had been incapable of any further effort.

Of the officers Morton Johnson was killed, Allen was killed, Worthington was shot through the right lung and had his left hand shattered; Walker was blinded in both eyes, Horley had his shoulder smashed, Kerry had a severe scalp wound, Hook and Morris were knocked out with machine gun wounds in the legs; Faux had his arm taken off by a shell splinter, Barr had his jaw smashed by a rifle bullet; Prestwich and Swaine were hit early in the advance, Slack was wounded by the same shell that killed his servant, Hanscombe was blown up by a trench mortar shell and had severe concussion, Megson got a machine gun bullet through his leg and Elstob had a slight wound in the neck; these two were able to carry on.

Most of our specially trained bombers and Lewis gunners had been knocked out. The ranks of our N.C.O.'s were badly depleted.

The Army Commander sent the Battalion a telegram of praise
and said that as a reward for our services he was going to pay
us the highest compliment he could, namely to put us into the
attack again as soon as possible ! The Brigadier came to say how
proud he was of us, and then the Divisional General told us what
fine fellows we were. Empty phrases - our thoughts were all with
the pals we had lost forever. The Times hailed the Defence of
Montauban as a remarkable feat of arms, but gave the credit of it
to Scottish troops ! !

Here is a newspaper account of the business:
"Manchester will ever have cause to recall with pride the opening
day of the Somme Battle.

"On July 1st. her lads, recruited mainly from the offices and
warehouses of the city, with the 2nd. Battalion of the Royal Scots
Fusiliers in support, not only captured the ridge and village of
Montauban, took several hundred prisoners and the first guns of
the Somme Battle, but reached a position further forward than any
on the whole battle front of some twenty miles, and held it
against all the counter attacks the Huns were able to launch
against it. Lord Derby's Division (as it is popularly known) which
included the Manchester and Liverpool Brigades, was on the extreme
right of the British line joining up with the French at a point
to the north of Maricourt.
"
For several days previously the attack had been practised in
an area behind the line, the assembly trenches, the Hun system of
trenches, the Glatz Redoubt and the village being laid out on the
ground in their several positions. Every man knew exactly what was
expected of him, and on the day no man failed; the whole operation
proceeded like clockwork. At 7.30 a.m. on July 1st. after a
tremendous bombardment in which every available gun and trench
mortar took part, the Liverpool lads rushed forward and overwhelmed
the Bosches. They, when the barrage lifted, along with another
Brigade whose objective was the Glatz Redoubt, gave the Huns little
opportunity of bringing out machine guns. An old general a few
months previously had remarked "These Lancashire lads, given a
fair chance, will run through the Bosches", and so it proved.
"
The objectives of the two Brigades having thus been attained,
at 8.30 a.m. the order was given for the Manchester Brigade to
advance on the village, a difficult operation as the Brigade had
to pass through a narrow defile prior to extending to the foot of
the slopes leading up to Montauban. This was aggravated by the
Brigade on their left being unable to get forward, which exposed
their flank to the German machine gun fire.
"
The two leading Battalions of the Manchesters suffered heavily
but they pressed on and wave after wave moved up the slopes and into
the village. On the further side of the village there lay a German
"communication trench known as Montauban Alley.There they consolidated;
and while prisoners were being collected and dugouts cleared
Captain Morton Johnson (killed the following morning) went out into
the open and chalked the number of his Battalion upon the first
guns captured; these some day should find a home in Manchester."
(This statement is inaccurate. Johnson did not go out himself to
do this; it was a task of little importance and no danger. The gun

crews had abandoned their guns at our first onslaught. Johnson
sent Aldous and Price to mark the trophies).

The casualties of the Brigade were eleven hundred, slightly
more than one third of its fighting strength. The Army Commander
reviewing the situation wrote as follows:-

The assault of the front system of trenches and the capture of
the village of Montauban was a feat of arms deserving the highest
praise and has not been excelled by any division of the New Army.
Their capture of Bernafay and Trones Woods, and the heavy fighting
which took place in the latter, shews a tenacity, a valour and a
fighting spirit that are wholly admirable.

The co-operation of the artillery with the infantry has been
most satisfactory and the way in which the two arms have worked in
unison, both previous to and during the Battle of the Somme, shews
that a very high standard of training has been reached. When the
full story comes to be told it will be found that Manchester lads
played no small part in what was perhaps the greatest battle in
history, regarded by those competent to judge as the turning point
of the war."

Beach Thomas, the war correspondent of the Daily Mail, wrote:-
"Perhaps it gives a wrong impression to treat the attack on July 1st.
as a separate event, but it will always remain a day of days in our
history. Waterloo is an episode compared with it. The battle of
July 1st. was a great victory, though our losses were great and the
success small over more than half the front - the crowning success
was at Montauban. Here two Brigades recently recruited from
Lancashire towns, especially Manchester, faced some very stalwart
Bavarian troops. The soldierly qualties of the men were illustrated
as much in defence as in attack. The trenches they fortified by
Montauban had been so ploughed and harrowed by our artillery that
they were little or no protection. But the work of consolidation
went so quickly that an hour or two later they were able to throw
back with terrible losses to the enemy and small to themselves
the most determined counter-attack delivered by the Germans at any
part of the field. On the victory here the successes of the following
days, weeks and months were founded."

All words, empty praise that will never give back to us the
comrades we have lost for ever.

The evening of July 3rd. found us still bivouacked in the
Happy Valley; the troops were tired and disappointed as we had
hoped to go into billets to refit and re-organise. Rain came during
the night and we all got unpleasantly wet. The troops were still
without blankets or shelter of any kind, just lying in the open.

On the morning of the 4th. we found that we were very short of
non-commissioned officers and especially trained men for bombers and
machine gunners. Knox asked me to ride with him into Heilly, where
we saw hundreds of German prisoners awaiting trains to take them
into internment camps.

On July 5th. we were ordered to provide a party of a hundred
and fifty men with three officers, to proceed to the battlefield
and help bury the dead, a truly ghastly business. To make matters

worse it was our own dead we had to bury. So it came about that our
men had to collect the shattered fragments of their own comrades,
often of their brothers and cousins. By this time the bodies had
begun to decompose and the stench of the battlefield was appalling.

I got permission to go up to Montauban to search for Johnson's
body, but could not find it although I had no difficulty in finding
the place where he was shot. On the 6th. and 7th. the entire
Battalion was engaged upon this work of burying the dead. By this
time we despaired of getting the rest we thought we had earned and
on the 8th. of July we were not surprised to get the order to stand
to arms and be ready to move into the battle line again at half an
hour's notice. We had never left Happy Valley and still had no
blankets or shelter; it had rained incessantly for four days: but in
spite of it all the spirit of the men was splendid and we were ready
to get on with the job.

We had left behind ten officers from the first battle and these
helped to fill our depleted ranks, but we had no reinforcements for
the N.C.O.'s or men. Engaged as we had been in the job of burying
the dead, there had been no chance of training men to replace the
specialists we had lost.

At 11a.m. on the 8th. of July we received orders to move at 1 p.m.
The attacks on Trones Wood had not gone well, and the 90th. Infantry
Brigade was to take the Wood. As my own Battalion had borne the brunt
of the heaviest fighting on the 1st. of July and had suffered most
casualties, we were placed in Brigade Reserve and our job was to act
as carrying parties. Our orders were to move up to our old assembly
trenches and remain there until 3 a.m. At this hour we were to go
forward to the old German front line known as Valley Trench and await
orders.

I had been commanding C Company but when the Colonel heard that
we were going into action again he insisted upon my returning to
Battalion Headquarters Staff in order that I should be with the
Adjutant and himself. This did not mean that I was in a position
of greater safety as of course we were in the line with the rest of
the Battalion, but I was rather fed up at the time; but I did not show
my discontent, and realised later that evidently I was considered to
be of greater use at H.Q.

We móved off, 265 men all told; men who had not been under any
covering for 10 days, men who had already fought against heavy odds
and achieved success, men who since then had been exclusively occupied
in cleaning up the previous battlefield.

Petrie, Sotham, Megson and myself constituted Battalion H.Q.;
with the companies were Elstob, Oliver, Davidson, Payne, Smithers,
Stafford-Badger, Jackson, Venner, Scudamore, Hoskins and Caiger.
The last six were entirely new to us. Smithers and Badger had come
from our 11th. Battalion and the others from the Royal West Kents.

We left Happy Valley at 1 p.m. and spent an uncomfortable night
in the assembly trenches. At daybreak we moved forward and the
various platoons were detailed for carrying parties, taking up
ammunition, water and barbed wire to the attacking troops. It has
hardly seemed worthwhile to mention it, but of course the German
artillery had been pounding away at us all this time. Most of its

fury had been directed on the battle front, but full measure had been devoted to Happy Valley and the other approaches and bivouacs.

Megson and myself wandered up and down Valley Trench inspecting the German sniping posts and concrete machine gun posts. Then I sat down near the field telephone to write a letter home. A message came through that Whytehead, commanding the 17th. Manchesters, had reported that the 17th., 18th., Battalions and the Royal Scots Fusiliers had captured the Wood but were being subjected to very severe shelling and would have to retire.

Petrie was anxious to see what was going on; from Valley Trench we could not see Trones Wood, but by going up to Glatz Redoubt which stood on rising ground he hoped to command a view of the Wood. We were under fairly heavy fire in Valley Trench, but the Bosches were basting Glatz Redoubt like blazes. Sotham tried to dissuade the Colonel from going but Petrie was a very obstinate sort of a chap and in spite of Sotham's insubordinate remark that it was sheer madness, the Colonel turned to me and said "What about it, Nash, I AM going forward to that sanguinary redoubt, will you come too?" Well, naturally I would; I thought it damned silly as I felt sure that we should not be able to see what was going on but it was no part of my job to argue with the Colonel.

So off we went, leaving Sotham blaspheming behind. Together we left the trench and the shelling was certainly pretty hot, but we managed to make our way about a mile forward to the higher ground, the shrapnel getting worse the farther we went. In point of fact it was the most thrilling journey of my life; I did not think we had an earthly chance of getting back and of course when we did get to the redoubtwe could not see anything of the attack on Trones Wood. I forebore to say "I told you so" and after Petrie had admired the surrounding view for the space of a cigarette, we turned round and walked sedately back. The Colonel was inclined to be a little portly, built for comfort rather than speed, but he was full of courage.

On our way back a German five point nine shrapnel shell burst with a clap of thunder just above our heads. I found myself lying on the ground and wondered why, until I saw the blood gushing from my right arm. There was very little pain, just a nasty draining sort of feeling. The Colonel had started to run, but came back when he saw I was hit. He helped me up and together we tried to make our way back to Valley Trench.

We had made but little progress before I collapsed and fainted from loss of blood. He dragged me into a shell hole that was handy and went off for help. When I came to again I found a Highlander tying up the arm, and for some stupid reason fainted again. When I regained consciousness I found that a Medical Officer of the South African Brigade had shoved on a tourniquet, and later on two stretcher bearers carried me back in state to Valley Trench.

As I was lying there with the Medical Officer fussing about with more dressings, Sotham came along to see me and was awfully nice; he was furious with Petrie on account of his foolhardiness and in fact the Colonel had been a grave responsibility to us both. After what seemed a very long time Hibbert and I were put on a

funny little light railway track and taken back as far as the Talus
Boise. The jolting rather upset things and when I was again able
to take notice we were at the Dressing Station on the Peronne Road.
Here several labels were tied onto me and I was put into a horse
wagon and jolted almost unbearably to Bronfay Farm. I was then put
into a motor ambulance and recovered conciousness at Bray. Here I
was shoved into another ambulance and taken as far as the Mat Double
on the Bray-Corbie Road, where I was inoculated with anti-tetanus.
After an eternity of time we got to Corbie and spent the night at
No. 5 Casualty Clearing Station. Here my devoted Hibbert had to
leave me.

At mid-day on the 10th. I was sent on to Daours and put on the
train for Boulogne. My arm was not giving me much pain, but they
laughed at me when I tried to get back to my unit. Late at night I
reached the 14th. General Hospital at Boulogne.

My trouble began when they dressed my wound at Boulogne. It was
excruciatingly painful. The shrapnel bullet had gone through the
biceps of my right arm, missing the bone by a hair's breadth. For
a long time I had a beastly glass tube in my arm and for several
days I was kept at Boulogne although every bed was urgently needed.
On the 13th. however the hospital had to be evacuated and I was put
on the boat for England. At about midnight I was admitted to the 4th.
London General Hospital at Denmark Hill.

Thanks to a decent constitution and with my proverbial luck my
wound made good progress and as wounded were pouring in at a rapid
rate I was discharged from hospital on July 27th. My wound was still
open and needed daily dressing but I was thankful to get away.
At Denmark Hill hospital I saw Worthington and also of all people,
Sotham who came in two days after me. I was awfully sick about this.

Sotham told me the story of the subsequent operations at Trones
Wood. The other three Battalions of our Brigade had been forced to
retire from the Wood, in accordance with Whytehead's intimation.
The Germans then re-occupied the Wood. At 10 a.m. orders came through
from Brigade. Three Battalions of the Brigade jointly had been unable
to hold Trones Wood. The 16th. Manchesters would re-capture the Wood
and hold it until relieved.

First of all we had to collect our various carrying parties
which were scattered over the face of the earth. Despatch runners
were sent off to get into touch with them and instruct each party
to assemble on a sunken road south of the Wood.

Little parties of men came up one by one until at last all that was
left of the Battalion was present.

Our original two hundred and sixty five men had now been reduced
by casualties to two hundred and twenty eight. This assembly of
isolated parties under the tremendous shell fire spoke well indeed
for the discipline of the men. A Lance Corporal in charge of ten
menwould receive orders to find his way to the assembly point.
Nothing would have been easier than to just fail to turn up,
to go to earth in some safe dug-out until the job was done, but in
every single case the men came along.

Petrie took the Company Commanders out to reconnoitre the ground over which they were to attack.

Three Hills.

There is a hill in England,
Green fields and a school I know,
Where the balls fly fast in summer,
And the whispering elm trees grow,
A little hill, a dear hill
And the playing fields below.

There is a hill in France,
Heaped with a thousand slain,
Where the shells fly night and noontide,
And the ghosts that died in vain:
A little hill, a hard hill
To the souls that died in pain.

There is a hill in Jewry;
Three crosses pierce the sky;
On the midmost He is dying,
To save all those that die:
A little hill, a holy hill
To souls in jeopardy.

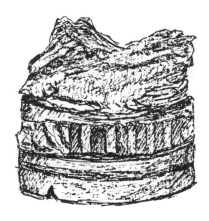

A piece of Enemy Shrapnel and a
British Mills Bomb.

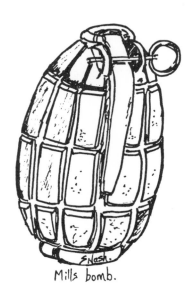

Mills bomb.

The War of 1914-1918.

Manchester Regiment

T/2nd Lt. T. A. H. Nash, 16th Bn.

was mentioned in a Despatch from

General Sir Douglas Haig, G.C.B., K.C.I.E., K.C.V.O., A.D.C.

dated 13th November 1916.

for gallant and distinguished services in the Field.

I have it in command from the King to record His Majesty's

high appreciation of the services rendered.

Winston S. Churchill

Secretary of State for War.

War Office,
Whitehall, S.W.
1st March 1919.

Citation of Mentioned in Despatches
from General Sir Douglas Haig on the
13th. November 1916 and signed in 1919
by Secretary of State for War,
Winston S. Churchill.

Chapter Thirteen.

Sick leave. Cleethorpes. To France again. Commanding B Company.

> To Odin's challenge we cried "Amen";
> We stayed the plough and laid by the pen,
> And we shouldered our guns like gentlemen,
> That the wiser weak should hold.....
>
> Then lift the flag of the last Crusade,
> And fill the ranks of the last Brigade;
> March on to the fields where the World's remade
> And the ancient dreams come true.

It was delightful to be at home and I appreciated the peace and quiet of Kingswood Grange after the infernal racket of war. I did absolutely nothing for a few days, just slacked and tried to recover my mental poise, and then when my arm was less painful I went down to Bristol for a week. I had a very pleasant time there and on August 11th. went back to Kingswood to find that my valise had followed me from France.

Hibbert had packed up all my belongings and had given the valise into the Casualty Clearing Station to be sent on after me. Like the wise lad he was, he first took a complete inventory of all my stuff and told the R.A.M.C. sergeant that he had done so ! To his foresight I attribute the safe arrival of every article of kit that I had. My despatch box had also arrived, containing the accumulation of my labours as Intelligence Officer, maps, operation orders and documents of the highest interest to me.

I then went up to Altrincham to see the mother of my dead friend, Captain Morton Johnson. She was very nice to me and glad to have someone who could tell her about her boy. Johnson and I had been fast friends; we billetted together whenever possible; we used to attend Holy Communion together we had held Montauban, but sadly the better man had been killed.

The remainder of my sick leave passed very happily and on September 7th. I attended a Medical Board at Birmingham University. They examined my arm and told me to report for two months' light duty with the 3rd. Battalion of the Manchesters stationed at Cleethorpes.

Cleethorpes was a little seaside town at the mouth of the Humber and after a long and tiring journey I found the Battalion under canvas. After one night in a tent I saw the Medical Officer and from him received permission to live in billets. I am not fond of being under canvas, especially in a camp. It is a great deal too uncomfortable.

I was attached to B Company and found rooms at 27 Grant Street where I was fairly comfortable. B Company was composed entirely of men back from the front and I enjoyed being with them. I found one or two old friends from my own Battalion; C.S.M. Berry and Corporals Waldron and Clayton among them. The two last named had been wounded at Montauban.

I did not take kindly to the 3rd. Battalion. It was my first experience of a Reserve Battalion and being myself still "hot from the Somme" I could not understand why it should contain at that time so many who had never been overseas. Men who had been in France for over a year and who had been wounded two or three times were yelled at by N.C.O.'s who although regular, time-serving soldiers, had been content to let apparently the volunteers go and fight while they stayed behind in safety.

I, who had been to France twice and had done over ten months' hard fighting, had the privilege of attending lectures on trench warfare delivered by officers who had never been out of England; and for an hour daily a young physical training officer taught me how to "go over the top" on a bayonet fighting course. I was not amused !

It appeared that an intense jealousy of the Expeditionary officer existed in those days; we knew too much and in the opinion of those at home, the best place for us was back at the Front, and the sooner we went the better.

The foregoing remarks may seem bitter, but I have never been able to see how so many Regular Officers could have been content to remain in England or in jobs of absolute safety at the Base while the volunteer officer was doing the job and the fighting for which after all the regulars had been paid and trained during long years of peace. For example, of the hundreds of officers employed at the War Office early in 1916 I do not believe you would have found a dozen who were not Regulars.

I went on with ordinary routine work until September 18th., when I contracted a violent attack of asthma, brought on by the cold east winds and sea fogs. On the 22nd. I was so bad that the Medical Officer insisted upon my being granted leave until my next Board and I was accordingly sent home. I returned to Grimsby for my Board on October 7th. and although my wound had not yet healed I prevailed upon them to pass me fit for Active Service so that I could get away.

At midday on November 6th. my orders came. I was to embark at Folkestone on November 9th. at 10.35 a.m. and until then I could go where I liked. While at the Orderly Room I heard that Major Knox had been killed on October 13th. at Flers while commanding my Battalion. I was awfully sorry as he was a gallant officer and a very dear friend of mine.

On November 7th. I went to London to see my Mother. On the evening of the 8th. I found myself at Paddington with a few hours to spare and conceived the idea of paying a flying visit to Bristol to see Nancy. I had changed most of my money into French notes and had just enough English money to pay my fare to Bristol if I travelled third or got a half fare voucher from the R.T.O. to travel first. As it was against regulations for an officer to travel by third class I went to see the R.T.O. He was a Lieut-Colonel of some Scotch Regiment and an obstructionist of the worst type.

He refused to give me a half fare voucher, to which I was entitled, so I replied politely that I had travelled third as a civilian and should do so on that occasion. He then threatened me with arrest if I should attempt to travel 3rd. class and sent his orderly to instruct the booking office clerks not to issue

me a 3rd. class ticket as I was an officer. I saluted and left
his office but could have cheerfully killed him. There was he a
regular officer who had never been overseas during the war, drawing
a fat screw while a lance corporal did his work for him, and placed
at Paddington for the purpose of assisting service men, and yet
behaving in such unwarrantable fashion.

I got a civilian to get me a ticket to Bristol and from the
corridor of a 1st. class carriage saw this damned fellows Military
Police going from one 3rd. class carriage to another looking for me.
As soon as the train left Paddington I moved along to a third class
carriage. On my return to France I reported the incident to General
Shea, commanding my Division, who had the swine badly rapped over
the knuckles.

Do you remember those bitter verses of Siegfried Sassoon?

> "If I were fierce and bald and short of breath,
> I'd live with scarlet Majors at the Base;
> And speed glum heroes up the Line to death.
> You'd see me with my puffy, petulant face,
> Guzzling and gulping in the best hotel,
> Reading the Roll of Honour. 'Poor young chap',
> I'd say, 'I used to know his father well-
> Yes, we've lost heavily in this last scrap'.
> And when the war is done and youth stone-dead,
> I'd waddle safely home, and die - in bed".

I returned to London in time to catch the 7.20 a.m. train
for Folkestone. At Charing Cross I met Hook and MacDonnell, two
former officers of the 16th. Battalion who were also going out again.
We were tremendously keen to get back to our own crowd, but our orders
only took us as far as the Infantry Base Depot at Etaples. Once there
we were at the disposal of the Officer-in-Charge of Re-Inforcements
who could send us to any Battalion in need of officers. I had however
taken the precaution of telegraphing to the Colonel of the 16th.
saying that we were on our way and would like to get back to our
own Battalion.

I went on board at Folkestone and had just sent a telegram saying
that we were off when orders came to dis-embark. The Channel was
closed on account of submarines. However on the 10th. November I
left England for the fourth time and frankly never expected to return.

We left harbour on the S.S. "Onward" at 11 a.m. The Channel
reminded me of a busy thoroughfare at home, with destroyers acting
as police, controlling the constant stream of traffic as the hospital
ships, leave boats and supply convoys passed to and fro. I arrived
at Boulogne at 1 p.m. and left again for Etaples at 6.30 p.m. reaching
my destination at 9 p.m. There I reported to the 30th. I.B.D. spending
the night under canvas.

At the Infantry Base Depot all the re-inforcing officers, including
those who had been overseas before, had to attend a series of instructional
parades in a training area known as the "Bull Ring". As this was my
fourth time out, I very much resented being put under the orders of a
non-commissioned officer, and insisted upon falling out. It was really

too much of a good thing for majors and captains to be called to attention by a sergeant and marched about by him.

However that did not last long, and on the 12th. Hook and MacDonnell and myself received orders to rejoin the 16th. Bn. of the Manchester Regiment and we were all very happy at the thought of getting back to our own men. Major Knox had written to me when I was wounded and had promised to give me command of a Company when I returned to the Battalion; I thought it likely that Elstob who had succeeded him in the command of the 16th. would see that this promise was fulfilled and it was therefore in a state of great content that I left Etaples at 5 p.m.

After the usual dreadful train journey we reached the railhead at Saulty late at night on the 13th. Twelve hours after our departure from Etaples we had covered exactly twenty one miles. All through the weary night we were bucketted up and down sidings and shunted all over the place. We were in a third class carriage which had no cushions and only hard deal seats, and we were not amused.

At Saulty we met Megson who was going home on leave and we found the Battalion Mess Cart, with Pearson driving, waiting for us. Pearson was an old friend of mine and it was delightful to be welcomed back again. We drove eight miles along the straight French roads, and as I saw the poplars silhouetted in the moonlight, and the Verey lights and star-shells going up in the distance, I hugged myself with glee at being back once again. I felt just like a kid going home from school for the holidays.

We eagerly questioned Pearson as to the Battalion and learned that there were very few of the old originals left, and most of those who had joined the transport section so as to keep together. Colonel Elstob was in command and Major Roberts had returned as his Second-in-Command, while Captain Gibbon was Adjutant.

The Battalion was then holding a line of trenches in front of Bretencourt, and opposite the German villages of Ficheux and Blaireville. The troops were in the front line for six days and then went back for six days to Bellacourt. The transport lines and QM Stores were at Bailleulval, and here we spent six days a month in the Divisional Rest Billets.

We spent the night of the 13th. at Knowles's billet in Bailleulval. He was then Transport Officer; he was an old Carthusian and his language as he described the new conditions in the Battalion was worthy of the best traditions of Charterhouse. Knowles was a particular pal of mine and it was splendid to see him again. The entire Transport Section, including many men whose faces I hardly knew, turned out to see us off to the trenches in the morning and I had a really wonderful reception from the old members of the 16th. Bn. The comradeship which existed between the men and officers of the original Battalion cannot be imagined by anyone outside. It was our chief asset in all our fighting life. I would prefer to be judged by the standard of the men who fought under me than by any other opinion.

We drove another six miles through Basseux and Bellacourt to Bretencourt, where we went through communication trenches to the Battalion Headquarters. Colonel Elstob gave us a hearty welcome. I liked him immensely, but sometimes wondered whether, (despite having his complete confidence as an officer), perhaps my previous close association with Colonel Petrie and Colonel Knox, had resulted in a suspicion in his mind that his command of the Battalion would be contrasted with theirs.

Hook was sent to A Company and MacDonnell to C Company, whilst I was put in temporary command of B Company. Without further delay I made my way up to my Company's sector accompanied by Scudamore, from whom I was to take over. This officer eventually transferred to the Royal Flying Corps.

The Battalion held a long line divided into three sectors, named respectively Osiers, Ravine, and Epsom. Each sector was held by one company, and the fourth company was held in reserve at Chancery Lane. The opposing German trenches ran in front of Ficheux and Blaireville, and were some two hundred yards away. Sometimes afterwards as it transpired we were to renew our acquaintanceship with these two villages. We had an outpost line formed by long saps, which were a considerable source of anxiety, especially at night.

My Company held the Ravine Sector. There were only two subalterns, as the Battalion was very short of officers. One of these, Scudamore, had joined the Battalion after Montauban, and in civilian life had been a planter in Jamaica. He had volunteered when war broke out and obtained a commission in the Royal West Kents. He was a very delightful chap with an irrepressible chuckle, and served me loyally and well. My other subaltern was H.R.W. Smith, who had been a Professor of Classics at some Canadian University, and still looked the part. He was awfully absent-minded and untidy although a very pleasant companion and a good conversationalist.

My Company Sergeant Major was my old friend Haslam, from Montauban Alley, and Winning was still Company Quartermaster Sergeant. Lance Corporal Coxon was the Orderly Room Clerk. Evered, my new batman, was a former A Company man. My old friend and servant Hibbert was very much alive but had been looking after the Battalion Medical Officer, Heathcote, and as this was a safer and softer job than I could give him in the line, I would not let him join me. Heathcote had taken over Fletcher's job as Medical Officer before the Somme fight.

One of our officers did not come back as Elstob had taken a dislike to him, founded on the fact that he had left behind in the trenches during relief a man of his who had been killed instead of bringing him out for burial. In the Sixteenth we made a point of never leaving a man behind us. In the Maricourt days we never forgave one Battalion for leaving one of their officers buried under a foot of mud in a trench.

Before lunch I went round the Company's line with Scudamore and found that there was much that needed attention. The trenches were unsafe and dirty. The troops looked neglected and unwashed. The sentries were slack and the sentry posts were ill-placed. The truth of the matter was that the majority of the officers then with the Battalion had joined us just before or just after the Somme Battle, and they had had really no chance of experiencing normal trench warfare. Everything seemed to have been let slide with disastrous effects. Even in my first casual inspection I saw that there was much to be done. The Bn. had altered.

We returned to Headquarters for lunch. This consisted of the usual 'Macnochie' rations, with tinned apricots and perhaps a cup of camp coffee to follow. Company Headquarters were in a dug-out opening out of a communication trench, a dozen steps from the front line trench. It was a fairly comfortable dug-out but very cold. After lunch I sent for C.S.M. Haslam and talked with him long and well for the good of the

Company's soul. Then I took him with me round the line and shewed him what I wanted done. Fire-steps were to be re-constructed to enable the troops to use them; new and more sanitary latrines had to be dug, parapets heightened, the men's shelters improved and the disposition of the sentry groups altered. By tea-time much had been accomplished.

Night set in and the troops stood to arms for the hour of dusk during which the German trench mortars sent over one or two bombs, otherwise all was quiet. I arranged that the two subalterns and the Sergeant Major should divide the watches of the night. For my own part I got precious little rest at all during the six days we remained in the line. I was at the time only a second lieutenant and the responsibility of commanding a strange company was a heavy one. Later when I knew my men and had tightened up the discipline I had an easier time. Until then I had to be all over the shop all the time, and many were the difficulties I encountered.

After the Battalion's terribly heavy losses, one of our main difficulties was the lack of experienced N.C.O.'s. We had been made up to strength by drafts from other regiments, East Surreys, Sherwood Foresters, Border Regiment and so on; and men joined us as sergeants and corporals who had never been overseas before. The Border Regiment were a very good crowd.

When any Battalion had suffered exceptionally heavy losses, it usually lost its identity and the remnants were posted to other regiments. It was a considerable compliment to the 16th. Manchesters that they remained as a Battalion and were re-inforced instead of being absorbed.

C.S.M. Haslam had been given too little assistance. C.S.M!s are very human and are subject to their likes and dislikes as are others, so to prevent the same men from usually manning fatigue parties, and to ensure they all have an equal share, duty rosters need to be instituted.

The troops were not getting adequate rest during the day and in consequence did poor work. I harangued the N.C.O.'s at some length and ordered that every man in my Company should have at least four hours consecutive sleep during the day. It was extraordinarily difficult at first to enforce that rule but it was carried out. It was my invariable question to sentries and to men I met on fatigue duty "How much sleep have you had to-day?". The troops did better work and I never once had a case of sleepy or inalert sentries. That was not the case with one company where during one tour of duty in the trenches, one of our officers found no less than three sentries fast asleep at their posts. They were put back for trial by court-martial. At the trial it was proved that they had had no definite time allotted for sleep during the forty eight hours previous to their offence and all three got off with a reprimand.

The winter of 1916 was a severe one and many cases of trench feet had occurred. To combat this, I arranged for my Company to have five hot meals or drinks a day and also for every man to have his feet massaged once a day in the stretcher-bearers' dug-out, where dry socks were also supplied.

For meals, hot tea was brought up at 5 a.m. and breakfast followed at 8 a.m. A hot meal came up at 12.30 noon; tea was at 4.30 and at 10 p.m., hot soup was available. During that very hard winter I had no sickness among the troops, and not a single case of trench feet.

My next job was to tighten up the discipline, and I insisted
upon clean ammunition and rifles, and decently kept trenches. I had
very little trouble. The troops learnt that I was prepared to do all
I could for their comfort, providing that they did their job thoroughly.
After all, a soldier's life depends upon his weapons, and a clean rifle
is no use if the cartridges are dirty; a single round of ammunition
which jambs at a critical moment is quite a sufficient passport to the
next world. Stale food thrown on to the floor of the trench is a
handicap which is quite unnecessary when combatting disease.

I found that the trouble lay with the slackness of the non-
commissioned-officers, and I adopted a drastic policy. Seniority was
flung to the winds, and I tolerated no N.C.O. if he were proved
incompetent. How well this policy was justified was shewn later when
the Battalion went into action. Colonel Elstob wrote "B Company did
very well... they fought magnificently. I want you to know this
because I consider that it is due to your efforts and hard work that
the Company proved itself so efficient". And Major Roberts wrote
at the same time and said "Your lads did the best work".

Strangely enough no instance of dis-satisfaction came to my
notice and the sergeants and corporals I had to supersede bore me
no grudge. They were occupying positions of heavy responsibility
for which they knew jolly well they were unfitted at that time.

THAT EVENING STAR-SHELL
" Oh, star of eve, whose tender beam
Falls on my spirit's troubled dream." — *Tannhäuser.*

NO POSSIBLE DOUBT WHATEVER

Sentry : " 'Alt ! Who goes there ? "
He of the Bundle : " You shut yer ———— mouth, or I'll come and
knock yer ———— head off ! "   Sentry : " Pass, friend ! "

It is believed the Author of this Diary knew the
Artist Bruce Bairnsfather. Ed.

Chapter Fourteen.

A changed spirit in the Battalion. Wounded again.
In command of A Company. My second Christmas in France.

Shaken from sleep, and numbed and scarce awake,
Out in the trench with three hours' watch to take,
I blunder through the splashing murk; and then
Hear the gruff muttering voices of the men
Crouching in cabins candle-chinked with light.
Hark ! There's the big bombardment on our right
Rumbling and bumping; and the dark's a glare
Of flickering horrors in the sector where
We raid the Boche; men waiting, stiff and chilled,
Or crawling on their bellies through the wire.
"What? Stretcher-bearers wanted ? Some one killed?"
Five minutes ago I heard a sniper fire:
Why did he do it ?...Starlight overhead -
Blank stars. I'm wide-awake; and some chap's dead.

On the morning after my arrival Colonel Weber, Chief of the Divisional
Staff, came right up to the trenches to see me and to wish me luck. He was
the Staff Officer I had taken round the Maricourt trenches.

In the evening the Germans began again to send over a lot of trench-
mortar bombs. These are a pet abomination of mine; They move so slowly
through the air that you can actually see them coming, and burst with
the force of an eight-inch shell. They do an extra-ordinary amount of
damage and that night blew-in long lengths of our parapet.

On November 17th. the whole of my Company line was badly knocked
about and I had several casualties. Sergeant-Major Haslam had a
narrow escape; we were hard at work building up the parapet and he
had just gone to the latrine which was a few yards back from the fire
trench. A trench-mortar bomb landed within a few feet and literally
blew him five yards. Luckily he did not even get concussion. At night
I took the opportunity of going out in front of the line to inspect
the barbed wire entanglements, much to the troops surprise. Apparently
it was not the custom now for Company Commanders to go out into
No Man's Land. I found the wire in shocking condition, in spite of
the reports I had received from those who had been out on patrol.
A Corporal had reported it in good order only two days before. I had
this man reduced, to shew the others that I was not going to be fooled
by falsehoods.

On the 18th. we were relieved and went back to Bellacourt.
As a Company Commander I was a mounted officer and had a pony.
After seeing the men comfortably settled into their billets,
I had a tub and changed my clothes.

The following day was Sunday and I went to the Padre's service
as a matter of principle. Bellacourt was hardly ever shelled and in
the afternoon I went round to the various Messes to look up old friends
in the Battalion and to make the acquaintance of the new officers.
In the Sixteenth we had been accustomed to our officers being not only
gentlemen, but men of efficiency and courage who invariably studied the
comfort of the troops before their own convenience. Generally if an

officer proved he was unable to carry the heavy responsibility of
commanding men in battle, then ideally he would be found another post
away from the front. Instances were spoken of when perhaps in the middle
of action an officer might lose his nerve and try to bring his men back,
sometimes only being prevented from doing so by a man of greater moral fibre.

When we attacked on the 1st. of July 1916 if any single officer had
found himself in front of the enemy line with only three men left, he
would still have gone on. If every man had been knocked out, he would
still have gone on to meet the death that they had suffered. There was
no coming back unsuccessful. If you were lucky you did your job and
returned; if not, you did your job - and died; but there was no retiring.

The Sixteenth had perished gloriously on the Somme. Regimental officers
who had joined us since and who had survived the fighting were good
fellows such as Wright, Heywood, Kershaw and Rylands, but had still to
acquire their experience which would be so valuable to them. The Battalion
had been made up by drafts from other regiments and officered by men who
had only recently come out from England where already the reserve of
officer material had been depleted. Hook and I determined to do our part
in restoring the spirit of the old Battalion. Upon some natures, fire
and the test of war have a refining influence; upon others the opposite
effect may occur.

Battalion Headquarters had changed somewhat too. Colonel Petrie used
to command the Battalion. He feared nobody and had already established
his reputation as a fighting man and had won the D.S.O. in the days
when it was not easy to do so. Although sometimes not much liked by the
officers of the Battalion, he had earned the undying admiration of
the troops. He did not encourage advice from his subordinate officers,
but his orders were explicit and he expected to be obeyed without question.
Major Knox as second-in-command had been a veritable tower of strength.
Captain Sotham may on occasion have been unpopular with the officers as
Adjutant, but he breathed efficiency and the whole regiment stood in
wholesome awe of him.

Sotham was certainly not conciliatory and it is possible that being
himself a Regular, he expected too high a standard from his officers.
On the other hand, the troops swore by him. His taciturnity and apparent
rudeness can surely be excused by the fact that he was often in very
great physical pain; but he never let his infirmities interfere with
the discharge of his duties.

I found Sotham very just; it was wise to do as you were told
without unnecessary palaver if you did not wish to be snubbed
and it was idle to expect praise for doing your job; but if he did
say "That was well done, young feller", his praise was worth more
than a Military Cross. I may be biassed because I liked the man and
enjoyed a greater measure of his confidence than most others.
But after all if we civilians entered the Army it was surely to do
our bit in the orthodox manner and I for one did not expect to be
asked "Please, Mr. Nash, will you very kindly take twelve men out on
patrol to-night, if it is not too much bother and providing that you
have no other engagements ?".

Colonel Elstob was a man whose courage was beyond question; he had
a charming personality and was a delightful companion; he was above
all else tremendously loyal to the spirit of the old Sixteenth, but in

his endeavour to improve Battalion Headquarters he had of necessity
to make some changes.

Under Petrie, the Company Commanders were never consulted and their
opinions might have seemed to be brushed aside; whereas Elstob encouraged
his Company Commanders to air their views and sought their criticism
and suggestions. With the original officers of the Sixteenth, the scheme
might have worked well, but with those serving at this time it was in
my opinion uncertain. Elstob hated hurting people's feelings and
whereas Petrie or Knox would have blasted any delinquent into efficiency,
he was inclined to make excuses for them.

Colonel Elstob strove hard to restore the old spirit in the Battalion.
He was a very gentle knight, sans peur et sans raproche. Ben Elstob's
inspired end at Manchester Hill in March 1918 when he gained the
Victoria Cross and the Battalion's stand upon that fatal occasion
surely justified his methods of training. I believe too that he was
one of the few commanding officers to retain command of his Battalion
during the whole of that disastrous period between the Somme and the
Retreat. It is because I am not made of such fine stuff as he that I
might have treated differently and broken those who proved inefficient.

The troops, God bless them, were the same staunch-hearted fellows
of old, and were genuinely pleased at my return. My own Company was
employed on fatigue work during our rest, but I saw that they had as
good a time as possible and got them better billets and more food.
And on November 24th. we went back to the trenches in quite a good
mood with each other.

We went back to the same sector and found that the Hun had been
carrying on the good work with his trench-mortars. On the 26th. one
of my sentry groups was being much shelled at the foot of Lancaster Sap
and I went along to them to move them out of danger. Whilst I was
giving orders to the N.C.O. in charge a shell burst right on top of us.
Three men were killed,two fatally wounded and I was buried and had a
slight wound. It was unpleasant waiting there buried during the
remainder of the bombardment, half suffocated, indeed I should have
been wholly suffocated if it had not been for two of the poor fellows
who had been blown in on top of me.

If it had not been for the slight cut I received, I should not
have counted as a casualty but it had to be dressed in case of tetanus
and I collected another gold stripe.

On November 28th. Captain Wilson returned from a course in England.
He had been Transport Officer but had been sent home for an operation
just before the Somme and now re-joined the Battalion and was given
command of B Company, myself becoming his second-in-command.
Elstob explained, quite unnecessarily, that Megson had A Company,
Agnew C Company, and Wickham D Company and as all three were senior to
me, he could not help sending Wilson to B Company. Wickham was another
of the officers who joined us after the Somme; he had come to us as a
full lieutenant from England and had been given an acting Captaincy.
I was still quite glad to be with Wilson; we were old friends and as
he knew nothing of trench war-fare, everything was left much in my hands.

On November 30th. we were relieved and went back to Divisional
Rest Billets at Bailleulval. It was a long march back from the trenches
and the troops were tired by the time we got to the village.

On December 1st. I went to the Divisional Baths and dropped down
in a dead faint. My long-suffering heart was beginning to get some of
its own back. The Medical Officer hurried me off to bed on a stretcher
and on the following day he told me that I must go back to England at
once or he would not be answerable for the consequences. As I had only
just re-joined the Battalion and was anxious to do what I could, I
pleaded with him and finally he consented to let me remain on condition
that I should go to him every week to be sounded. He knocked me off
smoking and warned me against losing my temper or becoming excited !

On December 3rd. I went to look up Thompson who had been my Scout
runner, and was then a corporal in D Company. He was looking very
fit and we yarned over old times and the risks we had taken together.
He has since been killed, but he was a ripping fellow and a very dear
friend of mine.

On December 4th. I went into Doullens to look for Major Baker
whom I had left there engaged upon Staff work. He had moved on and I
found another in his place. I had been to Doullens just about a year
previously. It was a nice little town but not to be compared with Amiens.

On the 7th. we were in the trenches again. It may be news to some
folk that we have late dinner in the trenches. Better late than never,
say I. On this particular date I had some thin smoked soup, meat and
potatoes, with tinned apricots and coffee. Everything is cooked on a
Primus stove or on your own evil-smelling brazier. Braziers are the
only things to keep a dug-out warm, but the coke fumes are filthy.

H.R.W. Smith met the Divisional General in the trenches on the 8th.
Smith had lost his own tie and was wearing a strip of sandbag in its
place. General Shea was a great fellow for wandering round the line,
and the following dialogue took place:-
The G.O.C. "Good morning. Who are you ?"
Smith.   "2nd. Lt. Smith, Sir, B Company 16th. Manchesters ".
The G.O.C. "And what were you before the war?"
Smith.   "Classical Professor, Sir, at a Canadian University".
The G.O.C. "Indeed. Then I suppose your head is filled with Horace".
Smith.   "My head is filled with the minor horrors of war, Sir".

On the 8th. of December I heard from Sotham that he might be
returning to the Battalion; alas he did not. C.S.M. Haslam went home
on leave. In the afternoon I was called round to C Company Headquarters
and found Agnew very disturbed and shaky. When I got back to my own
lines I found Sergeant Sutton, who had been the Battalion Orderly Room
sergeant but was now at the Base. He had come up to see me and we had a
chat over old times.

On the 10th. the Germans shelled us literally all day long;
they started at 7 a.m. and went on without ceasing until 6.15 .
The troops were rather jumpy in consequence and I spent most of my time
going up and down the fire-trenches. The next day all was quiet on the
Western Front, and we were able to repair the damage to our line.

On the 12th. we were relieved and took over a series of strong
posts in rear of the front line and about 800 yards from the German line.
There were four redoubts, named from left to right Orchard Post, Burnt
Farm, Shrapnel Corner and Starfish point and each was held by a garrison
of one platoon and two machine guns. Their purpose was to hold back
the Bosche should they ever penetrate our front line.

- 110 -

Relief nights always meant a welcome bath and change of clothing. Wilson and I had our headquarters at a farm house and on the 13th. I went along to visit the redoubts. At 6.30 p.m. the Germans commenced their evening hate, a bombardment lasting about an hour and a half; to add to our joy we were aroused at midnight by a gas alarm.

The week passed uneventfully and we had really quite a good rest. The houses around had been much damaged by shell-fire and we were able to use the fallen timber for fuel. The civilians were still fairly close to the line and we were able to buy eggs and milk.

On the 18th. of December we took over Epsom sector of the line which had been much harried by trench mortars and which had a very evil reputation. These trenches were badly constructed and were in rotten repair. We were moving under observation practically the whole time, especially in the support and communication trenches.

As usual the Company moved up by platoons at two hundred yards intervals. As one little group passed me I heard one cheery soul say: "Eh, Bill, what are soldiers for ? To hang things on, of course". Joking apart the burden an infantryman carries with him is tremendous and increases as the war goes on. It is easy to march or to fight light. It is another matter when you are carrying a load of sixty or seventy pounds.

German aeroplanes returning in the dusk spotted our relief and we were promptly shelled, escaping however with comparatively few casualties. The relief of course should not have been carried out until dark; it is one of the elementary rules of trench warfare: I often made myself unpopular at Headquarters by responding too frankly to invitations for suggestions and criticism. It was customary to have frequent Company Commanders' conferences when we would be asked our views. If we were told to do some really exceptionally foolish thing, and my opinion was invited, I gave it.

Taking over is a funny proceeding. After toiling through endless communication trenches, usually up to your waist in mud and water, in a crouching position that is aided by the weight of your pack upon your shoulders, you arrive at the Company Headquarters dug-out, stumble down the dark steps, fall into the charcoal brazier, and picking your shrapnel helmet out of the mud on the floor, chuck your gear thankfully off and blink stupidly for a minute or two in the sudden blaze of one candle. You say politely "Cheero. What a hell of a night. My lads are just coming in". Then it is the other fellow's move./ He shoves a whisky and chloride of lime at you and says "Well thank goodness, you've come. We have had a pretty hectic time. You will find that the Bosche is - (here follows a long story of German work, new trenches, barbed wire, snipers posts and so on). You might sign the trench store list. Here is the log book. Have a fag ? You will find that No. 18 bay is no longer safe and the Huns have spotted the loophole in No. 13 Fire Trench. We had seven men killed in the Bay last night at stand-to but we've got them out. The General has got the jumps over their new sap; keep an eye on it. What's that, Sergeant Major? All in? Excellent, there's no need for me to wait longer. Cheero. I have left you some candles and a little whisky. I'm afraid you will find the rats rather noisy; they seemed to be having some sort of revolution last night, an awful scrap. Well, good-luck and don't sit up too late".

You are left with the care of the trenches and the safety of the
line dependant upon you. It is the etiquette of reliefs to leave behind
a fire in the brazier, a few newspapers or magazines, at least one
candle and a little whisky; it does not matter how little..

Megson, commanding A Company, was taken ill, and on the 20th. the
Colonel sent me to take charge during his absence; things needed doing.
The Company was in reserve at Chancery Lane, covering Martinet's Wood.

We had delightfully comfortable dug-outs and those days were really
the most comfortable I had in France. We had little work to do and
Company Headquarters were palatial, as far as a dug-out can deserve
that name. Dixon was an excellent cook; he had been Oliver's batman
and was a charming fellow. He had been a game-keeper before the war,
and when Oliver was killed at Trones Wood Dixon became cook to
A Company's Officers Mess. He had a wonderful cat, a very Goliath of a
tabby with gloriously sleek fur and a magnificent moustache; although
he followed the Company wherever they went, even into the trenches he
looked very prosperous and shells did not worry him one bit.

The weather was bad during our stay in Chancery Lane. On the
evening of the 23rd. I watched a raid taking place further south.
The night was as dark as pitch, with a strong wind and driving rain.
A tremendous bombardment was going on; the flash of the guns stabbed
the darkness; at first only the German guns were shooting. No Man's
Land was lit up by Verey Lights and star-shells; then up went our
S.O.S. signal of three red rockets and quickly responding, our
artillery soon thundered into their barrage fire.

The general way of a raid is this :- During the day, the
communication trenches leading from the support line to the fire
trenches have been lightly shelled by the German batteries in order
to make sure of the range, a few shells have been dropped near
Company Headquarters for the same reason and one or two into the
barbed wire. This is called registering, and the Bosche forward
observation officer watches where the shells go and directs the fire
of his battery until he gets them where he wants them. The registering
may be done one or two days before the raid. Then on a dark night,
preferably a rough and stormy one, the enemy begin to cut our wire,
in other words destroy our entanglements with high explosive shells
and trench mortars.

Then our front line is extensively and heavily shelled for half
an hour or so, also the communication trenches in order to block them
and prevent the arrival of supports. Under the cover of his barrage,
the Hun infantry get up as close to our wire as they can and when
that barrage lifts, in they hop to our trench chucking bombs right
and left. The telephone wires are probably all cut, and the Bosche
drops a few more shells around Company Headquarters to keep the people
there happy and occupied.

In the meantime a frenzied Company Commander after a futile effort
to use his telephone, consigns it to the devil and tries to signal to
his artillery by means of rockets. These are usually damp or duds.
If he succeeds in firing them, they explode ignominiously in an
adjacent latrine.

After half an hour's brisk excitement, the enemy are driven back
to their own trenches; some are kept as specimens, others have been

killed, and the artillery on both sides dies down. "Normal conditions
are resumed", as you report to Battalion Headquarters. Then there's
the call for stretcher bearers; some poor fellows have got blighties:
others luckier have gone to Kingdom Come. Rifles are cleaned and
everything made ready again while the trench garrison repairs the
damage. You have been living in an inferno of noise and wounded,
covered with blood and black with powder, and when it is all over
some immaculate swell comes along and says "I thought I heard some
rifle fire; has anything exciting been happening ?".

Of course things are not always cut according to pattern.
Brother Bosche is a wily fellow and rings the changes, although he
is usually consistent. Sometimes just as the raid is over and we
are licking our sores, he will hop back again without troubling
to tell you he is coming.

I had a narrow squeak on the morning of the 23rd. I was going
down to Battalion Headquarters with my runner, to one of those
conferences, and passed a party of men working in a communication
trench. The Hun was shelling rather badly. When we came back half
an hour later we found that one man had been killed and two severely
wounded just five minutes after we had passed them. They were the
11th. South Lancs. working in Forest Street.

On the same day Colonel Weber, the Chief of the Divisional Staff,
offered me the command of a Divisional Training Company which was being
formed. It was a good and safe job behind the line, but like a fool I
felt constrained to say "No, thank you".

We left the trenches on Christmas Eve and got back to rest billets
at Bailleulval. The troops were in billets above ground but the Bosches
used to shell the village heavily at odd times so all the platoons were
apportioned to bomb proof shelters with orders to repair to them at
once in the event of bombardment.

I saw the Company to their billets and paid them in the afternoon,
going to bed very tired at 9.30 p.m. I was billetted in the school,
with Gill of the 18th. Battalion. The tour in the trenches had been a
long one and I was thankful for the chance of a rest. I was still in
command of A Company.

At 11.30 p.m. the Germans started to shell the village with
exceptional vigour, so I felt it incumbent upon me to roll out of bed,
slip into gum boots, and a British Warm and make sure that the troops
had vacated their billets and taken shelter in the appointed places.
On my way I collected the Sergeant Major and together we went around.
The streets were being very heavily shelled. We found that all but
one platoon had taken to their shelters; these had remained in their
billet, a large barn, in the centre of the village.

Most of the men of this platoon were sunk in a heavy drunken sleep
and the stentorian bellow of C.S.M. Potter failed to rouse them.
Shells were falling all around the barn and we had to go to each
individual man and strive to kick them back into a sense of their danger.
It's surprisingly difficult to deliver a good kick in gum boots and if
I hadn't thought of sticking a safety pin into them one by one, I doubt
if we should ever have got them out. One by one they stumbled out of
the barn to their shelters; the Sergeant Major and I were the last to
leave and before we had gone twenty yards, a crump of four shells laid
that barn as flat as the road.

With my own men of B Company, who would jump to do my bidding at a
beckon of the finger or a twitch of the eyelid, or with men of the old
Battalion, it would have been an easy matter to clear that barn in a
couple of seconds. I still have that nightmare sometimes, in gum boots
and pyjamas under a British Warm, kicking back into consciousness
drunken insensible men with shells rocketing around. And so my second
Christmas was as disturbed as my first. At 1 a.m. I went back to my bed
and slept the sleep of the dead.

<table>
<tr><td>

1.

No easy hopes or lies
Shall bring us to our goal,
But iron sacrifice
Of body, will and soul.

</td><td>

2.

There is but one task for all -
For each, one life to give -
Who stands if Freedom fall ?
Who dies if England live ?

</td></tr>
</table>

An early Heavy Vickers Machine Gun.

Machine Guns created heavy casualties on both sides.

A light Lewis Machine Gun.

Commanding B Company once again. Lewis Gun Course. Trench Fever.
Halloy. The coming Offensive. Open Warfare.

> Never look for strife, he's an ugly brute,
> But meet him whenever and where he likes;
> Only draw your gun when you mean to shoot,
> And strike as long as your enemy likes.
>
> Never force a fight on a smaller man,
> Nor turn your back upon a stronger clown.
> Keep standing as long as you damned well can,
> And fight like the devil when once you're down.

On Christmas morning I went to Church Parade and to Holy Communion
and in the afternoon the troops had a football match. In the evening
Elstob asked Hook and myself to dinner with the Battalion Headquarters
Mess. It was not a very cheery evening as I could not forget the men
we had lost since that last Christmas, but we got through it.

When the Battalion returned to the trenches Elstob asked me to mould
into shape a new draft of 150 re-inforcements who had just arrived.
In three days time however, I was sent for to take command of B Company
again as Wilson was going home on a long course. It seemed to me that
I had become a sort of general utility man and although it was a
compliment to push me into all these different jobs, I wanted to settle
in one Company. As it happened, I was to retain command of B Company
now for the rest of my active service.

I found them in Epsom Sector; the trenches were in a rotten state
and much work needed to be done. This tour of duty lasted for eight
days, and eight long dreary days they were too. Ravine Sector was
badly pummelled by trench mortars, and two dug-outs were blown in.
We had heavy casualties, the frost was severe and the enemy active.

On January 6th. I had a wire from the Adjutant congratulating me;
he did not say upon what so I vainly imagined that my D.S.O. had turned
up after all. It was however only my second pip. I had been promoted
lieutenant as from July 11th. 1916. As I had commanded the Battalion
in action on July 2nd., and since my return to the Battalion commanded
in turn A Coy, B Coy and C Coy I did not feel very excited about my
promotion. Soon after I was mentioned in Despatches for gallantry
in action.

On January 7th. we left the trenches for a long rest and after
a very long march arrived at a pleasant little village Warluzel, where
we were allowed to remain for a few days before proceeding to Dainville.
At this time the Brigade was commanded by a man called Lloyd - an unusual
looking fellow. Freddy, a relation of Frazer of the 18th. Battalion,
was still the Brigadier's messenger.

At the request of the C.O. I went on the 10th. to Le Touquet
to a Lewis Gun School for five days' instruction in Lewis Gun tactics;
I was very fed up as I hated courses and was anxious to get busy with
my Company, all the more so as Elstob told me that I should have
command of B Company permanently.

At Le Touquet we were really most uncomfortable. We were under canvas, four men in each tent; it was bitterly cold and our blankets and all our belongings were thoroughly damp after the first half hour and remained so for the rest of our stay. The Officers Mess was a huge barn-like hut in which we sat without fires of any kind. The meals were badly served and insufficient. The cold got hold of me and I had a severe heart attack on the 15th. The course was supposed to be up on the 15th. but continued to the 21st. I went into Etaples and Paris Plage occasionally, but thought them very dull and grossly over-rated.

While I was at Le Touquet the first Portugese officers made their debut in France. They looked slovenly and unreliable. While here I heard that my old Adjutant of the 4th. Gloucesters had been given command of the 12th. Bn. Gloucestershire Regiment. At last we were released from those filthy sand dunes and I got back to my Battalion on the 21st. of January, feeling absolutely ill. Colonel Elstob told me I had been appointed Acting Captain.

On January 22nd. General Shea inspected the Battalion and then called me up to him. "I like the way you handle your Company, Captain Nash; I am sure you will lead them well in action".

On the 23rd. I was sitting on a Field General Court Martial. Very severe weather set in and weakened as I had been by my stay at Le Touquet, I was quickly knocked over with a weird disease called trench fever. I took to my bed and under piles of trench coats and tunics tried to get warm. My temperature went gaily up to 104 and then down to 96 a few hours later and then up again.

Two new subalterns joined my Company, Haighton and J.A.Smith. There were now three Smiths with the Battalion, J.L.L.Smith, H.R.W. and J.A. Haighton and Smith were fresh from England. MacDonnell who had been acting as Lewis Gun Officer was returned to the Company so I had six officers all told.

The Battalion moved up to Dainville to do fatigue work, and I was left behind as I was too ill to be moved. I had a perfect damn fool of a batman by this time, a fellow who was quite useless and could not even find fuel of any sort to keep me warm. It was so cold that wild boars were driven from the woods into the village streets. It was a dismal job.lying there by myself, the only Englishman in the village except for my batman. A doctor used to come over from a neighbouring village and twice sent the ambulance to take me down to the Base, but I was anxious to retain command of my Company and refused to go into hospital. I ached all over and my heart gave me a very bad time.

On February 1st. the Battalion left Dainville and on the 2nd. spent the night at my village en route for Halloy. Determined to accompany them this time, I rose from my bed and rode on horseback at the head of my Company into Halloy, a very sick man. Halloy was about 4 kms from Doullens. Here we were to make a long stay, working on the second line that was being built on the railroad from Doullens to Arras. There were many native troops in the village - Indian cavalry mostly.

Company Sergeant Major Haslam had returned to a Cadet School to be trained as an officer and I promoted Sergeant Heap to take his job. Heap was one of the Border Regiment men who had joined us, a young fellow but most efficient.

I secured good billets for the troops but our own quarters were poor.
The cold weather continued but my trench fever was getting better.
In those early days of February I went through my Company very carefully
and weeded out any weak links in the chain. It was common knowledge that
we should be attacking before long.

By evening lectures, inter-platoon competitions, boxing matches,
iron discipline and much good fellowship, I turned my Company into
a really serviceable weapon. The troops had plenty of hard work and
I managed to get in some ripping rides.

On the 9th. at 11.15 a.m. a long train of empty trucks was
passing down to Doullens past the Battalion who were on fatigue at
the time. Heap, Leach and Gosling were sitting on the bank well clear
of the line when an open door of one of the trucks struck Gosling on
the side of the head and knocked him onto the rails. Ten or twelve
trucks had passed over him before we could get him clear. Mercifully
he was not killed but his right arm was badly crushed and had to be
amputated. Heap pulled him clear just in time to save his legs.
I twisted my ankle badly in the effort to get him clear. Gosling had
been a mess waiter in England when the Battalion was training. He was
a nice fellow.

Heap was complimented on his presence of mind by the Corps
Commander to whom I had the incident reported. He was the youngest
Sergeant Major in the Battalion, just as I was the youngest Company
Commander. We did well together; he was a Cumberland man, very tall
and very daring and absolutely conscientious.

Swaine, a subaltern who had been wounded at Montauban, rejoined
the Battalion and was posted to my Company. For the next week or so
I was much exercised in my mind as I was on the list for leave, and
wrote home to say that if I did not get leave within the next month
I should come home in a hospital ship, little realising the truth
of my prophesy.

Signs of the coming offensive around Arras were not wanting,
and the Battalion spent five days at Saulty Labret studying the new
formation of companies and platoons for attack. We were under the
instruction of Colonel Macdonald and had to carry out various exercises
under the supervision of General D'Oyly Snow. B Company did well
and on our return to Halloy my No. 5 Platoon was selected to give a
demonstration of the new attack to the rest of the Brigade.

Several new officers joined the Battalion; Ingram who was killed
later, Heywood an Australian, Ashe, Thwaites, Richardson amd Haines.
On the 28th. Dunkerley joined me as second-in-command. I was glad of
his services; he was an efficient second but did not enjoy so much being
later in command. Stonehewer who had been commanding C Company was also
attached to my Company.

Ingram told rather a good story against me; he had overheard a man
who had recently joined the Company asking one of my fellows what the
"Old Man" was like, meaning myself. This was the reply: "He's an artful
beggar, the Skipper. He came up to me in the trenches last time we were
in, and with a sweet (!) smile said 'Ah, Ryan, how are you?' - he knows
all our blinking names - 'What sleep have you had ? Breakfast all right ?
All well at home ? Splendid. Now let me look at your ammunition. This
won't do, laddie; a rusty clip like that might well be the death of you:

- 117 -

think of your family. I'm afraid I shall have to crime you; take his name, Sergeant. Good morning, Ryan, good morning', and off he goes to the next poor chap".

I was very well satisfied with my Company; with the prospect of a long offensive before us I had been making my preparations. My N.C.O.'s were acknowledged to be the best in the Battalion; they had been selected irrespective of seniority but had the confidence not merely of myself but what was equally important of the men under their command. Even the juniors were imbued with the spirit of leadership. They were taught to remember that in action an N.C.O. is a potential commander of his company and must be ready to carry on. I am a great believer in individual training and in the value of a contented mind. When the troops are fond of their section leaders and the Company Commander can keep the affection and respect of them all, you have a good fighting combination.

We had a company concert on the 6th. of March which was a great success. I scored the hit of the evening when thanking the artists. I regretted that we had not been able to secure the services of an impersonator who preferred to remain anonymous, and I told them the description of myself as overheard by Ingram. It was absolutely characteristic that the men howled with glee.

On the 10th. of March we went off to Grenas to practice an attack over some facsimile trenches of those around Mercatel. All the officers were billetted together in the Chateau, the first time we had had a full Battalion Mess since the Regiment left England. Here Lambourne who had become Regimental Sergeant Major fell down some stairs and damaged himself. He went home and Potter took his place.

After all the time we had spent in assaulting dummy trenches, news came that the Germans had retreated from Mercatel to the Cojeul River. On the 18th. we had sudden orders to pack up and be off. I thanked my stars for a company in good fighting fettle, and was a proud man when I rode out at their head when we left Grenas. We got on to the main Doullens-Arras road and spent the night at Bavincourt under canvas in the pouring rain.

On the 19th. we moved on to Monchiet. The main roads were crowded with troops, guns and limbers moving up to the front line. We passed a great many ambulance stations and many batches of German prisoners. At Monchiet we were housed in wooden huts. We were all very tired but in the evening a despatch runner came round to say that the Colonel wanted all company commanders at 8 a.m. the next morning for a long ride up to the line to make a reconnaissance before taking the troops up.

On the 20th. I rode through the rain to Battalion H.Q. where Megson, Wickham and MacDonnell and the Colonel joined me, and we pushed off. We rode through the much shelled village of Beaumetz and on the high road towards Arras, turning south at the Bac du Nord through Wailly to Agny. We rode easily, sparing our horses for we had far to go and the roads grew increasingly worse as we got nearer the front line.

It was strange to ride along roads which only a few days before had been swept by German rifle fire. The only danger now lay from our own mounts, maddened by the firing of our heavy artillery all along the road.

We rode eight miles to Agny where we handed our horses over to the grooms and made our way to the headquarters of General Stanley,

commanding the 89th. Brigade which we were to relieve. We found him
in a very deep and comfortable dug-out which seemed to be full of
cases of whiskey and large boxes of Fullers sweets. It is noteworthy
that neither then nor later when we returned after a six hours fatiguing
journey to the outpost scheme did he offer us any refreshment.

We had expected only to ride to Agny and back but on arrival found
that the outpost line which we were to take over on the morrow lay
four and a half miles farther on, over ground broken with trenches
and by gunfire. It was impossible to ride and we had to tramp it.
This was the perilous part of our journey; we left Agny and crossed over
our own front line system, now vacated as our troops had pressed forward
at the heels of the retreating Bosches.

We then proceeded to cross the former No Man's Land, now a
gruesome waste of barbed wire and decaying corpses, and crossed several
trenches of the German front line system. Our progress was rendered
the more difficult as the Germans had systematically blocked the roads
and mined the cross roads in order to delay pursuit. At one point our
road crossed under a railway bridge which had been blown up by the enemy.
As the line was of utmost importance to us a party of Royal Engineers
and a company of pioneers had been sent down to re-build the bridge.
This the Huns of course wished to prevent and they shelled that bridge
with 5.9 shells for three days without three minutes interval. We had
to scramble over the embankment and had the narrowest escape of our
young lives. The gunfire concentrated on that small area is unbelievable.
Dead-beat we still struggled on, with the despairing knowledge that we
still had the return journey in front of us. We reached at length the
Battalion Headquarters of the Battalion we were to relieve next day
and the various company commanders paired off and went to inspect the
section of the line we should take over.

As I read it the situation was this; the Germans had observed our
preparations for a big assault round Arras. They had been getting
their Hindenburg line ready to fall back upon with a view to
shortening their line and economising in man power, and they had
learnt from experience on the Somme that they could not resist the
onslaught of our men. They therefore decided to fall back in their
own good time to the positions previously prepared, and did it
amazingly well.

They destroyed everything as they went and did everything they
could to impede our advance. Trees were felled across the roads;
all crossings and bridges were blown up. Every dug-out was
destroyed and the evacuated villages of Mercatel, Boiry Becquerell
and Boisleux-St-Marc were laid waste with fiendish thoroughness.
The houses were razed to the ground, wells poisoned, young fruit trees
destroyed and everything of any possible economic or strategical
value done away with.

Booby traps abounded and a large part of our casualties were
caused by these slaughter traps. In some cases, dug-outs would be
left intact. A book would be left on the table; when touched it
detonated and blew the whole shop sky high. Coal in buckets was
mixed freely with high explosive. Stove pipes were charged to
blow up if a fire were started. The mere fact of hanging a
haversack on a nail left in the wall of a dug-out exploded a
concealed bomb. A shovel leaning against the wall detonated a mine

when removed. A branch of a tree obstructing the entrance to a
dug-out would set a time fuze to a mine which would explode several
minutes after the removal of the branch when the troops had gone
into the dug-out.

A chair would blow up if sat upon; attractive looking
souvenirs in the shape of helmets were sheer murder traps. Frequently
the explosions were retarded by means of clocks which ticked merrily
away for several days before setting off a fatal charge.

Roads that appeared in perfect condition would allow troops to
pass over them but would blow up as soon as a gun or limber passed
over them; sometimes a chamber with a thin roof was made under the road
and a heavy shell placed in it so that the detonator was exploded as
soon as a weight passed over it. I shall deal more fully with these
booby traps in my Intelligence Notes. For the moment let it suffice
that our friends the Bosches were never more thorough than in their
preparations for this well-timed retirement. They went back in their
own good time and established themselves in a splendid strategic position.

The troops in front of the old German trenches essayed a raid one
night and found the trenches empty. The battalions got orders to pursue
and left their trenches and endeavoured to get into touch with the enemy.
It was obvious that all the advantages lay with the Bosches. They knew
their ground; we did not. When we finally got into touch and sat down
to dig ourselves in, everything was in their favour.

The German artillery were in position, whereas our was out of range.
They were in prepared trenches, we were scratching holes in the earth
to find a little cover. They had picked the best spots, our forward
position was dominated by Telegraph Hill and Neuville Vitasse.
We had a big frontage to cover with troops wearied by trench warfare
and totally unused to open warfare.

Here is the situation as it affected our own particular front.
The 19th. Battalion of the Kings Liverpool Regiment was holding an
outpost line from the Cojeul River north of Boiry Becquerelle to a
point on the Beaurains road a thousand yards south of Mercatel; (as on
reference sheet 51.b.SW.Ed.4a.) This frontage of two thousand yards
was held by two companies, split up into eight outposts each of one
platoon. The support company had two platoons in some disused gunpits
in s.6.a. and two more platoons dug in on each side of Nagpur trench
and in rear of the main Beaurains road. The reserve company was occupying
an old German trench in S.5.a. and c. while Battalion Headquarters were
at the cross roads in M.35.c., over two thousand yards back from our
most advanced troops.

The right hand company in the front line held from the Cojeul
river to a point two hundred yards north of Nagpur trench. The left
company swung round from there on to the main road.

The right company had one outpost a hundred yards north of Nagpur
Trench, another astride the trench, a third halfway between the trench
and Boiry Bacquerelle and the remaining post in Boiry itself. The left
company had two platoons holding the main road and the other two
thrown forward of the sunken road T.I.a.

On the Battalion's right were London Territorials and on the left
the Royal Scots Fusiliers. There were no troops in support, and as
the Colonel of the 19th. said "God knows where the Germans are";

that was all very well but we ought to have known as well. They had
not found out; they thought they must be somewhere in front because
if our men moved at all, they were immediately sniped. None of our
artillery had been able to get beyond the railway line and the enemy's
main body were well out of range of our field guns. The German guns
on the other hand were very active and were well placed.

When we had tramped round the outpost positions we re-assembled
at Battalion Headquarters for our weary journey home. Six miles we
marched to reach our ponies, and then rode the seven miles to Monchiet.
We were tired when we got there. There remained many preparations to
make for the morrow and I spent the evening with my subalterns and
sergeant-major in order to have everything clear.

At last after a frugal meal of sardines and army biscuit I turned
in, only to be disturbed six times during the night by despatch
runners with fresh and ever increasing orders from Battalion H.Q.

The 1st/4th (City of Bristol) Battalion
the Gloucestershire Regiment.

The marriage took place on 28th. July, 1917,
of Thomas Anthony Havelock Nash
and Nancy Esther Agnes Reynolds.

Chapter Sixteen.

In the Outpost Line. The Exposed Flank. March 24th. Relieved.

Our Dead shall not return to us while Day and Night divide -
Never while the bars of Sunset hold;
But the idle-minded overlings who quibbled while They died,
Shall they thrust for high employment as of old ?

Shall we only threaten and be angry for an hour ?
When the storm is ended shall we find
How softly but how swiftly they have sidled back to power,
By the favour and contrivance of their kind ?

    The operation orders concerning the movements of the Battalion
on the 21st. of March and the nine subsequent days are to be found in
the appendix.   We left Monchiet at noon on the 21st. and marched to the
trenches at Agny. The roads were still full of traffic and the surface
was bad. In some places the entire Battalion had to march in single
file. Guns and ammunition were being got forward as far as possible.

    We reached the Agny trenches at 5 p.m. and settled down for five
hours rest before proceeding over the top to the outpost position
six miles off. Guides came from the 19th. Kings to lead us but after
the manner of guides lost their way. The last stages of our journey
were pretty bad; our path led us over a network of abandoned German
trenches and laden with our heavy kit we had to slither up and down
precipitous sides. There was a steady drizzle and continual shelling.
Ordinarily we should have been in position easily by 1 a.m. Thanks to
being led off the track it was already light when we reached the
positions we were to take over. We were led to the outposts under
the direct observation of the Germans.

    I took over from a captain of the Kings Liverpools and then
started off with my Sergeant Major and a runner to see my platoons
into position. Company Headquarters were in an anti-aircraft dug-out
in the sunken road and it was a long walk across a couple of fields
to my nearest troops.

    As the three of us were going down the Boiry road, we heard an
aeroplane above us and looking up discovered that he was a Hun.
We have heard a lot of rubbish about the British having the supremacy
in the air. There was no evidence of it during the ensuing fortnight.
The Bosche planes did just what they jolly well liked. We noticed that
this particular fellow was firing what we thought to be lights.
We soon found however that he was using tracer bullets from a machine
gun and directing his fire upon us.

    Tracer bullets are phosphorus coated, the idea being that the
manipulator of the gun can see where his shots are going. In an
ammunition pan there are usually two tracer bullets to ten others.
They make a very nasty wound.

    We took what cover offered, cowering in a ditch and ostrich-like
trying to protect our whole bodies with our shrapnel helmets.
For twenty minutes that Hun airman slowly circled over our heads firing
steadily and just out of range of rifle fire from the ground. Then I

suppose he thought it was breakfast time and popped off home; but talk
about a toad under the harrow !

We got round to our various sentry groups and returned to the
Company Headquarters without further mishap. It did not take me long
to realise that we were in for a remarkably unpleasant time. Our field
guns and, for some reason, our aeroplanes were useless. The Germans
from Telegraph Hill and other high ground overlooked all our dispositions
and if we moved a hand by daylight we were at once shelled.

All work had to be done at night, and even then if it was not well
camouflaged the Hun planes would signal its exact position and the
artillery would destroy it. Every morning the Hun planes flew low over
our lines, looking for signs of fresh trenches and working in praiseworthy
co-operation with the German field-guns. In the meantime of course not
a single British machine was seen.

On the 23rd. I moved my Company to take over the right of the
outpost line, moving of course before dawn to the decreed positions.
I took over from Megson who had established his company headquarters
at the junction of Nagpur trench with the main road. There was a
comfortable dug-out there but it was too well marked to be safe and
was not sufficiently central. I accordingly moved my Headquarters
farther up Nagpur trench. It was not comfortable in the open trench
but I was more accessible and as luck would have it the alternative
position was smashed to atoms by the German heavies; they had known
it would be a probable company headquarters.

I was severely handicapped by the absence of my second-in-command
who was away on some damned course of instruction. As a result I had to
remain glued to my Company Headquarters in case the Colonel wanted me
on the field telephone or anything urgent came in from one of my outposts.
My platoons were scattered over a thousand yards frontage and to visit
them by daylight was only to draw fire on their positions. Except for
one visit a night to each sentry post I hardly ever saw my men and was
dependent upon my subalterns for all information.

In the ten days of open warfare I had just twelve hours sleep and
was not able to wash or shave once during that time. Water was more
precious than gold. Rations had to be brought by mules over eight
miles of broken country. This seems an opportunity of paying tribute
to Knowles's work as Transport Officer. He and Ball, who was Quartermaster,
did wonders and never failed to get rations to us during the whole time
we were in France.

Battalion Headquarters used to ring up about every ten minutes
and in addition flooded me with documents, some of which I have
retained to the day. I was not amused.

At noon on March 23rd. I had a message from Headquarters that
the battalion of London Territorials on my right had withdrawn
"temporarily" and that consequently I had an exposed flank. That is a
singularly happy sensation and one calculated to increase the peace
of mind of any company commander. I was holding a thousand yards
with a hundred odd men and was now told that there was no one on
the right of me. Our London friends had got fed up with the constant
shelling and had just packed up out of it. Our flank was only in
the air for a couple of days, but it put years on to me. The enemy
could have walked through us at any time they liked.

Our first obvious business was to find out where the Germans were; their whereabouts had been the exclusive knowledge of the Almighty for long enough. To do this we sent out patrols; that's another sweet job, to send men out with their lives in their hands when you are not allowed to accompany them or share the risk. I did not enjoy detailing men for work which I was not allowed to do myself. It's one thing to say "Well, come on, lads, let's go and have a look around". It's a different pair of shoes to say "You go out and get into touch with the enemy, while I stay behind talking to Battalion Headquarters on the telephone".

As a result of our patrols we learnt that the Bosches were still holding Henin strongly and had actually a battery of field guns there. This was a village just in front of us that had been reported as evacuated; we found further that they were in force in the cemetery to the right and had deep dug-outs on the sunken road in front of the cemetery. They had a strong post in Nagpur trench only two hundred yards away from us and in the same trench as my Company Headquarters. We pushed up a bombing post as near as we could get without establishing contact.

We were heavily shelled during the night and the men fatigued. The Colonel had assured me that we were to be relieved from the front line every twenty four hours but he changed his mind and kept us in the same position. This was a compliment but one which the tired troops did not appreciate; however they were very good and cheerful. I had difficulty in obtaining definite instructions as to what we were to do in case of attack. There seemed to be some division of opinion at Headquarters about this, but finally I was told to hold on until every man had been wiped out, simple but explicit.

At 11 p.m. an order came through to start putting up a wire entanglement along our entire front. Apparently German cavalry had raided our neighbours and Brigade thought that a single strand of wire would afford us great protection. We put up all the wire we could get. Rations did not get up until after dawn on the 24th.

After an entirely sleepless night, bitterly cold, I had just sent in the Situation Report at 3a.m. when a platoon runner came dashing up and gave me the following message on a scrap of paper: "We are attacked from left. J.A.Smith. 2/Lt. O.C. 6 Platoon".

After my sleepless night this message made me think that I wished they would not choose dawn for this sort of thing. Luckily Major Roberts, the second-in-command of the Battalion, turned up just then, so after telephoning to H.Q. to have the reserves ready if needed, I left Roberts to answer the phone, and made my way to the platoon attacked. On my way another runner met me with : "They're through, Sir, the Bosches have broken through". Now was the chance for panic, so I told the man not to be a bloody fool and pushed on as quickly as I could, expecting to meet the Germans at every turn of the trench, with my own runner behind me and clamouring "Let me come in front, Sir, let me get in front". Not a bad lad, that.

On arrival I found the situation well in hand and the excitement practically over. When we had driven the beggars off I found out from Haighton, the officer in charge of the No. 7 platoon, what had happened.

No. 7 Platoon, astride Nagpur trench, had three outposts by day and two by night. One which was held by day and night was the bombing post established in Nagpur trench itself. Shortly before dawn the night outposts were withdrawn, and Haighton was taking their reports when bombs and shouts were heard from the bombing post, some sixty yards ahead of the main body of the platoon. In the dim light a large party of Germans were seen outside the trench with re-inforcements behind them. The Lewis gunners immediately opened fire and Haighton hurried down with supports to the bombing post.

Here Corporal Watson was in charge. Some 40 or 50 Germans had crept along the sunken road, crawled along the trench top sheltered by the parados, and bombed our post in the trench. The first bomb wounded five out of the seven men constituting the post; one was at once despatched to take word to the platoon commander. The sixth man was badly wounded by the next bomb. Private Ryan, already wounded, dragged himself out of the trench on to the parapet in order to be on the same level as the attackers, while one of his wounded mates passed him up bombs. For six minutes that heroic little soul kept the Germans at bay. Three times was he wounded; so weak that he could no longer stand, he continued to hurl bombs at the enemy when he was lying on the ground. He succeeded in keeping them at bay until the remainder of the platoon reached the scene of action. The Germans were beaten back with great loss to themselves and without attaining the object of their raid, capturing a prisoner for identification purposes.

We got the wounded away; Cadman, Cartwright, Dimsdale, Redford and Ryan. Ryan succumbed to his wounds later in the day; this little undersized Lancashire warehouseman had fought like a lion and died a hero. I tried to get him a decoration but in spite of much urging could not get it through.

I established another bombing post farther forward and relieved some of Haighton's N.C.O.'s. He himself had done quite well as it was his first time under fire. Later in the evening we sent out a patrol into Henin but could find no trace of the Germans. It is to be supposed that their abortive raid was a final throw before their further retirement.

We were relieved by A Company in the evening and went into the reserve trenches. At 11 p.m. on March 24th. came the order to adopt summer time. We got clear of the outpost line by 2 a.m.

On the 25th. we had a fairly quiet day but in the evening it was very dark and we had to supply two working parties to help D Company with their trenches. D Company supplied the guides who could not avoid getting lost. In addition to having two platoons wandering about France looking for D Company, I had been asked to send an officer's patrol into Henin. H.R.W. Smith, my Canadian professor, was very anxious to go and I told him to select any two volunteers from his own platoon to accompany him. He chose Wright and Aldous, two very good fellows. He set off at 10 p.m. to get into Henin.

At midnight Wright and Aldous came back, and reported that no sooner had the three of them left our outpost line and having lost sense of direction they wandered round in a circle for an hour and a half and by that time no one of them knew where they were. Smith made up his mind to take his escort back to the outpost line and leave them there. This he did, and set off on his own for Henin.

They came back and reported to me. I promptly damned them to all eternity for leaving Smith, even on his own orders, but this did not ease my mind on his account. It was as black as pitch. At 3 a.m. he turned up, having got to Henin and finding that the Bosches had a few men there again. I damned him to heaps for venturing into Henin on his own. I could cheerfully have strangled all three.

In the meantime MacDonnell with No. 5 Platoon had carried out a very ticklish task as covering party to A Company who were digging themselves a new trench farther forward. We suffered no casualties. MacDonnell was an excellent young officer and did his work exceedingly well.

On the 26th. we sent guides back to the Railway line to learn the route thoroughly. We also received warning from Headquarters that the Germans were leaving spies behind them, dressed as British privates. These remained in cellars when villages were evacuated and then mingled with the troops after the British came in.

On the night of the 26th. we moved up to take over the left sector of the outpost line and I made my headquarters in an old gun-pit. Poor 2/Lt. Clarke of C Company, whose first time under fire it was, was hit by a shell which blew him inside out. Curiously enough C Company lost a runner in the same way later in the day. We had a large number of men killed by direct hits from shells. The gentle Hun used to snipe with his field guns.

The 2nd. Yorks were to relieve us on the night of the 28th. and we were all considerably cheered at the prospect. My outposts were in a nasty position and subjected to heavy shelling by day and by night. I was however able to visit them more frequently than I had previously been able to, as Megson commanding A Company came to share my headquarters, his own having been blown up.. and could take care of the telephone. The troops were wonderfully cheery, considering all they had gone through, but were very tired.

A patrol of the Scots Fusiliers nearly came to grief when they crossed our front. They were challenged by one of my sentries but thinking we were Germans, failed to reply and tried to creep away. In the midst of our difficulties we were ordered to send one officer from each Company into Bretencourt to witness a bombing display ! Also came the message "The C.O. wishes to have by 6 p.m. a written report from Company Commanders in reply to the following :-
          "What do you consider the most valuable lessons
          learnt during this past week of semi-open warfare ?"
                              R.Gibbon. Capt. & Adjutant.
We were expected to write damned essays now, when we hadn't washed for over a week ! My effort did not meet with official approval.

The shelling increased during the night and Sergeant Kelly, my good old sniper and intelligence man of July 1st, was wounded. A Company lost one of its runners and never heard of him again. I had from the first insisted upon all my despatch runners working in pairs. If one were wounded or killed, the other at least knew where to find the body. These runners had long distances to traverse in the open, and going singly a man might easily be wounded and bleed to death, never to be found again. Headquarters were a long way back and runners were constant going backwards and forwards from the Companies, not always on the same route.

- 127 -

As the evening wore on, we prepared to receive the 2nd. Yorks
and at about 9 p.m. I was ready to leave when I heard that Private
Kewer of No. 8 Platoon had been killed by a shellwhich had detonated
right on him, blowing him to bits. I gave orders for a burial party
and was just setting out to read the Service over the grave when the
Padre came alon so we set out together. It was really his job, but
I made it a practice to see the last of my fellows. It was shelling
badly too. We reached the spot where the poor chap had been killed
and reverently the pieces were gathered into a sandbag and a grave dug.
The Padre recited portions of the Burial Service. While we were there
the Germans put into our immediate area sixty light shells. We had
dismissed the burial party before the service as the shelling was so hot.
That we were not ourselves killed I can only ascribe to the nature of our
mission. One shell buried itself in the ground at our very feet, and
failed to explode. The Padre was a very brave man and I had been out a
longtime and had many narrow squeaks but we both owned that that was
the most unpleasant five minutes we had spent in France.

We got back to Headquarters; Captain Field took over my part of
the line; poor chap, he was killed shortly afterwards. We got clear
by about 10 p.m. and had a long march over the broken ground, through
Ficheux and Blaireville to Bellacourt. The men were walking in their
sleep by the time we got there. I saw them into billets and went round
myself with the rum issue. They had a hot meal and seemed very cheery
though there were many gaps in the ranks. It was 3 a.m. before we got
to bed, worn out and every nerve strained beyond endurance,
but not down-hearted.

Reference is made to the Dawlish Scouts on page 169.

Chapter Seventeen.

A further break-down. Invalided home. Cleethorpes. Hospital.

I see across the shrapnel-seeded meadows
The jagged rubble heap of La Boiselle;
Blood-guilty Fricourt, brooding in the shadows,
And Thiepval's chateau empty as a shell.
Down Albert's riven streets the moon is leering;
The Hanging Virgin takes its bitter ray,
And all the road from Hamel I am hearing
The silver rage of bugles over Bray.

Oh spacious days of glory and of grieving !
Oh sounding hours of lustre and of loss !
Let us be glad we lived you, still believing
The God who gave the cannon gave the Cross.

Let us be sure amid the seething passions,
The lusts of blood and hate our souls abhor,
The Power that Order out of Chaos fashions
Smites fiercest in the wrath-red forge of War.
Have faith ! Fight on ! Amid the battle-hell,
Love triumphs, Freedom beckons, all is well.

After a few hours of blessed sleep and a bath and a shave I
put on clean clothes and felt able to tackle the mass of office work
which had accumulated. The troops needed fresh clothing and their
equipment had to be thoroughly overhauled. I recommended Haighton
and Greening, for Mention in Despatches. They had done good work and
were worthy of special recognition. My report to Bn. H.Q. in regard
to Haighton took the following form:-

From O.C. B. Coy. To the Adjutant.   March 30th. 1917.
Please bring to the notice of the Commanding Officer the gallant conduct
of: 2/Lieutenant E.S. HAIGHTON
who in face of exceptional difficulty and danger displayed great
coolness and presence of mind. When his post was attacked on the
24th. instant by a superior enemy force, he organised a successful
defence with the troops at his disposal and beat the enemy off.
This officer had then only been in the line for one day. I should
like the Commanding Officer to recommend that he be Mentioned in
Despatches.
                          T.A.H. Nash. Captain. Cmdg. B. Coy.

Haighton had really done very well and deserved a little bit of
encouragement. It had been rather a trying ordeal for a new man out
and he had acquitted himself well.

It was my practice when out of the trenches to issue Company
Routine Orders in order to let the troops know what was going on.
Here is a copy of the Routine Orders for March 30th. 1917.

Company Routine Orders No.32 by Captain Nash.

March 30th. 1917.

1. Bn. Orderly Room............9.30 a.m.
   Company Orderly Room........5.30 p.m.
   Sick Parade.................10. a.m.

2. No. 6647 Pte. Maddocks   )
   No. 32959Pte. Whitworth   ) Appointed Unpd. Lance Corporals.

3. Lewis Gun course is cancelled.

4. All men to be in billets by 9 p.m. Lights out at 9.30 p.m.
   All lights in billets to be shaded so as to be invisible from outside.

5. Facilities will be give to Jewish soldiers to attend services
   in the area during Passover.

6. No. ?   L/Cpl. ?   is deprived of Lance stripe for absenting
   himself from fatigue without permission.

7. Working parties will parade as usual except the party
   for Shrapnel Corner.

                    T.A.H. Nash. Captain. Cmdg. B. Coy.

    I also sent in the "Essay" called for in the midst of all the fuss
and commotion of last week. As the notes shed an additional light upon
open warfare I reproduce them here. I did not get a prize for my effort,
and to be frank I expected a Court Martial, but even this was witheld
from me. I am afraid I was often at loggerheads with Battalion Headquarters.
I was very young, and besides knowing that my Company was the best in the
Division, I had been told so both by the Colonel and by the Divisional
General, so perhaps I was a little swollen-headed. I prefer to think that
because I was swollen-headed, my Company was the best. I insisted on
COMMANDING my Company and would brook no interference from anyone in
my own province. I had seen more active service than any officer with
the Battalion and life was too short to pander to other's every new whim.
If I could not agree I held my tongue, but if asked my opinion, I gave
a true one. Here is the answer to what we considered the most useful
lessons learnt during the semi-open warfare:-

    "I consider that the following points have been emphasized during
the past week's semi-open fighting.
1. The absolute necessity of camouflaging all freshly dug positions
and of suppressing all movement during daylight.
    The position of outposts have not been sufficiently disguised
and some that have been camouflaged have been given away by the
careless exposure of the troops. The men do not realise that
although the Germans are not within two hundred yards from them,
they are under complete observation.
    Constant streams of runners have given away the positions of
Battalion H.Q. and Company H.Q.; there has been far too much movement,
not only in the outpost companies but also with those in support and
reserve.

    The report continued, "Working parties have started before dark
and have made no attempt to conceal from the enemy the work on which
they were engaged. For example, fresh earth was thrown up by a platoon
dug in south of Nagpur trench during the night. German planes flying
low spotted this and fired off flares. Half an hour later the
entrenchments were heavily shelled with many casualties."

"Tracks are made by ration carriers. Galvanised iron sheets put up as shelters are conspicous unless covered with earth.
2. The vital importance of avoiding well defined positions marked on maps, such as road junctions, old gun positions, junctions of trenches. Much of the firing, especially night firing, is done by map. These tempting positions for Battalion and Company Headquarters chosen on account of the ease with which their position may be fixed should be avoided for that very reason. It is a folly to use a road when a side path will serve your purpose equally well.
3. The necessity of keeping the enemy under constant and careful observation. Every movement he makes should be known to us if we value the security of our line. He should never be able to take us by surprise. It is not sufficiently realised that an enemy who is always under observation is not a very dangerous enemy.
There is a tendency to sit fast in one position - after having made it as secure as possible - and to go to sleep. Advanced observation posts should be established well forward, even if the risk of loss be large, the gain is proportionately greater.
4. There are many small points to guard against such as :-
     a. Runners working singly.
     b. Advanced posts and scouts carrying anything which might lead
         to their identification if captured.
     c. Tendency to accept existing conditions without attempting to
         improve them.
     d. Too few patrols.
5. Most important of all is the necessity for establishing the upper hand over the enemy; he should never be allowed to rest in peace. Harrassed by every means in our power, efforts should be made to destroy his morale. He should be raided every night and kept busy all day. Hounded by snipers, patrols, raids, machine guns and artillery, he should be in a constant state of unrest.But he isn't."

On March 31st. I went for a ride with Hook in the afternoon and called in to see Knowles. Wilson was expected back from England and it was common knowledge he would take over C Company. Hook and I rode as far as Basseux and for a few minutes listened to the band of the 18th. Manchesters. In the evening I had a sharp heart attack and had to be put to bed.

April 1st. was a Sunday and the Battalion turned out in full force for Church Parade. It was the last time I was to command my own B Company, had I but known it. The memory of that last parade will not leave me easily. Afterwards I went to Holy Communion.

In the evening I had another heart attack. This time the M.O. was insistent; I must go into hospital.

Both the Medical Officer and I had forgotten the arrangement about the weekly examination and my fool heart had been getting steadily worse. It seemed like desertion to me, but when the M.O. pointed out that not merely my own life was in danger, but that a sudden collapse in a crisis might involve my men in needless danger, I did not argue any more.

I will not speak of my intense disappointment at being no longer able to lead into action the Company I had trained so carefully. Nor will I dwell on my last farewell to them, my good-bye to the N.C.O.s, my groom Holland snivelling like a child and my last ride

on Tommy. After saying farewell to the Colonel and to Roberts, I went
into the Field Ambulance on the morning of the 2nd. There was a heavy
snowstorm and it was bitterly cold. I went from there to No.32 C.C.S.
and on to No.20 General Field Hospital at Camiers. After a few days
I went on to England, the doctors at the Base finding me unfit for
even light duty. I was fearfully fed up at going home "sick".

I crossed the Channel on the s.s. "Stad Antwerpen" and was sent to
an hospital in High Street Manchester which was like a work-house
infirmary. I got away from there as soon as I could and after a brief
period of sick leave wangled my way back to the 3rd. Battalion at
Cleethorpes, hoping to get back to the Front again.

In the meantime, things had gone badly with the Battalion.
They had attacked Heninel on the 23rd. of April, losing five officers
killed and eight wounded and suffering 250 casualties in the ranks.
The three other Company Commanders, Hook, Wilson and Megson were among
the killed.

Elstob wrote:-
The battle did not go very well.......the men behaved most gallantly
.......Sgt. Leach of B Coy has been awarded the D.C.M. Sgt. Gleave of
B Coy, Cpl. Profitt of B. Coy, and L/Cpl Coxon of B Coy, have been
recommended for honours and B Coy's Lewis Gunners did exceedingly well....
B Coy, Nash, did very well indeed...we were held up by rifle and machine
gun fire. B Company were scattered about in shell holes all day.....
they fought magnificently..I want you to know this, Nash, as I consider
that it is due to your efforts and hard work that the Company proved
itself so efficient... I am sorry you were not able to lead YOUR company
into action...." which all things considered was very handsome of
the Colonel.

Major Roberts wrote:- "Hook was in charge of your lads and they
did the best work; some of them staying out and going forward with
fresh troops and remaining fighting with them".

Balleine the Padre who considered himself a student of war wrote
the following commentary to me in a letter: "The battle was much as
might have been expected. The Bosche in a strong position did not mean
to give it up without a serious fight. The old Brigade of last June
could have done the job easily...as it was while nothing went seriously
wrong, nothing went quite right, and when once the attack had been held
up and fallen behind its barrage, Master Bosche had it all his own way
with his machine guns".

Such was the melancholy story.
Captain Wilson who had only just returned from England had been killed;
Captain Megson who commanded A Company had been shot through the head
and died instantaneously;
Captain Hook who had taken over from me was killed.
Ingram and Rylands were also killed.
To me the tragic part of the whole thing was that Wilson, Megson, Hook
and myself were the only surviving officers of the old 16th. with the
Companies. Ball, Knowles, Roberts and Elstob were all with Battalion
Headquarters and we were the very last of the fighting officers left.

It was an extraordinary act of Providence that sent me home just
a week or so before all my contemporaries were killed. Harvey, Wickham,
Laughland, J.L.L. Smith, H.R.W. Smith, MacDonnell, J.A. Smith and
Caiger were all wounded.

It was the middle of May before I got to Cleethorpes and there I found Major Grimshaw in command, who had once been Quartermaster Sergeant of the 16th. Battalion. Davidson of ours was there too. On April 24th. I learnt that I had been promoted from acting captain to substantive rank.

I found fairly comfortable billets in my old quarters at 13 College Street and on May 18th. had some more leave and went down to Bristol. Davidson went to a Cadet School at Rhyl and Madden of the 17th. Battalion joined us. He and I spent a lot of time together.

I was posted to the command of B Company which consisted solely of men returned from the Expeditionary Force, most of them straight from hospital or convalescent homes. I had seven hundred men under my command and was allowed to keep none for more than six weeks. As soon as men were drafted out, others took their place. I got on very well with the troops but again ran foul of my Battalion Headquarters.

My men came straight from hospital, many of them with open wounds and yet they had to sleep on hard tent boards with only two blankets apiece. A large number of them were suffering with jaw wounds, and were manifestly unable to tackle the ordinary diet and yet they were provided with the ordinary regulation food.

I had a serious row about this and failing to achieve any improvement I reported the condition of affairs through an indirect channel to General Von Donop who was commanding that area. After that more was done for the bad cases, but of course I got into hot water with the C.O. for taking the law into my own hands.

Another scandal was the haste with which men were sent out again to France, long before they were fit. I have seen men sent out who had only one eye, who had completely lost the use of one leg, who had a withered arm, who were stone deaf. I sent in protest after protest without avail.

I thought my heart seemed much better by now and applied for a Medical Board in order to get out again.

Failing this I decided to apply for a transfer to the 92nd. Training Reserve Battalion, whose Colonel was Crawford, who had been the first Commanding Officer of the 16th. Battalion. I was tired of the business where many officers and N.C.O.s appeared to be scheming to remain at home. The proposal which I think was usually made to any officer who was considered would be useful was tantamount to saying "If you are good, I'll keep you in England out of danger".

The War Office issued instructions that officers who were fit for active service should only be retained with a home Battalion for a maximum period of six months in any one capacity. This idea which had for its object the sending out of the able-bodied shirkers was defeated by officers swopping positions. For instance a man might be in command of a company for six months and at the end of that time he might change places with the Adjutant, or the Second-in-Command might swop places with another Company Commander. So they would ring the changes.

Sotham was with the 4th. Battalion at Tetney and I saw quite a lot of him. He and Slack and Madden and I held a Montauban Celebration dinner on July 1st. We had a great and glorious do. On July 25th. I

got six days leave and went down to Bristol and on the 28th.
Nancy Reynolds and I were married. I thought I was sure to go out to
France again.

At the end of August I had the most damnable asthma. I obtained
sick leave and went down to Bristol. My heart was still behaving
badly. On October 11th. I had a special Medical Board at Grimsby with
a very big gun as the President, a Colonel Tatham. He said my heart
was worse and would never be much good. He told me I should never be
fit for overseas and gave me six months light duty and offered to get
me invalided out. My transfer to Colonel Crawford's battalion had
just come through so I decided to carry on.

The new Battalion was at Chiseldon, near Swindon, and having found
comfortable rooms we hoped we were going to settle down. Alas for
human hopes and aspirations; we had been there just two weeks when the
Battalion was ordered to Lark Hill, Salisbury Plain. I got a day's
leave in which to look for rooms. We hired an old Ford car and loaded
it with our possessions and went down to Shrewton, the nearest village
to the camp. We could not find a single corner and had no choice but
to continue our journey to Bristol, where Nancy remained and I returned
to Chiseldon.

The end was drawing near; on Monday October 29th. the Battalion
was to move to the Plain. On Saturday I paid a flying visit to Bristol
and had a slight attack of asthma. On Sunday, having returned to
Chiseldon, my asthma was much worse and I had to be moved into the
Military Hospital. On Monday I watched from my bed the departure of
the Battalion to entrain for Lark Hill !

I remained in hospital for a week and on November 5th. I was sent
off in a motor ambulance to the Red Cross Hospital at Ramsbury in
Wiltshire, between Hungerford and Marlborough.

It was a jolly little village and the hospital contained about
twenty officers. It was the old vicarage. Moore was the M.O. in charge.

One of the principal excitements was to hire a pony and trap and
drive into Marlborough or Hungerford for lunch. It was a very pretty
spot, everyone was most kind and I looked forward to spending a very
pleasant three weeks there. Actually I was there for three months.

Nancy came to join me and we found comfortable rooms in the village.
Later on Miss Langford, who was Matron of the hospital, suggested that
she should come and help there, which she did, and lived in the hospital
itself. My heart went on in the same silly way, getting no better but
just a little worse; and now my stay in hospital lengthened from weeks
to months. Nor must it be denied that we were very happy there.
We loved our little drives and folk were very kind to us both.

After Christmas I had another Medical Board with Colonel Hall
as President, this was on January 8th. The doctors composing the Board
pulled a long face when they sounded me and after a very thorough
examination, I was sent into another room while my case was discussed.
In five minutes I was called in again; Colonel Hall said that they had
come to the conclusion that I was never going to be well enough to fight
again; in other words I was no longer of any use. He told me to go back
to Ramsbury and await the official intimation of my discharge from the
War Office.

On the 29th. of January that intimation came; Nan and I left for Lapworth, very sorry to leave our kind friends at Ramsbury. I got into communication with my Bank and learnt that I was to resume duties at Bristol. On February 20th. there was an announcement in the London Gazette which put paid to my military career: "Temp. Captain T.A.H. Nash relinquishes his Commission on account of ill-health contracted on active service and is granted the honorary rank of Captain".

Nan and I went back to Bristol and in a few days took up our residence in Stoke Bishop. In course of time I learnt that I had been granted a temporary disability pension of £105 a year and the beginning of March found me at work again. I had constant heart attacks for several months, gentle reminders that my idiotic disability still continued.

And so after three and a half years close packed with adventure did I find myself just where I had started ? Believe me, not exactly.

I am immeasurably richer in the possession of many friends; I have a storehouse closely packed with precious memories, pearls of countless price and rare worth. I have lived a life of rare adventure, such as is given to few men to live, - and still live. Gambling with death, I have forfeited my life many times, and yet keep it. I have learnt something of true values, in a land where life is no longer the most prized possession.

In my struggle for existence in years to come - for I am a very poor man - I have to strengthen me the memory of sterner fights and greater difficulties overcome. When I am sick of myself and of my fellow men, I have to cheer me the splendid remembrance of those horror-filled days when men's self-sacrifice shone bright and clear.

When I can no longer find satisfaction in what I am - just a glorified office boy - I shall find comfort and self-respect in what I have been, a leader of men, - and beloved by them too. I have lost my health but what of that ? How many more have lost their lives ? I am proud not to be scatheless in the day of national sacrifice.

It is true that my colleagues who have remained at home may have become rich; they have had opportunities and not neglected them. I tell you that poor and broken in health, I am richer than they. When I meet a chap hobbling along on crutches I need not look the other way.

Do you remember those lines written by a Press Correspondent who had gone out to the Front to write about the War ? He was writing about some troops he passed on the road :

> "They had done their trick in the trenches,
> They were coated and caked in mud;
> And some of them wore a bandage,
> And some of them wore their blood.
>
> The gaps in their ranks were many,
> And none of them looked at me....
> And I thought of no more vain phrases
> For the things I was there to see.
>
> But I felt like a man in a prison van
> Where the rest of the World goes free".

Copies of letters.

Some letters of interest to myself
arranged in chronological order.

In collecting these I have had to refrain from reproducing some of
the more interesting letters, as they are also the more intimate & personal.

From Private G.F. Hibbert to F.W. Nash.   10.7.16.

Dear Sir,
            It is with great regret that I have to inform you that
Lt. T.A.H. Nash has been wounded in the right arm. Mr. Nash is quite
cheerful and happy; I travelled with him as far as I could. From the time
he joined the Battalion at Grantham I have been his servant and have
always found him a thorough gentleman. His loss to the Battalion will be
missed greatly for he was respected by all officers and men.

            I feel his departure very very much for he has treated me
more like a brother than my superior and I sincerely hope his wounds will
cause him little trouble...

            Hoping for the best, believe me to be,

                    Yours faithfully,

                            G.F. Hibbert.

From Lieut. R.K. Knowles.   17.7.16.

My dear Beau,
            So glad you will be out of this for a time.
The Battalion is much as ever; we had 189 casualties in our last when
you were wounded; 89 missing: most have turned up but Oliver and Venner.
The former I am afraid is dead; nobody knows about the latter.
Smithers is dead. Joe Adj (Sotham) has gone collapse – Gibbon is
adjutant having been claimed from Brigade, they are trying to get Barber
as well.
            As a reward for our gallantry we have a week's rest,
and back again a la Divisional General; you could hear the cursing when
he said it. We have a draft of 50 or 60 men every day, mostly from the
Border Regiment; none from the Manchesters. The 17th. are about 1300
strong, they are making a mess of our drafts, the beautiful British Army.
We are about 500 strong still. One of our chaps who had a slight wound
on July 1st. is back in a draft to the 17th. Isn't it glorious ?
Royal Scots are with us, wounded on the same date. We have 4 new officers,
David you know was wounded and Ben is O.K. so is Megson.

            Reddy has died of his wound; I suppose his blood was in
a rotten state and he collapsed. He only had a bullet wound in the leg.
I do wish you were back here, however for your own sake I am glad you
are out of it. Doc. sends his best wishes. This is all at present.

                    Good luck, old man,

                        Yours,

                            R.K. Knowles.

TELEGRAMS: "SCOUTCRAFT, LONDON".

TELEPHONES: VICTORIA 8654 AND 8655.

IN REPLY PLEASE ADDRESS
    THE SECRETARY,
        AND QUOTE ....

THE BOY SCOUTS ASSOCIATION,

116, VICTORIA STREET,

LONDON, S. W. 1.

19th April 1917

Dear Captain Nash,

      I should like to congratulate you on being "Mentioned in Despatches" for gallantry.   This is an honour not only for yourself but for the 43rd Bristol Troop and also for the whole Scout Movement.   I am sure that all your brother Scouts would wish me to add their congratulations to my own.

      With cordial good wishes for your further success and all good luck,

        Believe me,

           Yours truly,

           Robert Baden-Powell

Captain J.A.H. Nash,
16th Manchester Regiment,
2nd Western General Hospital,
High Street,
MANCHESTER.

CS/AML

From <u>Colonel Hubert Knox</u>.   22.7.16.

My dear Nash,

          Delighted to hear you are going on fairly well.
We have been moving about a good bit since you left. The Colonel
has gone and I am in charge. Gibbon is Adjutant, only Big Ben and
Megson left out of the old lot. The usual gunning going on. Poor
Sotham very ill when he left.

          You are missed very much here by me, I assure you.
The drafts we got are from nearly every regiment under the sun,
Borders, E. Surreys, Sherwoods etc. However we will try to keep the
old spirit of the 16th. going.

               Very best salaams and hoping you are going on well,

                                   Yours ever,

                                   H. Knox.

From <u>Private Hibbert</u>.   4.8.16.

Dear Mr. Nash,

          I was very disappointed when I missed you at the C.C.S.
with your kit for I arrived with it at 2.15 p.m. and was told that you
had been evacuated at 2 p.m..... My next move was to their Q.M. stores
and the Q.M.S. arranged to send both your kit and Mr. Harvey's along.
I gave him your address and a full list of the contents of the kit and
impressed upon him that I was sending a further list along in a letter.
He gave me a look enough to poison me, but I didn't mind for I think
I had him beaten.....

          I gave D Company's old mess a visit. The old lady fed
me up like a fighting man and until I had filled my tummy she wouldn't
let me speak. When eventually I broke the news of your wound she
cried..... For the third time the Battalion has been in a big battle
but Pte. Thompson can tell you all about it as he was in it and I wasn't.
I got a slight dose of shell shock in the assembly trenches after helping
to bandage a few wounded men. It made me feel such a coward afterwards
for I got it at the last minute, but it made me feel awfully seedy for
a few days. As we were on our way up a shell dropped amongst D Coy's
machine gunners. Pte. Weilding was killed.

          Forgive me if I am asking too much but could you give me
permission to visit you if I do get home ? I am most anxious to know
how you are faring and I am dying to see you again; it seems so strange
you being away so long. With lots of love and kindest regards,

               Ever yours faithfully,

                                   G.F. Hibbert.

From <u>Private Thompson, my Runner</u>.   5.8.16.

Dear Mr. Nash,

          I told you in my last of the fight for the Wood.
After that we marched back to be re-organised..we were filled up with
men from every regiment but our own. After a few days we went back to
the line and bivouacked more to the left of our old assembly trenches.
We were there some days practising for the taking of our objective
(Guillemont) east of our captured Wood; on the 29th. we moved into

                              - 138 -

position, dug ourselves in and on the following morning made the attack. There was a low mist.

Our lads had to go forward out of the trench and then do a left wheel to face the village. Some lost direction; parties of men got to the outskirts of the village, as also the Scots. There was a lot of enemy machine gunfire and it was too hot to hold. The men had to retire and dig in, which position they kept during the whole of Sunday; to us it seemed as if every enemy gun had as its mark our new trench. Nearly every bit of ground received attention, mostly with 12 inch shells and the weather was terribly hot. We were not sorry to quit on the following morning. The General in his speech afterwards told us that the Germans had massed in that village eleven new and fresh Bavarian battalions for an attack on the wood we had captured and so cut off the right of our advanced line. Our attack frustrated theirs.. all our battalions suffered heavily..

Must now close wishing you health and a speedy recovery.

Sincerely yours,

E. Thompson.

Au Revoir !

From Captain R.H. Megson.   8.8.16.

Dear old Beau,

Your letter was great to receive....we sadly miss the old friends and I find it is a myth about people being callous.

You will have read what a spot we struck in Trones Wood with Huns up the trees with machine guns and bombs, but the Battalion was magnificent, as was only to be expected.

LED by the C.O. they did a really magnificent attack on the wood and we had a very strenuous twenty four hours which unfortunately left some more blanks.

Our last engagement was awful for we have now 8 inch and a few 17 inch shells to reckon with, and"they like me not".

Well, cheer oh and best of luck to you and any of the others you may see.

Ever your friend,

Robert H. Megson.

From Colonel Petrie. D.S.O.   19.8.16.

My dear Beau,

The W.O. ordered me to take over command of the 11th. York and Lancaster Regiment at Rugby Camp. I declined this and said I required some rest first. I was not keen to start work at once on some others after having had to deal with such a splendid lot as the 16th. Battalion..... I wish I could have stayed on with them but I don't think the Brigade liked me particularly.....it seems to me in this class of warfare that there is very little chance of

- 139 -

strategy and that all the credit should be given to the fighting
units for sheer slogging.

I hope the old 16th. will gradually get together again
and become once more what it was. It will take time.

With all good wishes to yourself,

Yours ever,

C.L. Petrie.

From <u>Major Elstob</u>.   25.8.16.

My dear Beau,

I hope that we shall soon have you back with us -
I know how you feel, old boy, about all the losses that the Bn. has
suffered. If you do come back to us, Knox will, I know, give you a
good job as he has told me so. At present I am acting as 2nd. in
command.....Knox and I have just come in from the new trench line;
we are feeling very hot and tired, two glasses of ale went down well,
Beau, I can tell you.

We will look after Thompson all right, I am working
him up as an N.C.O. Hawxby was killed four yards from me when we
were making a reconnaissance of Trones Wood before the attack.
Well, old boy, I hope the wound will soon heal.

Good-bye and come back soon,

Ben.

P.S.   Knox sends his very best salaams and says "Do not be under any
disillusions as to your command when you come back".

From <u>Colonel Petrie. D.S.O.</u>   30.8.16.

My dear Beau,

Thank you so much for your letter and expressions
of sympathy. I can't tell you how I miss and shall miss the old
Battalion. There can and never will be anything like it.

Whatever befalls I shall never forget the wonderful
lot of officers and men we had before the push - and how they
did in it.

We return from here to town to-morrow and I suppose
in a short time I shall be offered something again. I have no
heart left for tackling these reserve battalions. I am glad you are
so much better and do try and come and see us soon.

With all good wishes,

Yours sincerely,

C.L. Petrie.

From <u>Captain J.T. Ball</u>.   15.4.17.

My dear Nash,

        I am glad to hear you have arrived home and
hope that you will stay there — you have done quite enough in
this war, and more than your share. I my self am surprised you
were able to stick it for so long out here. Do look after
yourself and have a thorough rest; I fancy we have clipped the
Bosches' wings this time and that it will not last much longer.

                        Yours sincerely,

                              J.T. Ball.

From <u>General Baden-Powell</u>.   19.4.17.

Dear Captain Nash,

        I should like to congratulate you on being
"Mentioned in Despatches" for gallantry. This is an honour not
only for yourself but for the 43rd. Bristol Troop and also for
the whole Scout Movement.

        I am sure your brother scouts would wish me to
add their congratulations to my own. With cordial wishes for your
further success and all good luck,

              Believe me,

                  Yours truly,

                        Robert Baden-Powell.

From <u>Captain J.T. Ball</u>.   25.4.17.

My dear Nash,

        Many thanks for your welcome epistle; we are
in the thick of it.

        I am sorry to tell you the Battalion were badly hit
a few days ago.

        We lost Captains Wilson and Megson and Lieut. Hook killed.

        Wounded were Captain Wickham, young MacDonnell, Caiger,
the three Smiths, Harvey, Laughland and Rylands who died of wounds.

        About two hundred and fifty other ranks killed
and wounded.

        Both officers and men fought splendidly but it was
a tough nut to crack; however they gained the objective.

        I am sorry to say that a great number of N.C.O.'s
are in the casualties.

        I think it is about time we had a rest.

                  Best of luck, I remain,

                        Yours,

                              J.T. Ball.

From Lt. Col. Elstob, cmdg. 16th. Bn. Manchester Regt.   3.5.17.

Dear Beau,   On Active Service.

        I have been wanting to write to you ever since we came
out of the fight. To-night Major Roberts has shewn me your letter
in which you refer to our sad losses; to lose Megson, Wilson, Hook,
Ingram and Rylands in one show is very very hard and they were all
such gallant fellows.

        B Company, Beau, did very well indeed. MacDonnell and J.A.
Smith were wounded and I have heard from the former. We were held up
by machine guns and rifle fire; B Company were scattered about in shell
holes all day, I was able to get to some of them but movement was
very difficult. Sergeant Leach has just been awarded the D.C.M. for
gallant conduct before the battle. Cpl. Coxon, Cpl. Profitt, and
Sgt. Gleave have all been recommended for honours - they fought
magnificently. I want you to know this, Beau, for I consider that
it is due to your efforts and hard work that the Company proved itself
so efficient.

        H.R.W. Smith was also wounded. I am sorry you were not able
to lead your Company into action.

        Meggy, Willy, Hook, how can we speak or write of them.
I felt them all to be my friends and now they've gone.

        Of all the original officers of the Battalion
I am now alone with Knowles, and I sometimes feel it almost a sin
to be alive.

        We were able to bury all the officers in a neat little
cemetery and yesterday afternoon we held a memorial service for the
gallant dead in the warm spring sunshine under some budding lime
trees in a quiet French village away from the firing line.
It was not a cheerful ceremony but one was proud to be able to
hold sacred communion with our Friends and Comrades.
The end is not yet.

        Good-bye, Beau, this is going to be the year.

                With best wishes,

                        Yours very sincerely,

                                W. Elstob.

                                Lieut-Colonel.

From Captain Hubert Worthington.   4.5.17.

                                        Staff Mess,

                                                Crookham,

                                                        Fleet, Hants.

Dear Beau,

        Isn't this heartbreaking news - Willy, Meggy, and Hook -
all killed. Rest their souls, and 280 men casualties and 9 wounded
officers. Ben is all right, thank God. It nearly bowled me over.

I <u>am</u> so sorry to hear that you are bad, old thing.
This is the 21st. O.C.B. Parker is at No. 1 C.B., M.G.C., Bisley
Camp. I haven't seen him since I got here.

Let's know how you get on, old thing. I'm a platoon
commander after doing Company Commander from December 1914 -
rather nice I love the work. Let's see you if ever in these parts.

Ever yours,

Hubert Worthington.

From <u>Major R.E. Roberts.</u>   6.5.17.

B.E.F.

Dear Nash,

Am sorry not to have written you before....... it is indeed
a sorrowful ordeal that our Battalion has gone through.

Besides the three of the originals, two others also rest.

C.W.K.H. was in command of your lads, and they did the best
work, some of them staying out and going forward with fresh troops
and remaining fighting with them. I personally feel the loss of him
(Hook) more than any other. MacD is doing well, of others I do not know.

Hope you will get the doctors to give you G.S. Every day fellows
of your known ability are wanted more and more and it is generally
acknowledged that merit in the end gets its due.

The weather has been great, but the life seems more lonely
now. Get well soon.

Yours,

R.E.R.

From <u>The Revd. R.W. Balleine.</u>   11.5.17.

My dear Nash,

You are as fickle as the Elizabethan lover...
there should follow by rights a suitable quotation, were I
as apt at the classics as you - you must supply it yourself.

While with us you rail and declaim against the
fools and knaves in our midst and while keeping within the
due limits of parliamentary expression, use language curt
and picturesque about the Battalion's follies. When you
get away, your passion returns with all its old ardour.

Well, I don't wonder at it. Distance enables
one to focus attention on the essential qualities which go
to make up the unchanging core of a battalion's spirit.
Here we are too liable to put the superficial changes out
of perspective. It is certainly heartrending to see one after
another of the links with the original days disappear......

- 143 -

The battle was much as might have been expected.
The Bosche had a strong position and he did not mean to give
it up without a serious fight. The old Brigade of last June
could have done the job easily.... as it was though nothing
went seriously wrong, nothing went quite right, and when once
the attack had been held up and fallen behind its barrage,
Master Bosche had it all his own way for a time with his M.G's.

Megson, Wilson and Hook were all shot through the
head early in the day. The men individually did magnificently.
Proffitt - your Lewis Gun corporal - and his team remained out
firing the whole day, went over again with another battalion
after we had been withdrawn, and stayed out all the next day
as well.

We are out now, well behind the lines, doing
really useful training - long may it live.

The country reminds me of Oissy last year -
except that there are no strawberries and no Hotel Godbert
for you to entertain me in. The weather is glorious and
billets quite respectable.

All good wishes, my petulant Corydon; don't be
rash in trying to get out again in a hurry.

Yours,

R.W. Balleine.

From <u>Major Roberts</u>.   28.5.17.

My dear Nash,

We have been having a pleasant time lately.
The C.O. probably goes on leave to-morrow. Shea and Weber
left the Division over a month ago. We have a few new officers
but I don't know them sufficiently to form any opinion of them.
Heathcote has left us, sick, and Haynes went sick to-day.
J.T.B. is on leave at present.

The officers are in tents in a field together,
and in their mad young ways last night put young Hunter
(pyjamas included) into a neighbouring pond, as a peace offering
to the frogs whose chorus disturbed the night.

Clark - Gibbon's pal - looked us up the other night;
full of how he had won the battle of Arras.

Have you heard that C.S.M. Brown has the M.C. ?
Should you see Sotham, tell him that Dickinson has the M.M.

Well, cheer up.

Yours

R.E. Roberts.

From <u>Major Roberts</u>.   15.7.17.

My dear Nash,

      Am glad to see your Captaincy has appeared in the
Gazette, and as B Company is at present in need of someone to take
a paternal care of it, you must get those Boards at home to send
you back to us.

      Swain as perhaps you may have heard has been sent home
sick and I believe is at present in Whitworth Street; he had done very
well with the Company and is a loss to us. Laughlan is back again,
having recovered from his wound, and he is now our senior subaltern,
apart from acting captains and Stonehewer.

      I trust all goes well with you and that life at
Cleethorpes does not bore you to death. Balleine has departed
from us to be chaplain to some Corps school and we have rather
a pleasant fellow in his place.

      Corporal Simpson of D Company got the M.M. for
picking up a bomb and returning it to the Bosche; perhaps if he
had foolishly sat upon it he might have got a bigger honour.
We badly want a few of you seniors back, so let's see you soon.

             With best wishes,

                R.E. Roberts.

From <u>Lance Corporal Johnson, D. Company</u>.   5.8.17.

                    Sprottau,
                      Schlesien,
                        Germany.

Dear Sir,

      I have not had a chance to write to you before.
I am only allowed one postcard a week and a letter every fortnight.
I receive a fair number of letters but cannot answer them all.
I have had a hard and rough time but things are better now thanks
to the Red Cross.....I would like to tell you what I am doing but
am afraid it isn't allowed.....

      There are quite a lot of the platoon here, Chadwick,
Weekes, Higson, Martin, Sgt. Cosgrove, Burgess and Turner....
I wish I could speak to you about a certain officer of D Coy.
I don't know whether you would laugh or swear. Life is very
monotonous here, I wish I were with the boys again and chance
my luck. I should not get this far again, I would die first....

      I am waiting patiently for it to end and then I shall
make things hum for a while. I am able to speak quite well now.
I have still got the picture of Montauban in my head. I don't
think I shall ever forget it - it was as near Hell as I want to be.

      How is my cousin, I am afraid he keeps a lot from me,
he tells me he is not so bad but I am afraid he is a cripple
for life.

                    I shall always be pleased to hear from you.
                         I remain,
                              Yours affectionately,
                                   B. Johnson.

From Captain R.K. Knowles.   6.9.17.

My dear Beau,
               First of all I wish you very much happiness and
a long life with your wife...
               There is very little news here; fewer than ever of the old
lot left. Everybody seems to be suffering from war weariness.
We have a crowd of new officers here, half of whom I don't even know
by sight. They remind me of our good lance corporals of olden days.
               Well, I am very sorry to hear you are ill but hope
with rest you will be O.K. Remember, you stay where you are.
You have done your bit and you will never be fit to stand this
racket again.
                    Kind regards to your wife and yourself,
                         Yours ever,
                              Robert Knowles.

From Major Roberts.   November 1917.

My dear Nash,
               Your letter which I have just received makes me
feel rather a worm for not having written to you for such an age.
Let us dispel a wrong rumour. I have never left the 16th., in
fact during October I was in command, as W.E. was in England on
a month's leave; as Gibbon was also away on a three months show
at Aldershot - also Hunter, Kershaw and Dunkerly on leave or ill,
I had a busy time; we were in rather a tricky part of the line
at the time.....
               I am tired of being 2nd. in c. of a Bn. in a
Brigade where all the C.O.'s except one have sometime or other
been a good deal junior to myself.
               Gradually the old faces in the Battalion have
disappeared; illness, wounds or commissions, and you will not
know any of the officers here now except Guest who is Adjutant
and Ashe Hunter and Heywood who are the Company Commanders.
Kershaw has a soft job at railhead, paying odd men going on leave.
Dunkerly is in charge of some prisoners of war at some base.
We have tons of junior officers, every company rejoices in a
second-in-command, usually a fellow who has had a commission
fully a month.
               I find it getting damned lonely in the Battalion.
Ball and Knowles are usually some way off. The C.O. is usually

                              - 146 -

writing notes in his notebook, for the benefit of O.C. Coys at
orderly room, and the rest of the community are not very
entertaining. Do you remember Sgt. Cunningham ? He was bombing
sergeant at one time, he came into one of the Battalions in the
Division and was doing quite well, in fact was acting Company
Commander when his Battalion relieved ours in the line; he got
worried over paper or something of that sort and shot himself.

My brother who was in the 18th. has had to resign
his commission, the doctors in England not passing him fit for
Home Service owing to asthma. I am sorry your heart trouble
is still serious; I hope it will get normal again gradually.

Many thanks for your kindness in asking me to
come and visit you.....I shall look forward to seeing you
and meeting your wife some day when this dreary war is over.

        With all good wishes,

              Yours,

                  R.E. Roberts.

(Major Roberts died of wounds 21.3.18 at Rouen. Ed.)

From the Military Secretary at the War Office to
the Southern Command.

                          February 4th. 1918.

Sir,

I am directed to inform you that the Medical Board by
whom Captain T.A.H. Nash of the 16th. Battalion Manchester Regiment
was recently examined have expressed their opinion that he is
permanently unfit for military service.

In these circumstances it is regretted that there is no
alternative but to gazette him as relinquishing his Commission on
account of ill health contracted on active service and that he
should be so informed. The requisite notification will appear
in the Gazette in due course when he will be granted the honorary
rank of Captain, but such grant does not confer the right to wear
uniform except when employed in a military capacity or on
ceremonial occasions of a Military nature.

        I am Sir, Your obedient Servant,

                A. Keene. Colonel.

APPENDIX B.

Officers of the Battalion in November 1915.

Battalion Headquarters.

Lt. Colonel C.L. Petrie, D.S.O.	In command unti 10.7.16. Mentioned In Despatches. Left to command 1st. Gn. Bn. S. Staffs. Died suddenly in Portugal after war.
Major A.C. Kempster.	Fell ill at Couin after 3 days in France. Did not return to the Battalion.
Major Hubert Knox.	2nd. in Command until 10.7.16. In Command from then until 31.10.16 when he was killed in action at Flers.
Captain E.G. Sotham.	Adjutant until 10.7.16. Awarded M.C. Invalided 10.7.16. Subsequently wounded and P.O.W. Now with Tank Corps 4.12.29.
Captain F. S. Fletcher.	Medical Officer. Invalided home 10.6.16. Out again to 1/3rd. W. Lancs.Fd. Ambulance. Wounded. Died in 1928.
The Revd. R.W. Balleine.	Chaplain. Transferred to 3rd. Army Corps School in August 1917. Now has a parish in Manchester.
Lieut. L.F. Wilson.	Transport Officer; promoted Captain. Returned to England for operation June 1916. Came back to B Company in December 1916. Returned to England for Senior Officers' Course. In command of C Company April 1917. Killed in Action 23.4.17.
Lieut. G.P. Morris.	Machine Gun Officer. Tsfed to Bde. Returned to Battalion as Captain June 1916. Wounded on 1.7.16. Since employed in U.K.
Hon. Lieut. J.T. Ball.	Quartermaster. With Battalion until wounded 21.3.18.
Lieut. F. Behrens.	Bombing Officer. The first officer in the Battalion to be wounded. Lost leg at Hebuterne in November 1915.

A Company.

Captain Hubert Worthington.	Commanding. Wounded 1.7.16. Since employed in U.K.
Captain Elstob.	2nd. in Command of Coy. In May 1916 promoted to command of D Coy. Slightly wounded 1.7.16 and again 9.7.16. Promoted 2nd. i.c. Bn. 10.7.16. Given command of Bn. 31.10.16. Remained in Command until killed in action on Manchester Hill on 21.3.18. Awarded M.C., D.S.O., and posthumous V.C.

"The Manchester Regiment will defend Manchester Hill to the last".

Lieut. R. Megson.	Signalling Officer. Wounded 1.7.16 and 9.7.16. Mentioned in Despatches. Promoted Captain i.c. A Coy. Killed in Action 23.4.17.
Lieut. Mead.	Slightly wounded at Hebuterne Nov. 1915. Returned to home employment July 1916. Returned to France on the Staff. Killed in Action.
Lieut. R. Phillips.	Wounded 13.6.16. Since employed in U.K.
2/Lt. C.W. Hook.	Wounded 1.7.16. Returned to Bn. 10.11.16. Promoted Lieut. & Acting Captain i.c. A Coy. Jan. 1917. Commanded B Coy. 23.4.17. Killed in Action 23.4.17.
2/lt. E.S. Slack.	Apptd. Bombing Officer in Dec. 1915. Wounded 1.7.16. Since employed in U.K.
2/Lt. Henriques.	Spent a few weeks in France; never saw trenches. Invalided home in Dec. 1915.

B Company.

Captain F. Walker.	Commanding. Wounded 1.7.16. Blinded in both eyes.
Captain Payne.	2i.c.Coy. Took command 2.7.16 until 9.7.16. Wounded 9.7.16. Since employed U.K.
Lieut. Oliver.	Promoted Captain June 1916 & tsfd. to D Coy. Missing, believed killed 9.7.16.
2/Lt. Rhodes.	Returned to England before seeing trenches. Invalided Nov. 1915. Since employed in U.K.
2/Lt. Percy.	Apptd. Transport Officer May 1916 vice Wilson. Returned to Coy. Shell shock 13.5.16. Since employed in U.K.

C Company.

Captain Roberts.	Commanding. After many vicissitudes promoted 2nd in command of Bn. Died of wounds 21.3.18 at Rouen.
Lieut. Davidson.	2nd. i.c. Coy. Wounded 9.7.16. Since employed in U.K.
2/Lt. Gibbon.	Apptd. Adjutant vice Sotham 10.7.16. Promoted Captain & Major. Wounded and captured 21.3.18.
2/Lt. Knowles.	Apptd. Transport Officer vice Percy. Promoted Lieutenant and Captain.
2/Lt. Barber.	Transferred to T.M.B.

D Company.

Captain H.S. Greg.	Commanding. Sent home in May 1916.
Captain Morton Johnson.	2nd. i.c. Coy. Appointed O.C. C Coy, vice Roberts. Killed in Action 1.7.16.
Lieut. Dalgleish.	In valided April 1916. Jaundice and T.B.
2/Lt. S.R. Allen.	Apptd. Intelligence Officer; then returned to Coy. Killed while attempting to rescue wounded. Killed in Action 1.7.16.
2/Lt. T.A.H. Nash.	Apptd. Intelligence Officer vice Allen Dec. 1915. Assistant Adjutant Feb. 1916. Wounded 9.7.16. Promoted Lieutenant. Mentioned in Despatches 13.11.16. Returned to Bn. Nov. 1916. Wounded December 1916. (3rd. wound stripe & gassed previously). Promoted Captain i/c B Company. Discharged unfit 20.2.18.

Nominal Roll of Officers and other ranks

of B Company 16th. Battalion of the Manchester Regiment

March 24th. 1917.

Captain T.A.H. Nash. Cmdg. B. Coy. Invalided 3.4.17 and 20.2.18.

Captain R. Dunkerly 2nd. in C.	i/c P.O.W. Camp	
Lieut. Stonehewer		
Lieut Swain	Invalided	
2/Lt MacDonnell	Wounded 23.4.17	
2/Lt H.R.W. Smith	Wounded 23.4.17	
2/Lt J.A. Smith	Wounded 23.4.17	
2/Lt E.S. Haighton	Trench Fever	
2/Lt Scudamore	Tsfd. to R.F.C.	

43045 C.S.M., S.W. Heap

No. 5 Platoon

6702	C.Q.M.S.	T.A.Winning	Tsfd. to P.O.W. Camp
6738	Sgt.	T. Gammond	Band
7374	Sgt.	W. Gleave	Awd. M.M. 23.4.17 Wounded 31.8.17
6549	Sgt.	E.J.Reilly	Postman Rtd. for Comm. 10.4.17
6545	Cpl.	A. Proffitt	Awd. M.M. 23.4.17 L.G.
16421	Cpl.	H. Godwin	Signals Wounded 23.4.17
7235	L/Cpl.	W.F.Loxley	Division
32534	L/Cpl.	A. Sherwood	R.G.
43094	L/Cpl.	J. Stalker	R.G.
40888	L/Cpl.	S. Wilson	L.G.
43099	L/Cpl.	R. Langworthy	Bomber
40817	L/Cpl.	W. Lupton	L.G. Wounded 23.4.17
8042	Pte.	A. Ashworth	Bomber Wounded 23.4.17
41847	Pte.	H. Boon	L.G.
47516	Pte.	F. Berry	L.G.

41848	Pte.	E.F.Brown	S.B.
41849	Pte.	F. Brown	L.G.
41846	Pte.	A. Batchelor	
37201	Pte.	J. Casson	Batman
35488	Pte.	S. Campbell	R.G.
27307	Pte.	O. Green	R.G.
7221	Pte.	M. Griffin	Sanitary
18893	Pte.	J.E.Huddart	Signals
6499	Pte.	E. Hart	Transport
18600	Pte.	G.W.Harrison	R.G.
45077	Pte.	H. Holmes	L.G. Humane Soc. Medal
38431	Pte.	F. Hutchinson	Shoemaker. Gassed 31.8.17
7223	Pte.	R.J.Hall	Transport
27206	Pte.	W.J.Heyworth	Band
43007	Pte.	J. Hayton	Runner Wounded 31.8.17
6502	Pte.	A. Higginbottom	Band
41835	Pte.	A.E.T.Jeffries	Runner
41836	Pte.	G.W.Kent	L.G.
41837	Pte.	P.A.Kent	L.G.
35426	Pte.	B. Lewis	L.G.
7332	Pte.	F. Monks	Division
6526	Pte.	J. Meikle	Signals
29591	Pte.	F. Murphy	Transport
6535	Pte.	T. Ogden	Band
6544	Pte.	F.W.Potter	4th. Army Corps
6421	Pte.	J.L.Plant	Saulty
37148	Pte.	H.G.Pickles	Runner
36581	Pte.	J.E.Perry	L.G.
35503	Pte.	H. Parkes	Bomber
6547	Pte.	E.L. Read	Postman
35483	Pte.	W. Roberts	Batman
46650	Pte.	J. Ryder	Signals
37415	Pte.	H.H.Shroeder	Bombs
29061	Pte.	J. Simpson	Bombs
39556	Pte.	H. Sellors	R.G.
40864	Pte.	W.R.Saunders	Batman
34971	Pte.	A. Sutcliffe	L.G.
40868	Pte.	J.C.Salmon	Bombs
46647	Pte.	F. Schofield	Signals
37403	Pte.	H. Thackeray	Bombs
37755	Pte.	O. Whitaker	Bombs
6559	Pte.	E. Speed	Tailor

No. 6 Platoon.

7020	Sgt.	G.R.Lawton	L.G.
6475	Sgt.	J.R.Catlow	H.Q. Mess
	Sgt.	Joynt	
6570	Cpl.	A. Watson	Division
6676	Cpl.	G. Sheard	Gas
6534	Cpl.	W. Morris	Q.M. Stores
6553	Cpl.	A. Rushton	R.G.
6556	L/Cpl.	J. Travis	Cook
6560	L/Cpl.	W. Stafford	Transport
39647	L/Cpl.	O.S.Baldeston	Deaf
43101	L/Cpl.	L. Bunting	Bombs

17324	L/Cpl.	H.	Coxon	L.G.	Awd. M.M. 23.4.17.
40875	L/Cpl.	S.C.	Towle	L.G.	
27208	L/Cpl.	W.	Walker	Band	
37820	L/Cpl.	N.	Wild	R.G.	
5595	Pte.	A.	Atkins	L.G.	
1852	Pte.	F.	Barnes	B.	
35485	Pte.	F.W.	Benson	L.G.	
2041	Pte.	C.	Burgess	Div.	
6461	Pte.	F.	Battell	Trans.	
33222	Pte.	H.	Colley	B.	
38034	Pte.	J.F.	Casey	Batman	
6874	Pte.	J.	Cartledge	Trans	
27205	Pte.	W.E.	Coppock	Band	
28924	Pte.	W.	Cumming	B.	
35488	Pte.	J.	Dean	R.G.	
33219	Pte.	H.	Davenport	R.G.	
27241	Pte.	E.	Dunkerly	Winning	
27419	Pte.	F.	Dawson	R.G.	
35594	Pte.	A.	Ellis	B.	
18472	Pte.	J.E.	Ferns	L.G.	Wounded 23.4.17. Cleethorpes
33850	Pte.	J.	Garner	R.G.	
29628	Pte.	S.	Gardner	B.	
32640	Pte.	W.	Green	Scout	
11282	Pte.	G.	Grantham	L.G.	
41826	Pte.	A.D.	Gilbert	L.G.	
5539	Pte.	J.	Greenough	Cook	
6497	Pte.	E.	Hallett	Mess Cook	
21149	Pte.	A.	Harper	Sigs	
6505	Pte.	J.	Holland	Groom	
43014	Pte.	C.	Higgs	Bombs	
6504	Pte.	N.	Holden	Bde.	
7289	Pte.	H.	Howse	T.M.B.	
41834	Pte.	A.G.	Heath	L.G.	
6518	Pte.	J.	Lawrenson	Trans	
6520	Pte.	S.	Lomax	Trans	
37421	Pte.	S.	Mottershead	S.B.	
39445	Pte.	H.	Maguire	L.G.	
40848	Pte.	J.E.	Pearson	L.G.	
41842	Pte.	E.A.	Puddy	Pigeons	
37648	Pte.	J.	Pickering	L.G.	
41843	Pte.	S.V.	Parris	Pigeons	
35442	Pte.	P.	Qualey	T.M.B.	
6548	Pte.	A.F.	Rear	Trans	
34401	Pte.	W.	Rollston	R.G.	
25393	Pte.	J.	Ravenscroft	B	
27434	Pte.	F.	Stephenson	L.G.	
6677	Pte.	J.E.	Sinclair	Tailor	
43017	Pte.	J.	Thorogood	Storeman	
6439	Pte.	H.	Tollitt	Batman	
32608	Pte.	O.	Taylor	B	
40876	Pte.	B.	Thornewill	Sigs	
34629	Pte.	T.	Turner	Sigs	
34895	Pte.	J.	Wood		

No. 7 Platoon.

6832	Sgt.	H. Barton	Instructor at Base
6646	Sgt.	W.J.MacMinn	Killed in Action 31.8.17.
6700	Cpl.	H.A.Whittenbury	T.M.B.
7396	Cpl.	J.S.Banks	L.G.
6636	L/Cpl.	R. Jowle	Runner
4358	L/Cpl.	H. Bridson	L.G.
37929	L/Cpl.	G. Watson	Bombs. Wounded 23.4.17 Cpl. & Sgt.
30421	L/Cpl.	C.R.Rigby	R.G.
6575	Pte.	T. Airey	L.G.
6577	Pte.	H. Allen	Salvage
32952	Pte.	J. Boyle	B
32935	Pte.	E. Barraclough	R.G.
6346	Pte.	A. Broughton	Bde.
36393	Pte.	J. Cartwright	B. Wounded 24.3.17.
29111	Pte.	H. Cadman	B. Died of wounds 24.3.17.
33139	Pte.	J. Dimsdale	B. Wounded 24.3.17.
32984	Pte.	F. Dobson	L.G.
35575	Pte.	H. Eckersley	R.G.
38408	Pte.	J. Evans	R.G. Invalided
35439	Pte.	J. Fitton	Div.
45236	Pte.	J.B.Fairhurst	Band
29229	Pte.	F. Greenall	Runner
43105	Pte.	W. Gray	Salvage
6632	Pte.	J. Hulme	Div.
39637	Pte.	S. Harrison	B.
7230	Pte.	Houldsworth	M.P.
33475	Pte.	W. Harrisworth	L.G.
2824	Pte.	F. Hoskins	B.
43108	Pte.	J. Jinks	L.G.
33854	Pte.	G. Kendle	L.G.
29305	Pte.	J.D.Knape	L.G.
6642	Pte.	W. Lomas	Transport
6641	Pte.	H. Leonard	Salvage
6647	Pte.	J. Maddocks	Scouted. L/Cpl.
37988	Pte.	J. Moores	R.G.
43109	Pte.	J. Manger	Band
35853	Pte.	S. Mason	L.G.
40831	Pte.	F. Musson	S.B.
37937	Pte.	P. Nickol	S.B.
28547	Pte.	T. Ogden	T.M.B.
20947	Pte.	J.T.Ormerod	T.M.B.
38699	Pte.	F. Ogden	B.
6644	Pte.	C.W.Parker	Bde.
34205	Pte.	B. Parkinson	Runner
38700	Pte.	A.E.Ryan	B. Died of Wounds. Rec'd. M.M.
45240	Pte.	H. Razel	L.G.
37649	Pte.	G. Redford	B. Wounded 24.3.17.
40869	Pte.	A. Sells	L.G.
37655	Pte.	L. Stockton	Batman
32959	Pte.	E. Whitworth	R.G. Killed in Action.
46871	Pte.	J.H.Welbourne	Sigs.
34252	Pte.	E. Wild	B. Wounded
40887	Pte.	H. Whittington	R.G.
33562	Pte.	H.W.Whitehead	L.G. Wounded 23.4.17.

No. 8 Platoon.

43008	Sgt.	A. Leech	D.C.M. 23.4.17. Wounded 31.8.17.
6691	Sgt.	F. Thomas	Medical Orderly.
7355	Cpl.	W. Bell	B. Killed in Action 23.4.17.
43010	Cpl.	M. Quin	B. Wounded 23.4.17.
6597	L/Cpl.	W.H.Coxon	Coy. Clerk.
7056	L/Cpl.	H.F.Smith	Mess
6703	L/Cpl.	A. Williams	R.G.
35658	L/Cpl.	F. McDougall	R.G. Killed in Action.
43102	L/Cpl.	J. Barsby	L.G. Wounded 23.4.17.
43016	L/Cpl.	A. Patient	R.G. Wounded 23.4.17.
6579	Pte.	W.E.Austin	Bde.
33870	Pte.	J.W.Allen	L.G.
43002	Pte.	A. Aldous	.. . Wounded 23.4.17.
28901	Pte.	J. Berry	B.
20272	Pte.	T. Birtles	L.G. Wounded 23.4.17.
35459	Pte.	J. Blood	B.
6724	Pte.	R.E.Brunton	Chiropodist.
34844	Pte.	T.A.Beckett	
33115	Pte.	S. Bramwell	B.
6592	Pte.	E.C.Clark	Warluzel
30249	Pte.	T. Casey	B. Wounded 23.4.17.
43005	Pte.	G. Clarke	Sanitary
36514	Pte.	L.R.Collier	B.
34969	Pte.	R. Crompton	B. Wounded 23.4.17.
29623	Pte.	J.N.Davies	B.
6608	Pte.	H. Ellis	Sigs.
45151	Pte.	English	L.G.
40913	Pte.	F.W.Grattan	B. Wounded 23.4.17.
40911	Pte.	L. Goodwin	Sigs.
33385	Pte.	R. Gartside	L.G.
41833	Pte.	H.A.Heal	L.G.
6631	Pte.	J. Hoyle	Band
36959	Pte.	S. Jones	S.B.
29594	Pte.	C. Knight	B.
41838	Pte.	H.J.Kewer	Killed in Action 28.3.17 7p.m. M36 c97
29431	Pte.	C. Lancaster	B.
29001	Pte.	J. Lyne	S.B.
27216	Pte.	E. Lloyd	Batman
7469	Pte.	P. Maddaford	T.M.B.
41839	Pte.	A.P.Merriman	
40833	Pte.	J. Mould	L.G.
6649	Pte.	H. Maloney	Transport
31287	Pte.	D.J.Murphy	Salvage
41840	Pte.	J. Nisbet	
33644	Pte.	W. Rawcliffe	B.
41841	Pte.	B.S.Oldfield	
40858	Pte.	G. Randall	L.G.
21136	Pte.	A. Schofield	R.G.
47155	Pte.	E. Sheard	R.G.
41844	Pte.	F.J.Schewr	
13632	L/Cpl.	E. Shepherd	
33265	Pte.	H. Wright	B.
41845	Pte.	E.C.Walliker	B.
29778	Pte.	Wainwright	B.
25231	Pte.	W. Wolfenden	L.G.

APPENDIX C.

O R D E R S & M E M O R A N D A
relating to the
O P E R A T I O N S of March 21st - 29th.

Operation Order No. G.24.
<u>by Lieut-Col. Elstob,M.C.,cmdg.16th.(S).Bn.Manchester Regt.</u>

1. The 16th.Bn.Manch.R. will relieve the 19th.K.L.R's in   21.3.17.
   AGNY and forward trenches on 21/22 March 1917.

2. Disposition of Coys. in Outpost Line.
   A on left; D on right; B in support; C in reserve.

3. One section of the 90th. Machine Gun Coy. will be attached
   to the 16th. Manch. R.
   Disposition:- 2 guns in front line. 2 guns in reserve at Bn.

4. Route. Beaumetz - Bac du Nord - Wailly.

5. Starting Point. Crossroads Q.22.b.5.0.

6. Order of March. Hdqtrs. D.A.B.C. Lewis Gun Limbers.
   1 water cart. Mess Cart. Maltese Cart. Machine Gun section
   and transport, followed by the remainder of our transport
   which will halt in Wailly. Head of H.Q.Coy to pass starting
   point at 12.45 p.m.

7. O's.C.Coys to see that all ranks are acquainted with the
   name of the first destination "AGNY".

8. Guides to Agny trenches will be at Agny chateau at 3p.m.

9. Time of departure from Agny trenches to outpost will be
   2.30 a.m. 22.3.17.

10. Officers' valises to be at Q.M.Stores by 11 a.m. Officers
    are advised to carry shaving and washing materials in packs.

11. Mess kits will be collected at 12 noon.

12. A distance of 200 yds. will be maintained between Coys.
    on the march.

signed. R. Gibbon.

Capt. & Adjutant.

<u>C. Coy 19th. K.L.R.</u>   21.3.17.

List of Stores handed over to A Coy. 19th. K.L.R.

Bombs.	S.A.A.(bandoliers)
66	40

<u>C. Coy 19th.K.L.R.</u>   21.3.17.

List of Stores handed over to D. Coy. 19th. K.L.R.

Petrol Tins.	Bombs.	S.A.A.
2	80	23

C. Coy 19th. K.L.R.   22.3.17.

Dump List handed over to 16th. Manch. R.

Boxes of S.A.A.	6
Bandoliers of S.A.A.	15
Boxes of Verey Lights	2
Boxes of Bombs	5
Petrol Tins	10
Spades	62
Picks	1
Rockets	3
Bombs (loose)	18
Boxes Rifle Grenades	1

Artillery Instructions.

| A/150 | Major Fraser Tytler | J.T.43 |
| B/150 | Major Jacks | J.T.44 |

Both on same time which will be handed in to Coy. H.Q. each
evening and taken off by first signaller from battery in the
morning. Above two near Cemetery Boisleux le Mont.

| C/150 | Major Clifford |
| D/150 | Major Sarson |

From O.C. 5 Platoon. To O.C. D Coy. DIG.   22.3.17.

Relief complete. My H.Q. are at s.6.d.8.2.
No. 1 Sentry Group is at   T.7.a.I.8.
No. 2   "   "   is at   S.12.b.8.7.

Rations were received all right but owing to some mistake
we got the tea and No.6 got all the bacon. Also all the
Officers' rations were sent up to me so I am sending them
back and you can send me whatever I am supposed to have
please. We are digging in here. Cheery oh.

                                R. MacDonnell. 2/Lieut.
By Runner.

From O.C. 6 Platoon to O.C. B Coy.   23.3.17. 2 a.m.

I have taken over from D Coy (13 Platoon). We are digging in.
Sgt. Lawton and 6 men are patrolling in front.
Lewis Gunners have taken up position on Sunken Road in rear of
line about 100 yards to our right, in order to protect gap in
line. Can we have some solidified alcohol; D Coy seem to have
used it all, and if we can, dry tea rations would be useful.

By Runner.   John A. Smith 2/lieut.

From Adjt. to O.C. B Coy.   23.3.17.

Herewith 3 copies of the following maps (new editions):-
1/20000	51 b.s.w.	Edition	4a
1/10000	Blaireville	"	3a
1/10000	Beaumetz	"	2a

All previous copies are cancelled and should be returned to
H.Q. immediately. Please acknowledge.

S. Kershaw   2/Lieut.
Asst. Adjutant.

<u>From O.C. 6 Platoon</u> to O.C. B Coy.

I have taken over a box of S.A.A. and a box of bombs from
14 Platoon. A forward sentry group is posted in a trench on
which the working party have been engaged.

J.A. Smith   2/lieut.

<u>From O.C. 7 Platoon</u> to O.C. B Coy.   23.3.17.

Casualty Report: Nil. Front quiet. Working with all available
tools on consolidating and double blocking. Will you advise
as to time for Stand To please and are there any more spades
available please.

By Runner 2.50 a.m.   E.S. Haighton 2/Lieut.

<u>From O.C. 5 Platoon</u> to O.C. Coy DIG.   23.3.17.

Relief Complete. I have four posts:-

(a) 1 N.C.O. and 3 men in front about 300x in trench we are
    digging.
(b) 1 N.C.O. and 6 men Lewis Gun Post.
(c) 1 N.C.O. and 6 men out as picquet.
(d) A Gas Sentry.
Nos. a,c, & d come back to Sunken Road at dawn. No. b is a
permanent post. I haven't enough men for A Coy's Patrol.

R. de. C. MacDonnell

2/Lieut.

<u>To O.C. B Coy.</u>   R18.   23rd. Day.

Am informed that Battalion on our right has for the present
withdrawn their post which was on the S.E. point of Boiry-
Becquerelle AAA You had better watch your right flank
therefore turning back your right platoon a little.

R. Gibbon.   Captain.

From DIG. Time 1.5 p.m.

<u>To O.C. B Coy.</u>   RG12.   23.3.17. 12.1 p.m.

The C.O. wishes you to send out two patrols towards Henin to-night
each consisting of a good N.C.O. and four men. He suggests that one
should proceed by Sunken Road through T.I.c & d but does not wish
to interfere with any arrangements you may desire to make. As
mentioned over the phone this morning see that people on your
flanks are informed of your movements. Wire report of patrol
as soon as possible after each comes in.

R. Gibbon.   Captain & Adjutant.

To Adjt. DIG. N.10. 23rd. Day. In reply to RG 12.

My first patrol will move towards Henin via Sunken Road TI c&d
at 11 p.m. AAA My second will move towards Henin via S.E. side of
trench through TI a&b at 1 a.m. AAA Both patrols will consist of
1 N.C.O. and 4 men AAA Password BRICK AAA I am warning folk on
flanks will you tell artillery please AAA I understand from the
artillery officers that our neighbours are going to regain lost
ground on right to-night AAA I presume this will not affect
patrols AAA Please state if you still wish them to go out AAA
Have sent copies of your message re right flank to all platoons
and have ordered MacDonnell to get into touch at once falling
back if necessary AAA I will let you know his position directly
he tells me.

                          T.A.H. Nash. Capt. O.C. B Coy. 3 p.m.

To O.C. B Coy. R.21. 23rd. Day. In reply to N 10.

Re Patrols yes send them out aaa artillery knows re Henin.
Re your N13 - the Bn. H.Q. of Bn. onour right is by the
Railway at S.11.d.5.3. Don't know where their left Coy.H.Q. are.
                              R. Gibbon. Capt. & Adjt.
From DIG. Time 4 p.m.

To C Coy. N.11. 23rd.Day

Am sending out patrols towards Henin to-night at 11 p.m. and 1 a.m.
by different routes aaa password BRICK each patrol consists of 5
O.Rs aaaplease acknowledge.
                          T.A.H. Nash. Captain.

From B Coy. Time 3 p.m.

To Bn. on right of 16th. Manch R.   N12. 23rd. Day.

Have been ordered to send 2 patrols towards Henin to-night at
11 p.m. and 1 a.m. respectively aaa each patrol consists of
5 O.R.s aaa password BRICK aaa please acknowledge and let me
know what Bn. you are and what Coy.

Time 3.30 p.m.   T.A.H. Nash Captain. O.C. B. Coy.

The Adjt. .   N13. 23rd. Day.

Re. NLO. my runner has just returned from 2/Lt. MacDonnell who is
still at 5.12.b.8.7. aaa he has sent out to get into touch with
next Bn. aaa do you know where they are aaa I will send you news
when I get it.

From O.C. B. Coy. Time 3.15 p.m.T.A.H. Nash Captain.

To O.C. B. Coy. 16th. Manch. R.   7.15. p.m. 23.3.17.
From O.C. B Coy. 2/2nd. Londons.

Your message re patrols received aaa I am B Coy of the 2/2 London
Regt.

                          J. Newton. Lieut.

                          3.15 p.m.N14. 23rd.Day.

To DIG.

Situation unpleasant aaa much shelling from Telegraph Hill and
Neuville Vitasse aaa believe there to be a battery of guns in Henin
aaa men much fatigued but cheerful at prospect of relief aaa wind
fresh north westerly.

From O.C. B. Coy.   Time 3.15 p.m.T.A.H. Nash   Captain.

To O's Cmdg. Coys.   23.3.17.

Coys will remain in their present subsectors until to-morrow night.
O.C. A Coy will be asked to detail party for work on a communication
trench aaa particulars later.

                        R. Gibbon   Captain & Adjutant.

To O's i/c Platoons.   23.3.17.
From O.C. B Coy.

Please let me have here by 6 a.m. to-morrow sketches shewing the
dispositions of your platoons.   These are required by the C.O.

"The C.O. on going round this morning found positions not
entirely satisfactory with the advanced posts.   In many cases they
did not know who was on their flanks nor the approximate position
of same.   Careful attention should be paid to this.   Platoon
Commanders should know the difference between Patrols and
Sentry Groups".

     Anything of importance should be reported at once to
Coy H.Q. now at S.6.b.9.1.   Keep in constant touch with
people on left and right.   The C.O. says we must remain in
present sectors until relieved to-morrow night.

                        T.A.H. Nash.   Captain.

To O.C. B Coy.   By Runner.   4.10 p.m.   23.3.17.
          Casualty Report : Nil.

                        E.S. Haighton. 2/Lieut.

To O.C. B Coy.   23.3.17.

We have established a block and are on this side of it
lying low and all men in comparative safety.

We do not consider we can do anything at present but
may do later.   Personally I don't think it adviseable
just now.

Everyone very cheery.

We have had a lively time with "Percies".

                        E.S. Haighton. 2/Lieut.

- 159 -

Appendix 'D'.

Extracts from Gazettes and Printed Sources.

Mentioned in Despatches.
In the 2nd. Supplement to the London Gazette of Tuesday 2/1/17,
appears as Mentioned in Despatches under Manchester Regiment:
Petrie, Maj. (temp Lt.-Col.) C.L.R., D.S.O., Res. of Off.
Megson, Temp. Lt. (Temp. Capt.) R.H.
Nash, Temp. 2nd. Lt. T.A.H.
            also under the Wiltshire Regiment is included:
            Gillson, Maj. (temp. Lt.-Col.) R.M.T., D.S.O. who is
referred to on page 89 of this diary.

Relinquishes Commission.
In the Supplement to the London Gazette dated 19th. February, 1918
appears under Infantry Training Reserve - Temp. Capt. T.A.H. Nash
relinquishes his commission on account of ill-health contracted on
active service and is granted the hon. rank of Capt. 20 Feb : 1918.

Leave Passes.
1/4 Glouc. Regt. Danbury - 2571 Pte Nash T.A.H. from Rev. 18/3/15
to Tattoo 20/3/15. Signed Lt. Col. Davenport.

1/4th. Batt. Glos'ter Regt. recalled 2571 Pte Nash to report by
Rev. 22/3/15 or leave expiry date for Service Overseas.
Signed at Danbury on 18/3/15 by Lt. Col. Davenport.

16th. Bn. Manchester Regt. 2/Lt Nash T.A.H. from 13/4/16 to
22/4/16 Signed by (?) Capt. for D.A.A. & Q.M.G. 30th. Div. Xlll Corps.

In Roll of Honour.
Daily Mail dated 22/7/16. Wounded: 2nd. Lt. Nash T.A.H.
Manchester Regiment.

In Telegram from War Office Sec. to Nash, Kingswood Grange,
Hockley Heath, Birmingham. "Reg to inform you that 2/Lt T.A.H. Nash
Manchester Regt. was wounded 1st. Dec but remained at duty". 4/12/16.

In letter from Military Secretary, War Office via Southern Command
and the Military Hospital, Chisledon dated 4/2/18:
I am directed to inform you that the Medical Board by whom
temporary Captain T.A.H. Nash, 92nd. Training Res. Battn. (attached)
was recently examined have expressed their opinion that he is
permanently unfit for Military duty..... et cetera.

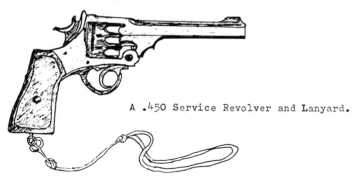

A .450 Service Revolver and Lanyard.

"Hints for Young Officers before Going to the Front",
is the title of a booklet compiled from a lecture by a Senior Major
which was delivered on 8th. January, 1915 and printed by Hewitt and
Rudge, Ltd., Whitley Bay. It was found among material belonging to
my Father such as his AB 64 Pay Book and Field Service Pocket Book,
which have survived 75 years.

It is my belief that its author was Major, later Field-Marshal
Montgomery, but it is not intended to enquire deeply into whether it
was indeed Monty's lecture. However, if one considers its lessons
were plainly understood and followed by this young - but experienced,
Unprofessional Soldier, (who had been on the 'receiving end', it might
be said), for the previous twelve months it should deserve a mention.

Page 29 of the Diary refers to Colonel Petrie D.S.O. taking over
command of the Battalion and a Montgomery succeeding him as Brigade
Major. Monty also had a D.S.O. by this time and like the author of
the booklet had returned from the Front in late October 1914; both
had been in trenches on the Aisne and both had the clear and precise
manner of speech and thought, which helped soldiers to feel that here
at least was someone they could understand and who understood them.
To my mind the following extracts typify his presentation:

Page 6 1(c). Dealing with qualities most useful in 'this' War.
(c) Cheerfulness on all occasions and especially in a very tight
corner. By this you will get very much more out of your men than
you otherwise would, and when things are really bad remember that your
men have got one eye on you all the time, e.g., if you are in a trench
under very heavy shell fire and losing men fast, a move to the rear
may be thought of, but if you're cheerful some man may say,
"Oh Mr So-and-So is laughing, we shall get out of this somehow all
right; they'll soon stop those d---d Black Marias," and the situation
may be saved.
(d) Cheerful endurance of hardships. - Don't think you're going out
to a picnic. There are many more pleasant things than sitting for
days and nights in very wet trenches, but you won't improve matters
for anyone by "grousing".

page 24 16 Billets.
paragraph 2 Remember to first select an alarm post before falling
out, post a guard, and you will generally have to place a picquet on
and barricade some road in your area, but the Brigade Major will
give orders as to this. Now you will remember that after a day's
hunting, even from the selfish point of view, it pays you to see your
horse groomed, fed, and rugged up for the night before you go and
have your food and a hot bath, so the same with your men. Before you
attend to your own comfort, go and see that all your men are
comfortable, that they have straw, water, fuel for cooking their
food and tea, etc. Next day you may be attacking and you'll be
proud of the way your platoon will behave. If you are a selfish
fellow you'll soon notice the difference in your men..... Ed.

A Zulu Knobkerrie used in night raids on the Enemy.

Manchester Regiment October 1915, Lark Hill.

Back row:	2/Lt Barber G.A.	2/Lt Slack E.S. Wounded	2/Lt Dyer Unfit	Lt Gibbon R. Wounded	Lt Phillips R.O. Wounded
Mid row:	Capt Elstob W. VC(Post), DSO., MC.	Lt Ball J.T. Wounded	Lt Behrens F. Wounded	Lt Wilson L.F. Killed	2/Lt Henriques Invalided
Frnt row:	Capt Worthington J.H. Wounded	Capt Walker F. Blinded	Capt Greg H.S. To UK 1916	Maj Kempster A.C. Ill	Lt. Col Petrie C.L. DSO

- 162 -

Lt	2/Lt	?	Lt	?
Megson	Allen	Unknown	Davidson	Unknown
R.H.	S.R.	to me. Ed.	W.S.	to me. Ed.
Killed	Killed		Wounded	
Lt	Lt	2/Lt	?	Lt
Knowles	Morris	Nash	Unknown	Fletcher
R.K.	G.P.	T.A.H.	to me. Ed.	F.S.
	Wounded	Gas/Invalided		R.A.M.C.
		Wounded		
Capt	Maj	Maj	Capt	The Rev.
Sotham	Knox	Roberts	Johnson	Balleine
E.G. MC	H.	R.E.	Morton	R.W.
Wounded P.O.W	Killed	Killed	Killed	Survived

A copy of the letter and photograph sent to Mrs. Johnson.

KINGSWOOD GRANGE,
HOCKLEY HEATH,
NR. BIRMINGHAM.

My dear Mrs. Johnson,

I have at last received my camera from France, and am sending you four copies of the last photograph ever taken of Morton. As a likeness it is bad, but it will show you that he was happy—he is distinctly smiling. You will notice that he is wearing Tommy's clothes, and his glasses. The trench is " Montauban Alley," which we consolidated and held after the capture and during the defence of Montauban.

On the right you will see round recesses in the side of the trench. These go back under the earth for six feet, and are supported by galvanised iron; the Germans used them as shelters. On the ground at the foot of them you will see some German equipment thrown hastily out. The cloth thing hanging from the side of the trench is a German indiarubber ground sheet. The floor of the trench is of wood. On the left, leaning against the side of the trench, is a trench ladder.

Morton and I had just been up to the extreme end of the trench to see if any Germans had been left in the dugouts.

The photograph was taken at about 12 noon on July 1st, 1916, and Morton went then to hold the right of the line, leaving me to hold the left.

Hoping Ronald is better,

Yours ever affectionately,
ANTHONY NASH.

MORTON, JULY 1ST, 1916.
In the German Trench at Montauban Alley.

This follows a letter of condolence sent to Mrs. Johnson on the death of her son Captain W. Morton Johnson on 1st. July 1916. This would appear to have been written by Second Lieutenant Anthony Nash whilst he was recovering in England from wounds sustained on 8th. July 1916, whilst attempting to view Trones Wood from the Glatz Redoubt with Lt. Col. Petrie D.S.O.

Fleur-de-Lis

Appendix 'G'.

Western Front.

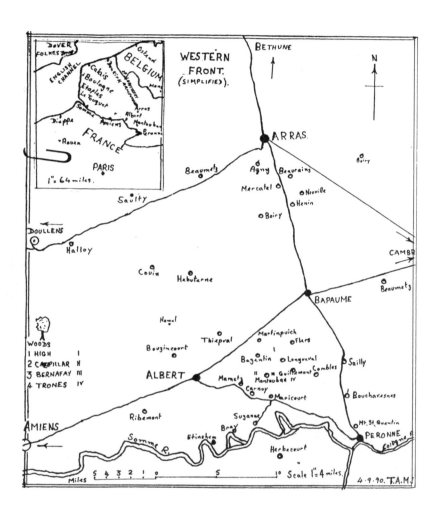

A simplified map indicating the
position of many of the places
mentioned during the period of
the Diarist's service with the
16th. Battalion Manchester Regt.

Lt. Cecil John Reynolds, 9th. Bn. Glos. Regt.,
and later R.F.C. with his sister Nancy - V.A.D.

Lt. Cecil J. Reynolds, Mesopotamia (Iraq).
Having been a member of the 9th. Service Bn. Gloucestershire
Regt., he was attached to the Regiment's 11th. Battalion in
the Balkan Expeditionary Force. Later as an R.F.C. Observer
and a 'sitting duck', he had an interesting time. When he
reported the arrival of a train-load of aeroplanes he was
disbelieved - which was a pity - because it turned out to be
Baron von Richthofen's Flying Circus 'showing the flag' from
the Western Front !

Ed.

APPENDIX H.

Pages bearing information relevant to T.A.H. Nash.

1 Pte 2571 enlisted at 3rd. attempt in 1st/4th. Bn. Gloucesters (TA).
9 Good friends Best, Shepherd, Young, Dunsford and Davies.
10 Marched 23 miles in 5¾ hours in full kit.
11 Made up to Lance Corporal 21/3/15.
13 Arrived France on 31/3/15 as part of Expeditionary Force.
15 Told unofficially of Commission in Glos. Regt. Special Reserve.
22 His fluency in French proved to be of considerable help.
26/27 Gassing & Dysentry. Commissions in 3rd Glos & 16th Manchesters.
28 Farewell to 4th Gloster Pals
30 To Grantham as 2/lt i/c 16 Pltn D Coy 16th (1st City) Service Bn Manchesters
31 Group photo taken at Lark Hill of Bn Officers.
    Arrive in France 9/11/15. Most junior subaltern but reported
    as, "Capable, self-dependant and conscientious" !
35 Asthma much worse.
46 Take over as Intelligence Officer and OC Snipers, on HQ staff.
52 Guide Col. Weber, Chief of Divisional Staff around the Front Line.
60 Informed of recommendation for DSO for Montauban.
71 Re-take duties and help to write-up War Diary for CO.
74 French Colonel asks for award of a Cross of the Legion of Honour.
81 Part of the 30th Division.
85 Posessed a Vest Pocket Kodak. Took photos of Train Alley.
    Montauban Alley is the scene where Morton Johnson was photographed.
88/89 Commanding beleaguered forces-relieved by Gilson CO 2nd Wilts.
90 The only officer to survive of the 3 Companies in the front line,
    he got his remnants of Montauban Alley safely back.
95 Glatz redoubt - Trones Wood; "Most thrilling journey of my life",
    was hit by 5.9 shell shrapnel.
    Saved by an Highlander and S. African MO and later 2 stretcher bearers.
96 F.D.S. - 5 C.C.S. Corbie - 14th. Gen. Boulogne - 4th London General.
99 Visit to Mrs. Morton Johnson. Med. Bd. send him to 3rd. Bn Manchesters.
99/100 Attached to B Coy at Cleethorpes. Some bitter remarks.
101 10/11/16 leave England for 4th time. Resentment at being put under
    orders of NCO's at Etaples 'Bull Ring'.
102 Comradeship existing between men and officers of 16th Bn.
103 In temporary command of 'B' Company.
109 Wounded by shell burst which killed five others. On 28/11/16 TAHN was
    2i/c of B Coy under Capt Wilson.
110 Collapsed with heart trouble.
115 O.C. 'B' Coy again. Disappointment re DSO - 2nd. 'pip' instead !
    Commanded Bn in Action on 2/7/16 and A, B, and C Companies since.
    Mentioned in Despatches.
116 Severe heart attack. Informed by CO he had been appointed Acting
    Captain. On 22/1/17 his Coy praised by Gen. Sir John Shea.
    Still ill with Trench Fever and Heart, he rode at head of 'B' Coy
    en route for Halloy.
117 'B' Company was selected for exercises under Gen. D'Oyly Snow
    and 5 Platoon demonstrate new attack to Brigade.
130 Essay. Loggerheads with HQ. Intense pride of 'B' Company.
    "Had seen more Active Service than any other officer with the Battalion".
131 Recurring heart attacks. Last time he was to command 'B' Coy.
    Other lives were at risk. Farewells. Journey from 32 Casualty
132 Clearing Station to 20 General Field Hospital Comiers, to High
    Street Hosp Manchester. Back to 3rd. Bn. Manchesters Cleethorpes.
    Colonel Elstob's report.

132   Wilson, Megson, Hook and Nash had been the only surviving officers
of the 16th with the Companies – now only Nash remained.
Ingram and Rylands who had also been frontline officers were also
killed. There were 250 casualties in the Ranks !
133   Applied for Medical Board to get out again; failing decided to
transfer if possible to Colonel Crawford's 92nd Training
Reserve Battalion. He had been CO of the 16th at the start.
Montauban celebration dinner on 1st July 1917.
134   28th July at Henbury marriage to Nancy E. A. Reynolds.
Severe asthma at end of August.
11/10/17 Special Medical Board at Grimsby.
6 months light duty.
92nd Training Reserve Battalion move to Lark Hill.
29th October 1917 back in Military Hospital at Chisledon.
5th November 1917 sent to Red Cross Hospital, Ramsbury.
Health worse, rather than better.
8th January 1918 Final Medical Board.
Appendix 'D' Government Gazette dated 19th February 1918:
Temp Capt T.A.H. Nash relinquishes his commission on account
of ill-health contracted on active service and is granted the
honorary rank of Captain 20th. February 1918.

THE BOY SCOUTS ASSOCIATION,

25, BUCKINGHAM PALACE ROAD,

December 1928.   LONDON, S. W. 1.

I should like to offer to you Dawlish Scouts my very
cordial congratulations on your winning the Duke of Connaught's
Challenge Shield.

This is a big feather in your cap seeing that you had to
compete against good teams from throughout the Empire and succeed
ed in defeating the South African team who were the last holders
of the trophy.

As a Cadet I was myself a fair marksman and have always
been thankful for the training it gave me not merely in being
able to hold a rifle straight but for the strength it gave to
my eyesight, to my nerve and patience, all of which have been
of the greatest value to me in after life.

Of course there are lots of people who will say it is a
vile thing for boys to learn Rifle shooting as it makes them
bloodthirsty and anxious to shoot people.

It is wonderful what piffle some otherwise well meaning people will talk.

If you are taught boxing (which is an art that every boy should learn) it doesn't follow that you therefore want to go about dotting people on the nose; but it means that you have exercised your body and muscles, have developed quickness of eye and action and have learned to keep your temper and to use courage and discretion.

At the same time it gives you confidence and ability to stick up for defence of the right.

And so it is, in a lesser degree, with miniature rifle shooting. If it really had the slightest tendency to make fellows blood-thirsty or eager for war I should be the last man in the world to encourage it, for I look upon war as a disgrace to civilisation, unChristian, and entirely out of date.

I cordially congratulate you on the good team work and patient practice which has enabled you to win the trophy.

Robert Baden Powell

Message of Congratulations from
Lt. Gen. Lord Baden-Powell
O.M., G.C.M.G., G.C.V.O., K.C.B.

LIEUT.-GEN. SIR ROBERT BADEN-POWELL,
K.C.B., K.C.V.O.
In 1908 Sir Robert Baden-Powell founded the organisation of Boy Scouts to promote good citizenship in the
rising generation, and in the Great War the members of
that organisation proved of great value.

POST OFFICE TELEGRAPHS.
GOVERNMENT TELEGRAM

N.º of Telegram _____

Date Stamp

A &

I certify that this Telegram is sent on the service of the Signature _____

Prefix	Time handed in	Charge			Sent at _____ m
		£	s.	d.	To _____ By _____

Office of Origin and Service Instructions

Words

The NAME and ADDRESS of the SENDER if to be telegraphed must be written at the end of the Telegram

TO { Lord Mildmay of Flete
Ermington S.O. South Devon

Please convey my congratulations to the
Boy Scouts of Dawlish for their
splendid win of my Shield which
has been held overseas for the last
two years. I am sure all the Boy
Scouts of Devonshire HAVE every
reason to be proud of this success
which must be due to an immense
deal of trouble their Scoutmaster, as
well as they themselves, have
taken.

Arthur

Message of Congratulations from
H.R.H. The Duke of Connaught.

- 171 -

Dawlish Boy Scouts and Empire Trophy.

Public Presentation. Messages from Chief of Scouts and Duke of Connaught.

The great honour which the Dawlish Boy Scouts have brought to the town by winning the Scouts all-Empire shooting trophy received honourable recognition in a special gathering at the Hut on Thursday evening. The presentation of Shield and Medals was made by Lord Mildmay, of Flete (Lord Lieutenant of the County), who brought messages of congratulation to the winners from two exalted personages, Sir Robert Baden Powell (founder and chief of the Scouts) and H.R.H. the Duke of Connaught (the donor of the shield).

The trophy has been held for the past two years by a South African troop, so that the Dawlish troop had the special distinction of recovering the honour for the mother country.

Mr F Hughes, J.P. (chairman of the Council), presided at the ceremony. Supporting the chairman and Lord Mildmay was Major Gen. Sir Edward May (County Commissioner) and Miss May, Miss Gonner (head of Dawlish Girl Guides), Messrs F G Avant-Washington and J H Lamacraft, the Officers of Dawlish troop and members of the winning

Councillors and prominent residents.

The Chairman warmly welcomed Lord Mildmay. They felt that the boys had brought great honour to the town, and they also felt extremely honoured by the attendance of Lord Mildmay amidst all his many activities in the county and throughout England—(applause).

An Example to England.

Lord Mildmay said nothing could give him greater pleasure than to take any part in the great victory achieved by the Dawlish troop, and of which the whole of Devon was proud. It was not a victory easily won, but meant that they had an infinite capacity for taking pains —one of the first requisites for the success of life—steadiness of hand, keenness, and the larger quality of nerve and patience. He congratulated them all the more because he was informed that the troop had been in existence only three years. They had already done what would be an example to the whole of England.

Wonderful progress had been made by the Boy Scout movement since it was started by Baden Powell in 1907. It had spread like wildfire. Now there was hardly a civilised country which had not taken it up. Last week he—Lord Mildmay—wrote to Sir Robert Baden Powell and told him of the success of the Dawlish troop, and he replied with a letter which he wished to have read.

Piffle and Well-Meaning People.

In his letter Sir Robert said he was delighted with the success of the Dawlish troop. It was "a big feather in their cap." After referring to his own experience of the great value of learning to shoot, Sir Robert proceeded:

There were a lot of people who would say it was a vile thing for boys to learn rifle-shooting because it made them bloodthirsty and anxious to shoot people. It was wonderful what piffle some otherwise well-meaning people would talk. If one were taught such things as boxing it did not follow that one would go about "knocking people on the nose." If miniature rifle-shooting had the slightest tendency to make fellows bloodthirsty he would be the last man in the world to encourage it, for he looked upon war as a disgrace to civilisation, un-Christian, and entirely out of date.

Lord Mildmay added that he had a communication which would carry still greater weight. He had also got into touch with His Royal Highness the Duke of Connaught, who had sent him the following telegram:

Please convey my congratulations to the Boy Scouts of Dawlish for the splendid win of my

shield, which has been held overseas for last two years. I am sure all the Boy Scouts of Devon have every reason to be proud of this success, which must be due to an immense deal of trouble by their Scoutmaster, as well as themselves.

True Standards of Success.

These two communications, said Lord Mildmay, ought to be kept in archives of the Dawlish Scouts (applause). Continuing, he asked "How was the success of human to be measured?" Certainly not span of years, certainly not by success acquiring riches, nor according to some of the other standards by which they were in great danger of being deluded times. No, it was to be measured by simpler test, the way in which men and women had spent themselves in unselfish effort in doing their duty to those around them and improved the lot of those amongst whom they were thrown —(applause).

Lord Mildmay concluded by a special word of congratulation to and praise the Scoutmaster, Capt A Nash.

Capt. Nash said he was calling up Lieut. W A Maunder (assistant scoutmaster) to receive the shield, because he was responsible for the training of the team, and success was due in no small measure to his efforts—(applause).

Lord Mildmay then presented the shield and medals, the members of the team being J Mitchell, J Burgess, L Tapper, T Jennings, E J Crapp and Burch.

Lord Mildmay was warmly thanked on the motion of Mr Avant-Washington, seconded by Mr J H Lamacraft.

A concert followed. Selections were given by Mr Geo. Willcocks' orchestra, with solos by the leader, songs by Mr Culmer Hodges and Mr A J Davey.

Dear Sir,—As my attendance on Lord Mildmay prevented me from publicly thanking the artistes at the conclusion of the concert yesterday, may I please express through your column the deep gratitude of the Scouts and myself to Mrs Culmer Hodges, Mr A J Davey, Mr Geo Willcocks and the ladies and gentlemen of the Orchestra who so kindly gave their services. I should like also to acknowledge my indebtedness to Mr A J Prince who organised the Concert for the Scouts.

Yours faithfully, ANTHONY NASH Red House, Dawlish. Dec. 21st.

Scouts win Empire Shooting Shield from South Africa.

Tribute to the Rank and File.

An eloquent address with a stirring final appeal to the highest citizenship was given by the president of the Legion, Capt. Anthony Nash, who opened with the words:—

"Let us with thanksgiving and all honour before God and man remember those who gave their lives in the service of their country."

He said one of the most depressing features of life since the war had been the publication of much ill-considered literature by men who should have known better. The impression derived from these diaries and biographies is that the conduct of the war was entrusted to scheming politicians and incompetent generals, and they were saddened by the thought that all their sacrifices might have been in vain. He would beg of them to be under no such delusion. The men who died saved you and saved England from a fate far worse than that which overtook those violated regions of France and Belgium. The men who won the war were the rank and file of fighting men, the private soldier and able seaman, and they turned with thankfulness from the picture of general intrigue and rottenness disclosed in high places to contemplation of the cheerful steadfast courage of the men whose sacrifice prevailed in spite of all.

We lost one million British dead in the war. Marching four abreast those men would cover 335 miles of road, from here through Bristol and Birmingham and Newcastle, right to the foot of the Cheviot Hills, and it would take them five days and five nights to pass you.

What could they say of them, these men of ours? "They died for their country"—yes, but they did so much more than that. Did they all realise the life of continual sacrifice they led before they died, while they were waiting to die, and the wonderful spirit of humanity and unselfishness that lightened it? At the call of King and Country they abandoned the sheltered security of their occupations and, giving up all that made life dear to them, entered upon a road of unaccustomed peril and hardship, the road which was to lead them to Calvary. Their life at the war was spent under conditions of appalling physical discomfort. To many the unaccustomed discipline must have been irksome; to others the anxiety of family affairs must have been mental torture. Yet with every nerve and sinew strained to the limit of human endurance—and how far that can be stretched only those of us know who have tried—they met every danger and hardship with quiet cheerful courage. It was comparatively easy to be heroic for an hour or two when you are feeling in the mood; it was not so easy in the waterlogged trenches or in a floating coffin at sea, day after day, month after month, seeing their best friends killed at their side, knowing that at any minute a similar fate might be theirs.

Those gallant souls who had passed on were not lost to them; they were

Remembrance Sunday 1927.

around them still; watching over them, living again when we think of them, trying to comfort us and guide us, trying to imbue us with their own spirit of humanity and goodfellowship. The "measure of God's mercy is broader than man's mind," and He had given them a communion of thought and love which not even death could destroy and which forgetfulness only could dim.

Remember the Living.

But when all was said and done the dead were beyond our aid. They could help us, and were helping us, but we could do nothing for them. What of their comrades who have survived? To those who did not in the war leave behind some actual part of themselves, their limbs, sight, speech, or hearing; "to us looking back the mountainous happenings of those days have acquired a dreamlike quality and have sunk in the distance;" but, in the hearts of the maimed, memory will not fade, nor from their seared fibre will disablement depart. They remained as limping monuments of a half-buried war, no longer upheld by the admiration of their countrymen nor much by their own consciousness of duty done, but having to make good with an unremarked gallantry greater than any they showed in the wet shell-searched trenches or charging a storm of bullets, greater because it must last so long—all the rest of their lives.

The man who begged in the street might be a waster—probably he was; on the other hand he might have fought by your own son's side and helped him in many a tight corner. "I don't think I should like to risk passing him by"—(applause).

Service for Others.

I would ask you now, as President of the British Legion in Dawlish, to do whatever you can for these men who risked everything for you. Do it in remembrance of your dead. "If you break faith with them who died, we shall not sleep."

Finally, let them always pray that Almighty God, who made them Citizens of this Realm, might enable them to be worthy of those who died for them; that He might grant them a willing heart to do whatever duty might be laid upon them; with gladness to serve the State and their brother men, and with undaunted faith in the good purposes of God to shew both courage and good cheer; that so by word and deed they may take their part in establishing that better world which their brethren died to win.

Honouring the Dead.

Profound silence prevailed in the town yesterday morning at the observance of the two minutes' silence, testifying to the cessation of activity in this brief pause to pay a tribute to the memory of the vast army of the fallen.

Round the War Memorial many gathered for a short service, conducted by the Vicar of Dawlish.

Poppies were sold in the streets during the day on behalf of Earl Haig's fund for victims of the war. This was organised by the British Legion.

The Midland Bank.

Mr. Nash transferred to Yeovil.

It will be cause for regret to Dawlish people to know that Mr Anthony Nash, the esteemed manager of the Dawlish branch of the Midland Bank, has been transferred to take charge of their larger and more responsible branch at Yeovil. Mr Nash leaves to take up his new appointment almost immediately. Whilst feeling regret at his departure, residents generally will warmly congratulate him on what is in the nature of a big promotion, because, although Yeovil is not a large place, the bank there has much wider ramifications than here, being the centre of an extensive district. Sorry as he is to leave Dawlish, as we know, Mr Nash himself cannot but feel gratified at this expression of confidence from the directorate of the Bank. He was appointed to take charge at Dawlish five years ago last March, and has considerably extended the scope of the local branch's business during that time.

As a private citizen Mr Nash has earned the gratitude of the town for his excellent work in connection with the founding and carrying on of the local Troop of Boy Scouts. It was only comparatively a few weeks ago that he resigned the post of Scoutmaster and has since acted as Hon. Secretary. The fine efficiency to which the Troop has attained is largely due to his efforts. Mr Nash is also the very active President of the local branch of the British Legion. In other directions he has shown his practical interest in town matters, and will be missed in many ways. Warm good wishes for good health and success will go with him.

'Going-On', from Dawlish to Yeovil.

Presentations.

At the weekly parade of the Dawlish Boy Scouts on Friday, the 3rd inst , there was a full muster to bid farewell to Capt. A Nash on his leaving for Yeovil, and also to make a presentation, which took the form of a "Thanks" badge in gold, and a silver match case inscribed " From the 1st Dawlish Boy Scouts to Capt. A Nash. In great appreciation."

Mr C Culmer Hodges (scoutmaster) spoke warmly and appreciatively of the work Mr Nash had done, both as Scoutmaster and Secretary, and of their sorrow at losing him. He asked his acceptance of these small gifts as tokens of the goodwill which the Troop had for him, coupled with their wishes for his future welfare.

The presentation was then made by Troop Leader G Doble.

Capt. Nash, in acknowledgment, said he felt very sorry indeed to be leaving Dawlish and particularly so when such expressions of good feeling had been made towards him. They had all been friends to him, and he should ever watch their progress with interest. After all, friendship was a thing they could take with them wherever they.went.

Concluding, Mr Nash said : " Mr Culmer Hodges has said some very nice things about what I have done for the Troop. The finest thing I ever did for you was to persuade Mr Hodges to become your Scoutmaster. I wish him and you all possible luck."

Long remembered kindnesses of Boy Scouts and British Legion.

Farewell Gift from the Legion.

The members of the Dawlish Branch of the British Legion assembled at their Club-room on Saturday evening last to make a presentation to their President (Capt. A Nash) on his leaving the town.

The Rev C F Baines (hon. secretary) said they felt they could not let Capt. Nash leave the town without showing some recognition of his services.

Major R C Campbell (chairman), who made the presentation, said Capt. Nash would be greatly missed by them, not only for his help in financial matters, but in many other ways. If anyone deserved promotion he—their President— did. He would now ask him to accept a little token of appreciation from the Dawlish branch.

The gift, took the form of a silver cigarette box, with the recipient's private crest on the cover, and the following inscription engraved on the side : " To Capt. A Nash from the Dawlish Branch of the British Legion, 1929."

Capt. A Nash, replying, thanked them very warmly "for this delightful token of remembrance." It was hateful to say good-bye, but it was fine to know that he had won their friendship, and, better still to know that this friendship would endure. There was in life one quality of greater worth than health or riches, prosperity or power, and that was just friendship. As he looked around that room he was proud to think that he had so many friends.

He would say, in conclusion, " Carry on, that is our password, yours and mine "—(applause).

A portrait of the diarist T.A.H. Nash taken
about 20 years after the start of World War One.
No longer an Unprofessional Soldier but a Banker,
he died some five years later before his 45th.,
birthday in 1939, largely as a consequence of
chlorine and phosgene gassing in the War.

OBITUARY

CAPTAIN T. A. H. NASH, DURDAR.

The death took place at his home, Crinan, Durdar, on Thursday, of Captain Thomas Anthony Havelock Nash, aged 44, manager of the Court Square branch of the Midland Bank, Carlisle. Captain Nash was badly gassed during his service with the 16th Manchester Regiment in France during the Great War, and had suffered constantly from the effects ever since. He had been unwell for about two years. During the last few months the effects of the gassing had become acute and were an indirect cause of his death.

Born in Sussex, Captain Nash was manager of the Midland Bank at Dawlish, Devon, and of the Yeovil branch, Somerset, before coming to manage the Court Square branch, Carlisle, in September, 1933, in succession to Colonel Soulsby. Although a man of the most courteous and likeable personality, Captain Nash took comparatively little part in local affairs and, in fact, during the latter part of his life in Carlisle was severely handicapped by illness. Nevertheless, he took an unremitting interest in the welfare of other ex-Servicemen and was a member of the Ex-Servicemen's Association. He was also a Freemason and a member of the Carlisle Rotary Club.

Captain Nash, who lived in Northumberland Road, Carlisle, until last December, when he removed to Durdar, leaves a widow and four children—Mr Morton Nash, who is employed in the Midland Bank at Penrith; Mr Megson Nash, at present in Southern Rhodesia; Miss Mary Nash and Mr Miles Nash, both of whom are in Carlisle.

The funeral takes place at 11 a.m. this Saturday at Wreay.

1. Obituary Notice : Capt. T.A.H. Nash.
2. Extract from Capt. Worthington's letter.

Dated July 2 - 1939

SOUTHWAITE 2
SOUTHWAITE.

Southwaite.
Carlisle.

Part copy of a letter received today from Captain Hubert Worthington.

This is just to tell you what I hope may bring you comfort.

Yesterday the City Battalion of the Manchester Regiment had their annual commemeration of the Somme Battle in the regimental Chapel at Manchester Cathedral, (which I attended). It was a very moving occasion. The Cathedral Choir sang beautifully There was a good turn up of the men and the relatives of the fallen.

The Archdeacon of Manchester made some very touching references to your husband-- and of his passing--- and how he was in our thoughts and prayers- -how brave he had been and how courageous on that July 1st. twenty twenty three years ago at Montauban.

I thought you might like to know that in such fitting surroundings he had been commemorated amongst his former comrades.

The price of being buried in a very pretty
village is to have the gravestones moved to
one side when being entered for a Best Kept
Village Competition.

The site of the graves of the Author and
his Mother amongst those of his friends.

Epilogue.

After the War my Mother and Father lived at Yealmpton whilst he was earning their living in Plymouth. My brother Morton, and I, Megson, were born there in a cottage which had been a baker's shop. (I believe that at times we were put in the window where fresh loaves had been exhibited - thus giving rise to the expression, Half Baked ?) Then evidently my Father having satisfied the Bank that he was worthy of greater responsibility, was given the job of opening a branch in Dawlish, thereby making him the youngest Midland Bank manager.

The following five years were amongst his happiest with occasional drives in a Pony Trap, Trojan and Morris Cowley and swims in the sea. His work was satisfying, and he also took very seriously the re-establishment and training of the Dawlish Boy Scouts Troop. A party of them went to France and Belgium to see the Battlefields and as may be seen from the news reports which follow this conclusion the Scouts won from South Africa the Empire Shooting Shield donated by H.R.H. the Duke of Connaught.

I am sure he would have been proud of all his young men who made a success of their lives irrespective of their eminence, but one in particular who is known to me is Peter Burdett the present Teignbridge District Commissioner. Another connection with 'Pop', is through his old Divisional Commander- General Sir John Shea, who died some time ago. He became the Chief Scout's Commissioner for London and presided at the World Jamboree in Kenya.

The affairs of the British Legion and Ex-Servicemen were a further matter of active concern to him in his everyday life and must have constantly reminded him of his lost Comrades. Regrettably Dawlish was to be the scene of his greatest loss, as sad to say Nancy our Mother died in 1928. The little bit of Dawlish next to her grave remains empty, as although purchased by my Father, he was to be later buried in Cumbria, with his Mother next to him when she died in the following year.

We moved to Yeovil for five years and then having in the meantime re-married, on his next promotion he left Somerset for Carlisle to take over from Colonel Soulsby who had commanded the 5th. Battalion Border Regiment, and who was now retiring from the bank. The move particularly pleased me because of the friends I made, including one I was to marry twelve years later, who was the Colonel's daughter Kay.

My Father loved the countryside but we had soon to move into the City when we were besieged at Southwaite by a plague of rats which came across the river.

At this time, Pop's health, which had so long been a problem, was deteriorating and not a day passed when he did not have to save himself from choking as a result of his wartime gassing with chlorine and phosgene. His heart was no better and although it probably did not matter, one could still see shrapnel in his arm.

Anyway, in June 1939, shortly before his 45th. birthday the combined difficulties eventually took their toll of him. I was by this time working in Southern Rhodesia on a cattle ranch and my good step-mother Phyl sent me the news with a copy of Captain Worthington's letter and Obituary Notice. Phyl and her children Mary and Miles were now left to face in Bristol, close to where Pop had his 'digs' as a single man, another World War.

The Army Medal Office confirm that the late Captain T.A.H.Nash
of the Manchester Regiment, formerly 2571 Lance Corporal of the
4th. Gloucester Regiment, was awarded and issued with the :

1914-15 Star   British War Medal   Victory Medal
                                        Mention in Despatches

Acknowledgements.

I wish to express my thanks to the persons named below for
the help they have given me in order that this Diary could be
published successfully thereby fulfilling one of my ambitions.

I should particularly like to high-light four ladies -
not as may be imagined, for their typing, as I did that myself -
but to Miss Elizabeth Shea on behalf of her late Father for
providing me with some initial stimulus half a century ago;
and Phyl, my late Step-Mother for her contradiction of the
popular image of unpopularity; Sue for her vignettes; and my
better-half Kay, for her patience and support throughout this
labour of love.

If my Father were alive he would assuredly wish to join me
in thanking David and Anne Picton-Phillips for their expertise
and gentle introduction to Publishing; whilst the interpretation
of my ideas for the Cover design cleverly executed by Jane Brett,
similarly deserve for her a vote of thanks.

Among other kith and kin are my brother Anthony and sister Mary;
Joyce and my late brother Morton; our sons Richard, Andrew and Chris,
with our daughters-in-law Pat, Ann and Sue; also Derek Reynolds and
Cheryl Dowdall.

Captain Robert Bonner and Major Ron Young of the Manchester
Museum Committee of the King's Regiment and Wendy Chandley -
Archivist; Lt. Col. Henry Radice, Archivist (Hon). Gloucestershire
Regiment.

Steve Evans of Ace Cameras; Peter Williams; Eddie Powell, Organist;
Peter Locke; Ronald Fraser-Milner; Heather Deans; and the late Bruce
Bairnsfather and'Monty', all deserve my thanks.

Finally I must mention my Colleagues of the Katharine Lady
Berkeley's School who presented me on my retirement with an
Olympia Traveller de Luxe which has served me so well, and
deserves a D.S.O.

T.A.M.N.

- 180 -

Tony Nash and Kay Soulsby shortly before
their marriage at the end of World War 2.

Their repatriation to Rhodesia saw the
loss of all their wedding presents and
worldly goods when the s.s. Fort Massac
sank off Middlesborough at the start of
the journey to the Cape; fortunately for
 them they were on the Isle de France.

16th (Service) Battalion Manchester Regiment.

Roll of Officers.

Lieut.-Col.	CRAWFORD, J. C.	2nd Lieut.	PHILIPS, R. O.
Major	COMYN, D. C. E. ff.	„	MEGSON, R. H.
Capt. & Adjt.	SOTHAM, E. G.	„	RHODES, E. L.
Captain	GREG, H. S.	„	PERCY, J. E. G.
„	WHEATLEY-CROWE, H. S.	„	HENRIQUES, G. L. Q.
„	ROBERTS, R. E.	„	KNOWLES, R. K.
„	WALKER, F.	„	HOOK, C. W. K.
„	PATEY, M. H. R.	„	MEAD, P. J.
„	PAYNE, J. J.	„	CLARKE, W. F.
„	WORTHINGTON, J. H.	„	HAYWARD-BROWNE, I. W.
„	GEARY, SIR W. N. M., Bart.	„	DYER, H. DE D.
„	TAYLOR, A.	„	GIBBON, R.
„	JOHNSON, W. M.	„	PRESTWICH, E.
„	ELSTOB, W.	„	BLES, G. M.
Lieutenant	BEHRENS, F. E.	„	BARBER, G. A.
„	WILSON, L. F.	„	ALLEN, S. R.
„	OLIVER, J. M.	„	SLACK, E. S.
„	DALGLIESH, A. B	Lieut. & Q.M.	BALL, J. T.
„	DAVIDSON, W. S.	Lieutenant	FLETCHER, F. S. (Med. Off.)
„	SINGTON, A. J. C.		*Attached.*
„	MORRIS, G. P.	Lieut.-Col.	LEDWARD, H.
		Captain	CUNLIFFE, H. H.

Brigadier-General WESTROPP, Major PETRIE, D.S.O., and the Chaplain (Rev. W. R. BALLEINE) also appear on the Photograph.

The following were not present when the Photograph was taken :—

2nd Lieut. CLAYTON, E. G.
   „   DAY, C. E.

2nd Lieut. O'CONNEL DE COURCY
   MACDONNEL, J. P.
   „   NASH, T. A. H.

Found amongst papers relating to Diary:

July 1 11.30 a.m. From Adjt. Elsie   To Lt. Nash
I am told that all Officers of A and B Coys are out of action.
Please investigate and if so take charge.

July 1 12.15 Noon From Lt. Nash   To Adjt. Elsie
I have taken over command of remainder A B and C Coys.
Am holding and consolidating M--- Alley.
Cannot get into touch with left division.
Need wire badly. If I can get some will put it out.
Am sending you 80 prisoners.

July 1 3.0 p.m. From O.C. Firing Line Lt. Nash To Adjt. Elsie
All going well. Men very exhausted but working hard.
Quite able to hold out. Artillery, rockets and Very pistols badly wanted.

July 1 4.30 p.m. From Adjt. Elsie   To OC Firing Line.
Have asked for rockets -3 tins. Know you will do all possible.

July 1 4.37 p.m. From O.C. Firing Line   To Adjt. Elsie.
We have at length established communication with Division
on our left. They have only just got up into position.
Our estimated casualties -
A Coy 3 Officers 79 ORs. B Coy 4 Officers 83 ORs. C Coy 3Offrs 42 ORs.
Enemy moving batteries from B to G Wood.
Can you send me water and more ammunition.

July 1 9.30 p.m. From Lt. Nash   To Adjt. Elsie.
Enemy attacking whole frontage. Estimated force two battalions.
Have sent S.O.S. Situation well in hand. What about that ammunition?

July 1 11.0 p.m. From Lt. Nash   To Adjt. Elsie.
Enemy counter attack has failed and he has drawn off into valley.
Our casualties during attack estimated 40.
Artillery rather slow in replying to S.O.S.

July 2 4.0 a.m. From Lt. Nash   To Adjt. Elsie.
Enemy have again attacked M--- Alley.
Small party have broken through between us and our right.
Have asked for bombers to get them out. Enemy massed for attack
in valley. Must have more grenades.

July 2 4.58 a.m. From Adjt. Elsie   To Lt. Nash.
HQ bombers were sent to left of our front but should be making
their way towards you now. Am sending up SAA and bombs now also
half Coy Scotties coming reinforce with an Officer.

July 2 5.30 a.m. From Lt. Nash   To Adjt. Elsie.
Situation well in hand now attack completely beaten off.
SAA and bombs not yet arrived.
Reinforcements did not turn up but are not needed.
Can we have some water. All serene.

July 2 7.45 a.m. From Adjt. Elsie   To Lt. Nash.
Battn is to be relieved by Wilts. Bring your Coys out and march to
Assembly trenches handing over all bombs spare SAA and tools to Wilts.

Supplementary to letter of Jul 4th. 1916:
July 2 3.45p.m. To Adjt Elsie. A B and C Coys relieved.
(On reverse of document in handwriting appears: Copy of letter from
Anthony dated July 4th. 1916).

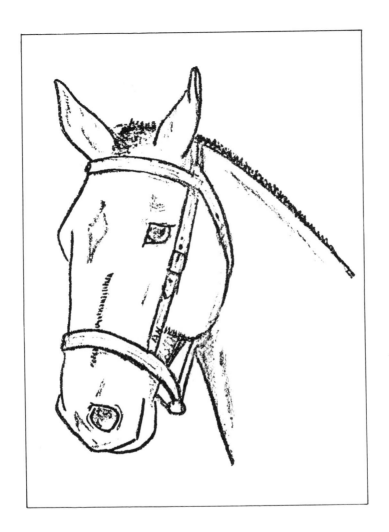

A reminder of 'Tommy', D Company's
faithful horse and equally faithful
Groom Pte. J. Holland.

INDEX.

2nd Bn Yorkshire Regt 127 128
York and Lancaster Regt 18 139

55th Brigade 86 88
89th Brigade 119
90th Brigade   31 91 94
Manchester and Liverpool Brigades 92

18th Division 83
30th Division 72 81 91
Lord Derby's Division 92

Territorials and New Armies 3

Canadians 15 24

French 44 83
Soixante Quinze Batteries 74
Colonial Troops 65
146 Reg. d'Infanterie 76
Artillerie 72
Iron Division 72 91

German Army Res Corps 62
6 Army Corps 79
104 Saxon Infantry 23
63 Regiment 67
87 Regiment 72
Artillery 77
62 Infantry Regt 80 87
Bavarians 93 138
Machine Guns 132

Portuguese 116

'B'
Bac du Nord 118
Baden-Powell Robert General 141
Badman 27
Bailey Major 18
Baillelval 102 113
Baker Major 10 15 27 28 41 110
Baldeston O S L/Cpl 151
Ball J T Hon Lt & Capt QM 31 124 141 146 148
Balleine R W Revd 31 38/9 43 74 108 128 132 143 148
Balloons observation German 81
Band 13
Banks J S Cpl 153
Barber 136
Barber Lt 31 34 149
Barnes F Pte   152
Barraclough E Pte 153
Barrett 51
Barsby J L/Cpl 154
Barton H Sgt 153
Basseux 102 131
Batchelor A Pte 151
Baths 10
Batman 116

Battell F Pte 152
Bavincourt 118
Beach Thomas 93
Beaumetz 118
Beauval 41
Beckett T A Pte 154
Bedfords 2nd Bn 78
Behrens F. Lt 31 38 41 148
Bell 45
Bellacourt 102 107 128
Belton Park 30
Benson F W Pte 152
Bernard M le Lieut 51
Berry CSM 99
Berry F 150
Berry J 154
Best Joe 1 7 9 11 28 39
Big Push 72 78
Billon Wood 76 78
Birtles T Pte 154
Blairville 102 128
Blears 84
Blood J Pte 154
Boiry Road 123
Bois de Canaples 37 44
Bois de la Hutte 25
Bois de Ploegsteert 21
Bois de Tailles 78
Bois de Vaches 54 55
Bombardment - see Shelling
Bombing 53 87 92 107
Bonneville 37-41
Booby Traps 119
Boon H Pte 150
Boots, thigh 44
Border Regt 60 104 116 136 138
Boulogne 12 13 34 62
Bowie L/Cpl 87
Boyle J Pte 153
Bramwell 154
Brasserie 21
Bravery 45 55 87 109
Bray 44 65
Breastworks 16
Bretencourt 102 127
Brewery 21 24
Brewery Yard 44
Bridson H L/Cpl 153
Brigade 55th etc - see Army
Briquesnesmil 78
Bristol 1 99 101
Broderick Cap 22
Bronfay Farm 58 76 78
Broughton A Pte 153
Brown Cpl 63 CSM MC 144
Brown E F Pte 151

```
Colonel  52  55  60  64/5  84/5  90  94 100
         112 118 132  138
Combles  80
Commission  10  15 27
Comyns Maj  30  31
Cook  3  110
Coppock W E Pte  152
Cosgrove Sgt POW 145
Couin   38
Court Martial  116
Coxon H L/Cpl MM   152
Coxon W H Cpl 103  132  142  154
Crawford Colonel  10  11  30 133
Crecy  34
Crompton R Pte  154
Crucifix  21  23  45/6
Cumming W Pte  152
Cummings  39
Cunliffe  29
Cunningham Sgt  146

'D'
Dainville  116
Dalgleish  31  34  43  150
Danbury  1  7
Davenport H Pte  152
Davenport Colonel  11  27  39
Davidson Lt  31  60  81 94  133  149
Davies J N Pte  154
Davi(e)s S 1  9 27 38
Dawson F Pte  152
Dean J Pte  152
Death  34 61
Deccan Horse  71
Decorations  54  60  74  108  115 129 132
             143  144/5
Depot Base Infantry  101
Detuncq  34
Devons  65
Dimsdale  126  153
Divisions - see Army
Dixon  112
Dobson F Pte  153
Doulieu  13/4
Doullens  39  110  116
D ouamart  63
Dowling  29
Drill  7
Dugouts  112
Dunkerly E Pte  152
Dunkerly R Capt  117  146  150
Dunsford  1 7  8  9  10  28
Dysentry  27
East Lancs  21
```

East Surreys 104 138
Eckersley 56
Eckersley H Pte 153
Ellis A Pte 152
Ellis H Pte 154
Elstob W Lt Col VC 31 65 87 90 91 94 101/5
          108/9 115/6 132 136 138 140 142
English Pte 154
Epsom 103 111 115
Equipment - see Supplies
Etaples (Bull ring) 38 101/2 116
Etinchem 44 74 78
Evans Lt 52
Evans J Pte 153
Evered 103
Exhiliration 61

'F'
Fairbank Sgt 59
Fairhurst J.B. Pte 153
Fargny Mill   56 64 67
Faucaert 37
Faux 91
Ferns J E Pte 152
Ficheux 102 128
Field Guns captured 85
Field Capt 128
Fire in Barn/shelled 113
Fire in Billet 42/43
Fitton J Pte 153
Flers 60 100
Fletcher Capt MO 31 35/6 52 55/6
          74 103 148
Fletre 14
Folkestone 12
Fowler Lt 76/7
Frazer 115
Freddy 115
French Field Marshal Sir John 41/2
French Army 52 55 59 63
French cuisine 43
Fresnes 62
Friends 135
Frise 53/4 68
Froissy 65
Fry General 71
Funerals 63 67 94 128 142

'G'
Gammond T Sgt 150
Gardner S Pte 152
Garner J Pte 152
Gartside R Pte 154
Gas 27 53 65/6 68 111
Gazette London - see App. 'D'
Geary Sir William 29

German formations - see Army
Geteschranks 68
Gibbon Lt 30 41 65 Capt 102 127 136 138 146 149
Gilbert A D Pte 152
Gill 113
Gillson Col 2nd Wilts 89 and App 'D'
Glatz redoubt 95
Gleave W Sgt 132 142 150
Gloucestershire Regiment - see Army
Godbert Cafe 65 74 78
Godwin H Cpl 150
Goldhanger 11
Goodwin L Pte 154
Gordon Highlanders 58
Gosling 117
Gramophone 43 74
Grantham 29 30
Grantham G Pte 152
Grattan F W Pte 154
Gray W Pte 153
Green O Pte 151
Green W Pte 152
Greenas 118
Greenall F Pte 153
Greening 129
Greenough J Pte 152
Greg H S Capt 31 35 37 39 43 53 65 150
Griffin M Pte 151
Grimsby - Med Board 100
Guard duty 10
Guest adjutant 146
Guides 79
Guillemont 60 138

'H'
Haig's staff 71
Haighton E S Lt 116 125 129 150
Haines 117 '144
Hall R J Pte 151
Hall Col Med Board 134
Hallett E Pte 152
Halloy 116
Hamilton Sir Ian 4
Hampshire Regt 21
Hanscombe 66 91
Hants Farm 23
Happy Valley 93/4
Hardships 7/8
Harper A Pte 152
Harrison G W Pte 151
Harrison S Pte 153
Harrisworth W Pte 153
Hart E Pte 151
Harvey Lt 60 90 132
Haslam Sgt/CSM 87 89 103 107 110 116
Hatfield Peverel 5

Havernas   37
Havre   62
Hawxby Sgt 30 39 60 140
Hayton J Pte 151
Headquarters 53 124
Heal H A Pte 155
Healey 78
Health - see Medical - Trench fever 116
Heath A G Pte   152
Heathcote Capt MO 103 144
Heap S W Sgt/CSM   116 150
Heaton Park 29
Hebuterne   9 38
Heilly   65   78 94
Henin 125
Heninel 132
Henriques Lt 31 37 149
Herbebois   62
Heroism   26
Heywood Lt   108   117 146
Heyworth W J Pte   151
Hibbert G F Pte Batman exceptional 30 73 79 84 90 95
                    99 103   136 138
Higginbottom A Pte   151
Higgs C Pte   152
Higson POW   145
Hindenburg   119
Hints for Young Officers-see App. A
Holden N Pte   152
Holland J Pte   131 152
Holloway Lt   1
Holmes H Pte   151
Hook C W Lt/Capt   31 91 101 103   108 115
                    131 132 142   143 149
Horley   85 91
Horses and "Tommy"   66 76 108 116 118 131
Hoskins F Pte   153
Hoskins Lt   81 94
Houldsworth Pte   153
Howse H Pte   152
Hoyle J Pte   154
Huddart J E Pte   151
Hughes   41
Hulme J Pte   153
Hunger   2
Hunters Avenue   23
Hunter   144   146
Hutchinson F Pte   151

'I'
Indian Cavalry   116
Ingram Lt   117 132 142
Intelligence   46 48 52 79/80/81 99 App. H
Interpreter   14
Irish Rifles - see Army   19

Le Cateau 52
Ledward Col 29
Lee Pte follows Barrett 52
Leech A Sgt DCM 154
Le Gheer 19
Le Mesge 78
Leonard H Pte 153
Le Touquet 116
Letters - App A
Lewis B Pte 151
Lewis Capt 7 38
Lewis Gun Sec 65 88 91 132
Liaison 48
Lice 24 25 110
Licientiousness 62
Listening tele aparatus 68
Liverpools 18th Bn 76
Lloyd Brig Bde Cdr 7/1/17 115
Lloyd E Pte 154
Lomas W Pte 153
Lomax S Pte 152
London Territorials 120 124
Longueval 80
Loxley W F L/Cpl 150
Lupton W L/Cpl 150
Lyne J Pte 154

'M'
Macdonald Col 117
MacDonnel Lt 101 103 116 118 127
                132 141/2 150
MacMinn W J Sgt Killed 153
McDougall F L/Cpl Killed 154
Machine Gun Corps 66 138
Machine Gun Wood 76
Maddocks J Pte 153
Maddaford P Pte 154
Madden of 17th Bn 133
Maguire H Pte 152
Maldon 4 12
Malony H Pte 154
Manchester Regt Bns - see under Army Brit
Manchester Hill 109
Manger J Pte 153
Mansell Lt 28
Maps see Appendix 'G'
Marching 9 10 13 14 78 App 'E'
Maricourt 44 46 51 52
Martin POW 145
Martinet's Wood 112
Mason S Pte 153
Mason's billet 4
Mat Double 96
May L C 11
Mead Lt 31 38 71 81 149
Medical Officer Capt Fletcher 31

Medical Officer Capt Heathcote 103
Medical Officer Capt Moore 134
Casualty Clearing Station No. 5 96
14 Gen Hosp Boulogne 96
London Gen Hosp Denmark Hill 96
Hospitals Camiers and Manchester 132
Medical problems Chisledon 99 100 105 109
Ramsbury and Boards 116 131/33 134/5 App 'D'
Megson R H Lt/Capt 31 34 43 60 74 90/91 94 102
        109 118 124 127 132 136 138 139 141 143 149
Meikle J Pte   151
Mercatel 118
Mericourt Ribemont 69
Merriman A P Pte 154
Mess Sgt Catlow 151
Mess purchases etc 46 74 102
Meteren 14
Meuse-Etain Warcq 62
Mist 60
Monchiet 118
Monks F Pte 151
Montauban 60 76 77 79 81 84 85 89 91
          99 117 133 145
Montgomery Major 30 71 App 'E'
Moores J Pte 153
Morale and Spirit 42 55 102 108 109 135 App 'E'
Mordy Pte 4th Glos 25
Morris G P Lt 31 34 41 91 148
Morris W Cpl 151
Mottershead S Pte 152
Mould J Pte 154
Mud 45/6
Murphy D J Pte 154
Murphy F Pte 151
Musson F Pte 153

'N'
Nagpur Trench 120 124
Naming Streets 44
Napoleon 13
Nash F.W. 136
Nash T A H Pte 2571 1
Nash further indexing in App 'H'
Naurs 37
N C O's 82 92 118
Neuville Vitasse 120
Newman 25
Nicholls 25
Nickol P Pte 153
Nisbet J Pte 154
Noise 79
No Man's Land 17 24
Norris Killed 77
Nuns 24

'O'
Oesterhove Camp 13 34
Ogden F Pte 153
Ogden T Pte 151
Ogden T Pte 153
Oissy Chateau 78
Oldfield B S Pte 154
Oliver Lt 31 60 81 90 94 112 136 149
"Onward" s s 101
Orchard Post 110
Orderly Room 47
Orders and Memoranda App'C' 155-159
Ormerod J T Pte 153
Osiers 103
Outposts 123
Oxford Copse 79

'P'
Palmer 41 84
Paris Plage 116
Parker C W Pte 153
Parker 142
Parkes H Pte 151
Parkinson Capt 38
Parkinson B Pte 153
Parris S V Pte 152
Patient A L/Cpl 154
Patrol 64
Payne Capt 31 41 60 67 81 94 149
Pearson J E Pte 152
Pearson 102
Pennington 84
Penny 28
Percy Lt 31 65 66 149
Periscope 18
Peronne Road 44 58/9 67
Perry J E Pte 151
Pests 24
Petrie C L Lt Col DSO 30 53 54 60 64 74
     94 97 108 109 139 140 148 App 'D'
Phillips R Lt 31 77 148
Pickering L/Cpl Scout killed 67 78
Pickering J Pte 152
Pickles H G Pte 151
Pioneers 119
Plant J L Pte 151
Ploegsteert 19 21 27
Plug Street Trenches 23
Pommiers Ridge 85
Pont de Briques 13
Pont Nieppe 25
Pont Remy 34
Pony 41 46
Poppies 71
Portuguese 116

Potter CSM 113 118
Potter F W Pte 151
Prestwich 29 91
Price 85 93
Prisoners 67 68 77 80 91 92 93 118 145
Profitt A Cpl 132 142 143 150
Pounds 27
Poynton Signaller 87
Puddy E A Pte 152
Pump - Bairnsfather 26
Purity Villa 23

'Q'
Qualey P Pte 152
Quartermaster 124
Queen's 7th Bn 66
Quin M Cpl 154

'R'
Raid 112
Rainbow 34
Ramsbury 134
Ramsden Capt 71
Randall G Pte 154
Rations 45 90 103 111 123
Rats 7 23 45 73
Ravenscroft J Pte 152
Ravine Sector 103 115
Rawcliffe W Pte 154
Rawson Capt Adjt 4th Glos 27 28 38 39
Razel H Pte 153
Reactions 84 85
Read E Pte 151
Rear A F Pte 152
Reddy CSM Killed 60 136
Redford G Killed 126 153
Registering 71 112
Reilly E J Sgt 150
Reliefs 55
Revolver 36
Rex or Rix 38
Reynolds C J Lt 10
Reynolds N E A 134
Rhodes Lt 31 37 149
Richardson Lt 117
Rigby C R L/Cpl 153
Roberts R E Maj 31 102 105 125 131 142 143
               145 146 149
Roberts W Pte 151
Rockets 88
Rollston W Pte 152
Rouen 62
Round Point 53
Royal Dragoons 55
Royal Engineers 119

Royal Scots Fusiliers   see 'S' or 'Army'
Rum 46 83
Runners 79 127
Rushton A Cpl 151
Ryan A E Killed   118 126 153
Ryder J Pte 151
Rylands Lt 108 132 142

'S'
Sailly le Bois 38
Saint Gratien 65
Saint Riquier 34/5
Saint Silvestre Capel 14
Salisbury Plain 12
Salmon J C Pte 151
Salvation Army 34
Saulty Labret 117
Saunders W R Pte 151
Savile Lt 4th Glos Killed 28
Saxon Infantry 104th 23
Scandals 133
Schaffgrezyt Paul POW   80
Schofield A Pte 154
Schofield F Pte 151
Schewr F J Pte   154
Scots Fusiliers Royal 59 77 81 92 95
                120 127 136
Scouts 67 79 88
Scudamore 81 94 103
Sellars H Pte 151
Sells A Pte 153
Sentries 17 51
Service Watchnight 10
Shackles 4
Shea General Sir John 60 71 92 101 110
                116 136 144
Sheard E Pte 154
Sheard G Cpl 151
Shelling 47 48 53 56 62 66 71 76 80 83
            110 113 118 119 127 139
Shepherd E L/Cpl 154
Shepherd 4th Glos Killed 9 28 38
Sherwood A L/Cpl 150
Sherwood Foresters 60 104 138
Shirkers 133
Shoeleather 44
Shrapnel Corner 110
Shrapnel Helmets 51
Shrewton 134
Shroeder H H Pte 151
Shropshire Light Infantry 17
Simpson J Pte 151
Simpson Cpl MM 145
Sinclair J E Pte 152
Slack E S Lt 31 53 64 91 133 149
Slag Alley 89

Sleep, 86 87 104
Smith-Dorrien Gen Sir H 14
Smith 84
Smith H F L/Cpl 154
Smith H R W Lt 103 110 116 126 132 142 150
Smith J A 116 132 142 150
Smith J L L 116 132
Smithers Lt 81 94 136
Snipers 24 46 59 60 64 79
Snow D'Oyly General 117
Snow 9 10 15 35 58 60
Somme 44 72 108
SOS 88
Sotham E G Capt Adjt 30 31 53 54 60 67
         74 76 84 86 90 94 95 110 136 148
South Lancs 11th Bn 113
Spandau 72
Speed E Pte 151
Spies 51 52 94
Spirit - Morale 42 55 102/3 108 109 135
"Stad Antwerpen" s s 132
Staff Officers 60
Stafford Badger Lt 10 94
Stafford W L/Cpl 151
Stalker J L/Cpl 150
Stand-to 17
Stanley General 118
Starfish Point 110
Stephenson F Pte 152
Stevens L/Cpl 79 84
Stevenson General 90th Bde 31
Stockton L Pte 153
Stonehewer Lt 117 145 150
Stotesbury Major 4th. Glos 1
Street Names 44
Supplies/Rations 15 26 45 86 90 94 103 111 124
Sutcliffe A Pte 151
Sutton Sgt 110
Suzanne 44 46 47 51 62
Swain Lt 66 91 117 145 150

'T'
Taking Over 111
Talmas 44
Talus Boise 79 80
Tatham Col RAMC 134
Taylor O Pte 152
Telegraph Hill 120 124
Tents 2 3
Tetney 133
Thackeray H Pte 151
Thigh Boots 39
Thomas F Sgt 154
Thompson Maj 39
Thompson E Runner exceptional 54 79 84 90

Whittenbury H A Cpl 153
Whittington H Pte 153
Whitworth E Pte 153
Whizz-bang Shell 46
Whytehead Colonel 95 96
Wickham Capt 109 118 132 141
Wielding Pte Killed 138
Wild E Pte 153
Wild N L/Cpl 152
Williams A L/Cpl 154
Wilson L F Capt Tpt 31 37 43 65 109 115
                131 132 141 142 143
Wilson Sgt 4th Glos 19
Wilson S L/Cpl 150
Wiltshires 2nd Bn 89
Winnezeele 13
Winning T A CQMS 103 150
Wire barbed 107
Wolfenden W Pte 154
Wood J Pte 152
Woodham Mortimer 11 12
Worcesters ,8th Bn 39
Worthington H Capt 31 64 91 96 142 148
Wounded 45 89
Wright H Pte 126 154
Wright Lt 108

'Y'
Yorks 2nd Bn 127 128
Yorks and Lancs 18
Yorks and Lancs 11th Bn - See Petri Col
Young - the best natured - 4th Glos 1 9 28
Ypres 25
Y Wood 68

'Z'
Zepplin 54

December 15ᵗ 1915.   France –

———— I am very tired, having
just returned from the trenches.
I am quite glad to be back in billets
I have marched twenty miles back
from the trenches. Wasn't it extra-
ordinary that I should come accross
my beloved Fourth Gloucesters? I
had a most enthusiastic reception
from rank & file, and the officers
were jolly nice to me. I had
dinner with Davenport, the Colonel,
and Major Thompson. Captain Rawson
is now Colonel commanding
Argyle & Sutherland Highlanders; he
was the Adjutant and a man I
admired tremendously. I saw
Best & Shepherd & all the others.
          The trenches are in an

appalling state, up to our waists
in mud. I went in for instruction
to the 8ᵗ Worcesters and they
were awfully decent to me. I
brought away a shrapnel helmet
as a souvenir of my visit there

Dec. 16ᵗ
          Morning! I feel much
fresher this morning and have bathed
shaved & had my buttons cleaned;
a tremendous asset to one's self
respect.
          I look like being the sole
survivor of the officers soon.
Major Kempster has gone home
with pleurisy. Captain Payne is
very ill at present. Belcher
has been badly wounded & has
had his leg amputated.

Fletcher the medical officer is slowly cracking up; Mead won't last long; he was hit by a piece of shrapnel, but his nerve had already gone. Henriques & Rhodes have both been evacuated sick to the Base, so that is four already gone & three likely to go. I am jolly fit. I enjoyed watching the others dodge the shells - it was great fun.

I am going over to see Major Baker tomorrow who is at D——. I had an accident yesterday & burnt my Burberry badly. They are awfully inflamable things. My men were topping - such cheery little devils.

An awfully nice hound has attached himself to us; a black & white fox hound.

I must be off now to inspect my platoon

Geoffrey

May 28th 1916

Mustn't tell you any news but cheers, & again cheers. I am supremely happy & run about with a broad grin on my face.

These rats are getting beyond the limit. They parade for rations every night now, & nearly killed the Quartermaster Sergt. yesterday because the rations were half an hour late & they had paraded too soon. Prestwich vows he went into the Ration this morning & saw 40 of them forming fours!